The Clinical Science of Mineral Therapy

The Clinical Science of Mineral Therapy

Leslie Fisher

THE
MAURICE BLACKMORE
RESEARCH
FOUNDATION

For Irene, whose enthusiasm for mineral therapy has most times exceeded my own, and for Juliet, who with the irrepressibility, innocence and dignity of a seven year old, has confirmed my belief that Peter Pan made the right choice after all.

Acknowledgements

I am indebted to Paul Callinan MSc, for the tremendous work that he did in establishing scientific support for the traditional principles of mineral prescribing. It is from his mammoth literature search that much of the chapters on physiology and biochemistry have been taken.

When I sat with Paul in a restaurant one Saturday evening in 1983 and outlined the areas that I particularly wanted him to cover, neither of us really believed that much would come of it. Well, we were both wrong, there was a lot more support waiting in the literature than either of us would have imagined. Paul's enthusiasm increased with each new nugget uncovered, so much so that he ended up with a pile of abstracts three metres high.

Regardless of all that, the information uncovered would have been very ordinary if it were not for Paul's genius for uncovering that which is not ordinary, to see relationships that are not obvious and always then to re-assess the situation from a lateral perspective.

My gratitude is also expressed to Blackmores Ltd. and the Maurice Blackmore Research Foundation for the funding of the above and many other projects that have ensured the very survival of this amazing therapy.

First published in 1991
The Maurice Blackmore Research Foundation
23 Roseberry Street, Balgowlah, NSW Australia 2093

ISBN 0 7316 8447 8

Set in 10/11 pt Times and Helvetica by Authoset, Hobart

Compugraphic output by, Desktop, Hobart

Colour separations by, K+H Lithographic Reproductions, Sydney

Printed by Dee Why Printing Works Pty Ltd, Sydney

Cover Photography by, Richard Eastwood, Hobart

Cover Concept, Design and Graphics by, Ray Langmaid, Hobart

Contents

Preface

This book looks at the important role that minerals play in contributing to the states of health and disease in the human. I must confess from the outset, that there is a definite naturopathic bias in the way that I have presented the material. This bias stems not only from my own beliefs and experience, but also the comforting knowledge that even where the most recent medical research is concerned, this bias is continually being confirmed and supported, not contradicted. The text is therefore a synthesis of the traditional homœopathic and naturopathic perception of the disease process and the role that mineral deficiencies play, combined with the more straight-down-the-line orthodox medical, biochemical and physiological viewpoint.

Regardless of the fact that the older views are generally supported by the newer findings, there will still be occasions though, where they do not entirely concur, or where the traditional claims pass beyond present scientific understanding. In this regard I can only suggest that the reader decide for himself whether to proceed on the basis of that which is traditional, having as it does, tremendous credibility conferred by time and empiricism, combined with whatever support modern research can provide, or the more narrow and self-limiting approach of waiting for scientific elucidation of these observations before proceeding at all. Personally I do not think that these technical and philosophical arguments ultimately matter, that is, apart from providing us with some cerebral comfort. It is the more practical common-sense issues associated with getting sick people well, that always seem to be casualties in these sorts of debates. Our first duty and perhaps loyalty is to our patients; to get them well by the safest and most efficient means possible. In this regard, new, has certainly not always proven to be better.

Whereas, for literally decades, there had been little or no change in the natural therapies, suddenly there has been a plethora of therapies with bold and extravagant claims to tempt the open-minded (some would say credulous) practitioner. On the positive side, time has provided for a definite shake-out of these newer therapies, so that only those with any true merit have survived. Many practitioners have also learned a thing or two from all this. One, that there is no such thing as a universal panacea; and two, that in the gaining of knowledge, effort is required. In this regard, the situation has also forced a shake-out within the professions as well. The temptation is within us all to get things the easy way if we can, but in the end, self-respect if nothing else, determines that we must work for what we get.

This text is therefore written for these second-wave practitioners as much as it's written for the novice. It seems that for those who are blessed with the quality of endurance, nature has a habit of balancing the excesses of man. Ultimately, if one waits long enough, the dross usually works it's way to the surface and can be cast off. That which is left is the pure essence, easy to see and impossible to forget or supplant. This approach to mineral therapy is one such essence, and if all this experimentation has done nothing more than to make it easier for those practitioners, who are genuinely searching for answers to find what they're looking for; then time has served a worthy purpose..

While a considerable amount of biochemical and physiological support for each of the minerals has been provided in the text, the temptation has been resisted to perform an overkill in this department. The technical information has been structured in such a way as to support the prescribing principles and to offer additional information and perspectives that would not normally be provided in the college, or be easily sourced by the graduate practitioner.

In the past, a lack of virtually any technical support for the theories of mineral therapy was a definite liability; one which thankfully has now been largely eliminated. This approach to mineral therapy, along with most other *old* disciplines such as homœopathy, have suffered unfairly through the years, from the criticism of being unscientific; and that is in spite of the overwhelming clinical evidence to the contrary. Quite frankly, it's been my experience, that those individuals who demand absolute scientific proof (whatever that may mean), very rarely go on to practise mineral therapy, and if they do, they invariably make a mess of it. For them, it then becomes a self-fulfilling prophesy; "they knew from the beginning that it couldn't work." This book is definitely not targeted at that market!

On the back cover of this book I have reiterated the statement that I made on the cover of the last book, and that is; "*for the most part, mineral deficiencies represent the lowest possible common-denominator to disease.*" Nothing has transpired over the time that causes me to question this belief.

To avoid unnecessary circumlocution I have used the male gender throughout the text. Having chosen this format, I wish to make it quite clear that no woman should feel the slightest tinge of offence; as none was intended.

Leslie Fisher
Hobart, Australia. January, 1991

Chapter one

Introduction to mineral therapy

Introducing *The Clinical Science of Mineral Therapy* presents somewhat of a dilemma, as there are so many interesting aspects that are worthy of consideration. The obvious objective of any author though, is to capture the interest and imagination of as many readers as is possible. In fulfilling this objective, it is very easy to concentrate on one aspect, whilst completely overlooking or diminishing another. One also knows that what may work well, by appealing to one reader, will not necessarily capture the interest of another. What follows then, is a thumb-nail sketch of mineral therapy, canvassing as many aspects as possible, but at the same time trying to establish it in the context of the total environment.

A therapy must be compatible with the total environment in which it will operate

One of the justifiable criticisms of modern technological medicine, would be, that it is almost totally divorced from the most important ingredient of all, and that is the patient. As all the component parts invariably feed off each other, the effectiveness of any modality is going to be diluted if there cannot be a symbiotic relationship established between, in this case, the patient, his environment and the therapy.

In this context, it is impossible to introduce these concepts, without pre-empting matter that will follow in later chapters and in much greater detail; but let us now look at those individual aspects, so that it can be seen how important they are in their own right and how they complement each other in the total sense.

The therapy and the practitioner

When is mineral therapy not mineral therapy?

The first point to be made is that all forms of mineral therapy are by no means the same. Mineral therapy is a general term that can be applied to a variety of dissimilar methods. Methods ranging from the present day orthodox medical use of minerals as electrolytes, to the older Schüssler homœopathic approach where minerals are seen as a complete system of cure.

Therefore, the present situation is quite confusing, because there are a number of distinctly different methods of prescribing minerals in vogue.

While each of these different approaches can be termed mineral therapy generically, they as different to each other as chalk is to cheese.

At this early point, it is important to state quite clearly, what this particular method purports to be and where necessary, canvass the salient differences between it and other methods.

Let us just assume for the moment that the rationale as to why we need to prescribe minerals has been accepted, because this aspect is much more complex and better left to the appropriate place in the text (see chapter Three, "The physiological role of minerals").

Important considerations

The minerals

The mineral salts employed are basically those that were originally identified by Dr. Wilhelm Schüssler, of Germany in 1873 (see chapter Two, "The history and principles of mineral therapy").

The form

This method considers that the mineral salts of Schüssler, are physiologically preferred forms, as they are natural to the earth and the food chain. The more recent development and use of non-physiological forms is seen to work contrary to the body's mechanisms for absorption and utilisation as they are designed to bypass normal body controls to increase their effectiveness (see pages 29-33).

The dose

The small pharmacological dose principle as introduced by Dr. Maurice Blackmore of Australia, is considered to be more effective than both the homœopathic preparations of Schüssler and some of the high doses that are used by other methods today (see pages 33-35, 38).

The safety

The inorganic mineral salts of Schüssler and Blackmore can be considered the safest because of their natural form and their low dose. Where safety is concerned, the dual aspects of *form* and *dose* cannot be separated. It is bad enough if we have a physiological form, administered in a dose that is too large, or a non-physiological form given in a low dose, but where we have non-physiological forms combined with high doses, we then have the potential to do harm (see pages 33-35).

The prescribing

When new is not necessarily better

The clinical prescribing method presented by the author is based upon an amalgam of, traditional homœopathic symptomatology, present day knowledge of biochemistry and his own clinical research (see pages 106-119). In keeping with Schüssler's original concept the method is also presented as a system of cure. The modern orthodox medical use of minerals has continued to be ad hoc, where they are seen only as being complementary to the general drug regimen, and never applied or thought of as a system of cure. Generally, the alternative use of minerals is also ad hoc, employing large doses of non-physiological forms and administered with an undisciplined approach to prescribing.

In recent times there has been a tendency to generally downgrade the importance of minerals, relative to some other essential nutrients. This situation has occurred more by default than design, but it has ensured that minerals are viewed by many practitioners as being passé. In a very real sense, minerals are now the *poorer cousins* of vitamins, trace elements, essential fatty acids and other nutrients, whose action is seen to be much more interesting and important. In time this attitude will be seen to be an error of judgement on the part of both researchers and practitioners alike. The importance of the other vital nutrients should not be diminished, but their role should only be established and appreciated in the overall context of the environment in which they operate. Ultimately it will be established, that unless the mineral status of the patient is established first, then a therapy may not be effective or only superficial in its action, due to underlying mineral deficiencies.

Poorer cousins

The method offers tremendous security to both practitioner and patient, based on the fact that it has been in use for over 100 years. When one considers, the all important aspects of efficacy and safety, there can be no better recommendation for a therapy, than the test of time. Unlike a lot of other *natural* therapies, the basic principles have been supported and confirmed, rather than denied by present-day scientific research. In fact, it is interesting to note that many of the symptoms that were ascribed to a particular mineral deficiency over 150 years ago, have only just been rediscovered or reconfirmed by modern research. The security that both the practitioner and the patient can take in such an unblemished and redoubtable history is enormous and should not be discounted.

Unfortunately, most alternative therapies on offer thus far, have not been *alternative* enough to represent a real challenge to the modern drug. Most alternatives are also limited in their application, which then necessitates additional learning and confusion on the part of the practitioner, in trying to manage his increasing armamentarium. The situation also leads to lack of compliance on the part of the patient, as *he* tries to manage his cure. Much better if we can employ one viable stand-alone method, if such a thing exists; one that can be every bit a match for the modern technological drug. Any practitioner who bothers to learn the method properly and apply it thoughtfully, will find that mineral therapy is well equipped to meet the drug brigade head-on. Undoubtedly, situations will arise, when a modern drug will work better than a mineral; but on the other hand, there will also be occasions when the action of a mineral will far surpass the action of a drug. Over all, minerals can be seen to work better than drugs, and basic commonsense dictates that we should opt for the most conservative method first.

To serve the patient's immediate interests, there may actually be the need to combine mineral therapy with conventional drugs. This marriage of strange bedfellows, does not seem to diminish the effectiveness of the minerals, with the minerals at times being seen to actually potentiate the effectiveness of the drug regimen. In cases where elective surgery is on the agenda, the minerals can be introduced so that surgically associated risks and recovery times are reduced, and the quality of healing is increased.

The argument as to whether minerals work better than drugs in the short-term is really not the most important issue (although it may seem so at the time; and there may also be considerable pressure from the patient for it to be seen that way too). What really matters is a treatment's ability to root out the cause of the illness, and thus protect the patient's long-term interests. In this regard the minerals stand alone.

Mix and match

There is virtually no other modality, orthodox or unorthodox, where mineral therapy cannot be combined to better serve the long-term interests of the patient. The physical therapies are a good example of how minerals can be combined to enhance the overall effectiveness of the treatment programme. The anti-inflammatory properties of the minerals for instance, can be exploited to enable manipulative treatment to begin earlier than would normally be the case. Where treatable underlying pathologies exist, manipulation can often be used to advantage in a palliative way, while the cause is being addressed by the minerals in the longer term. The interesting thing about all this though, is that as the practitioner becomes more experienced with mineral therapy, he begins to use it more and more as a stand-alone modality.

Side-effects are an all too common occurrence associated with the modern technological drug. While these adverse reactions are not totally confined to conventional medicine, it is still in that arena where they mostly occur. Regardless though of where and why side-effects occur, one factor is certain, and that is, that the management of a case is made much more difficult and time consuming. Mineral therapy on the other hand, is virtually free of any precautions, contraindications or side-effects, either in the short or the long-term (see "Acute reactions to treatment" on page 132). Apart from the obvious benefits that flow to the patient from such a situation, it also makes life considerably easier for the practitioner, because beyond basic commonsense precautions, he can devote his entire energies to getting the patient well. There are many situations, where putting aside the distress or harm that a side-effect may cause, it may also be difficult for the practitioner to continue treating the patient, because an equally effective alternative can not be found to replace the offending treatment.

Now and forever

Prophylaxis is another important and yet often overlooked aspect of a patient's treatment regimen. There are some patients, who for a variety of reasons, can never be made well, to stay well. Many modalities may be capable of providing a satisfactory outcome for the patient in the short-term, but keeping the patient well in the long-term, is another matter altogether.

Usually, long-term protection against a return of the original malady, is either by involving the patient in changes of lifestyle, such as diet, etc., or just leaving it to pure chance. Having got the patient well in the first place, it would be very nice if the very same therapy could be applied equally well as a prophylactic. Generally speaking, if mineral therapy is capable of getting the patient well, it is also capable of keeping the patient well. This may not seem to be an important aspect to an inexperienced practitioner, or to the average patient either; in fact it may seem negative to even contemplate such an outcome. Negative and all as it may first appear, having at your disposal an efficient prophylactic as part of your overall treatment strategy, offers tremendous security and confidence. The philosophy that can be applied to mineral therapy with regard to its maintenance qualities, is, *that which cures, can also be used to prevent.*

Treat the patient not the disease, treat the cause not the symptoms

The practice of mineral therapy also allows the practitioner to treat the patient as an individual. To *treat the patient and not the disease, to treat the cause and not the symptoms.* These are the very planks of naturopathic philosophy. There are many other naturopathic modalities that also make these claims, but in truth, most only pay lip service to the principles. For this philosophy to be fulfilled, a therapy must first of all have the ability to be able to conform to the principles of treating the whole patient and not the disease by name. Many naturopathic modalities are in fact prescribed in just the same ad hoc way as conventional drugs. The medication is worked out on the basis of the illness and there can be no accommodation made for the fact that not all patients suffering from the same disease, will suffer in exactly the same way. Practitioners who are new to this concept can be excused, if the principles are seen as just another example of the sorts of clichés, that are so often uttered by *fringe* practitioners. Actually, the principles do exist, have a firm foundation and can be demonstrated to work in practice. This particular method of mineral therapy demands that the practitioner assess each patient individually, regardless of the complaint. Often this involves making use of a lot of information that other modalities would consider to be irrelevant or unrelated. In this way the patient is analysed and treated as an individual, who just happens to be suffering from a disease that is the same as someone else's.

To continue to conform to this principle, it is also important that the process be ongoing and not just stop at the first consultation. The disease state is dynamic regardless of whether the patient is getting worse, or is getting better. Unless a modality can accommodate these ever changing states in the patient, then the claim to be treating the patient individually should not be made. Although the name of the disease being treated has remained the same, the patient certainly has not! It is one thing to have the will, it is another to have the tools and materials available, with which to express that will. This can even mean contemplating a change in a patient's treatment when the patient is already responding satisfactorily - a strange concept for some practitioners to understand. Why bother changing a treatment that is proving to be successful anyway? Regardless that the patient is responding, there can be no guarantee that the improvement will continue, or even be maintained, simply by continuing with the same treatment. It may be necessary to make minor adjustments, just as much because the patient is improving, as it would be if the patient were not responding or getting worse. This method of mineral therapy is able to accommodate those subtle grey areas of change and transform them, where necessary, into a more accurate prescribing package.

There is also another aspect of possessing a modality that is in conformity with the philosophy of treating the patient and not the disease. If the practitioner is limited to treating a disease label and the treatment isn't going too well, then the practitioner has no option other than to discard that particular treatment and try something else. At this point the business of healing starts to appear very hit-or-miss; and a miss is as good as a mile! On the other hand, if the treatment allows the practitioner to prescribe according to the totality of the patient's symptoms and signs, regardless of the disease, then the opportunity is there for an adjustment to be made within the modality, rather than a complete change of modality, that will bring the treatment back onto course again. This is just another example of how this system of medication differs from other forms of mineral treatment, and most other modalities as well.

Hit or miss healing

Before leaving the discussion from the practitioner's standpoint, it is important to identify some target objectives and markets, so that the student can be left with no ambiguity as to where the therapy is leading him. Rather than go into a discussion about specific diseases, it is more productive at this stage to simply determine the general areas where the therapy can be applied successfully and the principles that should be considered at the same time

To market, to market

The general areas where mineral therapy can be applied to great benefit, are, the psychosomatic disorders, the idiopathic patients and conditions of unknown ætiology. Collectively these categories could be summed up as; *the medical poor achievers!*

Medical poor achievers

Being able to target these groups successfully is one thing, but there are other important requirements, if not obligations, that we must try and conform to as well. These basic treatment objectives can be listed as follows:

Treatment objectives

1. To treat the cause of an existing illness.
2. To prevent an existing illness from becoming worse.
3. To prevent vague symptoms from developing into a fully blown disease.
4. To maintain good health in the present absence of disease.
5. That our treatment should do no harm.

The patient and the community

All the attributes already covered with regard to the therapy and the practitioner, should also be equally applicable and analogous to the interests of the patient. There are aspects of those issues though, that are worthy of further consideration, because to the patient they may have a slightly different meaning. In this regard, we are probably only considering the informed and thinking person and what this person may consider to be important, when required to seek medical attention.

Alternative spending

Without doubt, todays thinking consumer of health care, is chasing the greatest result, by the safest and most convenient means and in the quickest possible time. (Cost has not been included as one of the criteria, as it can be demonstrated that these consumers are usually prepared to spend more, for their *alternative* treatment). Orthodox, or conventional medicine is therefore, rightly or wrongly, losing this battle for the consumer, to alternative forms of medicine. There is a conflict of interpretation, terms and interest, between the way orthodox medicine views itself from the inside and the way its consumers view things from the outside. Orthodox medicine has been guilty of perpetuating a number of incestuous myths, which along with its inherent bureaucratic sluggishness and arrogance, has been responsible for not only the present state of consumer disenchantment, but also the rumblings from some of the troops within. One illustration of how this has come about, is to examine the antithetical logic behind the argument that orthodox medicine presents to denigrate its opponents.

When the pot calls the kettle black

We have orthodox medicine claiming that its own methods are sound, logical, scientifically proven, effective, safe and therefore, conservative, while criticising alternative methods as being; unsound, illogical, scientifically unproven, ineffective, unsafe and radical. Even a brief study of the facts will reveal that the difference between how orthodox medicine views itself and the reality of the situation, is to say the least, schizophrenic. Much of what passes for orthodox medical treatment today has dubious scientific support, is probably unsafe in the short or long-term and is not very efficacious. As for the claim of conservatism, implying a thoughtful, secure and safe approach to the patient, the converse again must be applied. Much medical treatment (drugs, surgery and investigative procedures) is radical to say the least, rendering at times, more risk to the patient than the disease being treated. In the general terms of morbidity and mortality, medical methods over the past 150 years can be demonstrated to have made little or no positive impact on the major scourges that have afflicted mankind.

There is also a growing realisation amongst a section of the community, usually learned through personal experience, that not only can they no longer rely upon orthodox medicine, as they had perhaps become accustomed to in the past (the disappearance of the old-style family doctor, saw to that), but that they can no longer put their trust in governments either. Governments all over the Western World are backing away from their traditional community health care commitments, as costs escalate. The message being given, loud and clear, is; *if you are middle class or borderline middle class, then don't think that you can go on relying on us!* Governments and the medical profession are now in the process of softening up the masses, lowering there preconceived expectations, ready for the big health care crunch of the nineties. This situation in itself is an interesting bit of circuitous logic to contemplate, because who educated the public to those expectations in the first place? Be that as it may, this situation only serves to demonstrate what should have been obvious all along and in that sense may have a positive rather than a negative outcome: and that is, that every individual must become more responsible for the maintenance of his own health. In this regard, this must not only be seen as a duty to oneself, but to the community as a whole. The notion that the maintenance of health is a State matter and responsibility, will by the end of nineties, be as dead as the proverbial dodo!

New lives for old

Some people are already beginning to piece things together and are making positive changes in their lifestyle. This is evident from the increasing interest in matters such as, better diet, exercise, meditation and the taking of food supplements etc. Now, these sorts of things on their own, are probably not sufficient to ensure that a person would never get sick and require treatment; but if every good citizen was prepared to institute these changes, then the present health care burden would undoubtedly be much lightened. It is also the duty of every doctor, to investigate the patient's lifestyle, so that errors may be corrected. If any treatment required can be seen as complementary, to the other positive elements in the person's life and vise versa, then a thinking patient has something that he can relate to. If on the other hand, any treatment is seen to be in conflict with those influences, or be seen to do nothing for the person's long-term interests, then it will be all the more difficult for that patient to cooperate.

There has always been a strange irony in medical utterances about the processes of health and disease, which has led to much confusion and misunderstanding, not only within the lay community but also within medicine itself. It is as if the states of health and disease are totally separate and incompatible entities, something akin to God and the Devil. Health is something one just has as one's birthright, while if one becomes ill, then one is an innocent victim of some negative force that is usually beyond one's control. Whether by design or default, this has proved to be a very successful marketing strategy on the part of our health advisers, but it is also one of the major reasons why the health care system is in the mess that it is today. Lay people, starting with small children at school have been educated to believe that if they become sick, then not only are they victims to be pitied but also that they must immediately place themselves in the hands of an expert to be fixed. The truth is of course, that every individual has the opportunity to make or break his own health. Real victims in this sense of the word are rare!

Philosophically, naturopathic medicine has never drawn these value judgement distinctions between the states of health and disease, the way orthodox medicine has done. Naturopathy has always taught that the two states are interchangeable and reversible according to how the individual chooses or is forced to live his or her life. If a person's life is in accord with the laws of Nature, then a state of health is promoted, but if there is contravention of those laws, then disease will be encouraged. There is an innate force, operating within us all, at all times, that given the right opportunities and conditions, strives for a level of perfection that can only be offset by our genetic inheritance. In this context, any doctor faced with a sick patient has a duty to ensure that his therapy is not only going to function in conformity with those immutable principles, but that he is also obliged to become involved in examining all aspects of the patient's life, so that the patient's future well-being is considered, not just the present.

Staking a claim for the communal good

Both the consumers of health care and the community as a whole, have a stake in ensuring that the physician treats the whole person rather than just the disease. Basic ignorance is still the greatest factor that keeps thinking people and even physicians on the wrong course, where errors of lifestyle are concerned. Once having been introduced to the principles of acquiring and maintaining good health though, there can be no further excuse for not giving the matter serious consideration.

Who would have believed twenty years ago that there would have been such a turnaround in the public attitude toward smoking! We have a situation in Australia today where smoking is banned in all government and public buildings, public transport, domestic airlines, some restaurants and most private offices. Legally there are actions being brought by lung cancer sufferers, against past employers, who unaware of the dangers, subjected their employees to the effects of passive smoking. Smokers have suddenly been made to feel like lepers and are squeaking and squealing that their basic rights have been taken away from them. Changing public attitudes and demands have brought this situation about. The individual must acknowledge his responsibility to the community, if any organised society is to survive. It is situations like this, that have further demonstrated to thinking people, that they cannot rely upon the experts and that they must safeguard their own interests, even if that means being somewhat of a pioneer.

Lepers that squeak & squeal

It is quite conceivable that sometime in the future we could see similar attitudes being expressed toward other sections of the community which are seen to be acting against the common good. People who refuse to lose weight, who refuse to exercise etc., could all end up being treated in much the same way as the smokers are today. Why should the section of the community which is prepared to assume responsibility for its health, carry the financial and social burden of those who are hell bent on destroying themselves.

So what are thinking consumers' of health care looking for and what can we as health care professionals do to satisfy their requirements? First and foremost, thinking people want to be well and remain well, but if they do become ill, then they want a simple, safe and yet efficient means to restore them to health; and if they do need to seek professional health care assistance, then they demand that the doctor be a *doctor* and not a *technician*.

Doctors or technicians?

This particular method of mineral therapy when combined with a sensible lifestyle, can almost always satisfy the needs of the patient and the practitioner. Philosophically speaking, if the interests of the patient are satisfied, then automatically the interests of the practitioner and the community are also satisfied.

The history and principles of mineral therapy

Minerals have been used in the treatment of human illness since the sixteenth century, when the Swiss physician. Philippus Aureolus Paracelsus (1493-1541) changed the face of medicine, by the application of chemistry. In slightly more recent times, research was conducted by Dr. Samuel Hahnemann (1755-1843), Physician, and founder of the Homœopathic System of Medicine. Hahnemann investigated extensively the physiological and pathogenic effects of the minerals, Sodium, Potassium, Calcium and Silica. Hahnemann had also evaluated dozens of other mineral, botanical and animal substances and in 1796 published an essay entitled, *A New Principle for Ascertaining the Curative Properties of Drugs*, in which he stated:

Dr. Hahnemann's principle of "like cures like"

> Every powerful medicinal substance produces in the human body a peculiar kind of disease - the more powerful the medicine, the more peculiar, marked and violent the disease. We should imitate nature, which sometimes cures a chronic disease by superimposing another, and employ in the disease which we wish to cure, that medicine which is able to produce another very similar artificial disease and the former will be cured, *Similia similibus* (like by like).

Hahnemann continues:

> Most medicines have more than one kind of effect - the direct one in the beginning, passing gradually into the second (I call it the indirect after-effect). The latter state is generally exactly opposite of the former.

Hahnemann's philosophy decried the use of "crude" substances (including minerals), when used as drugs. The Homoeopathic belief is that a *crude* substance should be first prepared by a process of mixing called "trituration" (serial dilution), before being administered as a drug. This involves the thorough mixing of the crude substance with a diluent medium, such as sugar of milk, alcohol or distilled water, followed by further mixing and further dilutions. The dilutions are conducted according to a decimal (1 part drug mixed with 9 parts diluent and expressed as the number of dilutions followed by an "x". Eg., 3x, 6x, 12x, etc.) or centesimal (1 part drug mixed with 99 parts diluent and again expressed as the number of dilutions followed by a "C", or "th". Eg., 30C or 30th, etc.) order. At each step of dilution, the mixture is ground or shaken vigorously (successed) for a time period of not less than two hours. The resultant medicine is then said to possess the healing forces originally contained within the crude drug but unleashed by the process of trituration. In this newly *potentised* form, the drug is considered safe to be administered as a healing agent. It is claimed that the homœopathic drug, following its dilutions and mixing, is assimilated, not via the gut, but directly through the epithelium and neurilemma of the mouth, pharynx and œsophagus.

The homœopathic preparation, testing and prescribing of a drug

Individual homœopathic medicines are tested and established by a procedure called "proving". The *proving* of a substance amounts to the controlled poisoning of healthy human volunteers by administering small doses of the drug and noting the effects. The symptoms and signs produced by such a *poisoning*, are meticulously noted by either the volunteers themselves, and/or trained observers, collated and then included along with all the other provings in the homœopathic *Materia Medica.* The drugs are then applied according to the homœopathic principle of *like will be cured by like* as originally established by Hahnemann. True homœopathic prescribing is the matching of *one* drug to *one* patient. The matched drug is then called the "similimum", because during a proving it has produced symptoms in a healthy person, that most match the symptoms presented to the doctor by the sick patient. The World's very first homœopathic *proving* of a drug was conducted by Hahnemann, using himself as the subject. By administering four drams of cinchona bark (from which the antipyretic, quinine is extracted) twice a day, Hahnemann was able to artificially induce symptoms identical to those associated with malaria. The bouts of intermittent fever, lasting from two to three hours ceased when the doses of cinchona were withheld and reappeared each time the drug was re-introduced. Richard Haehl MD, in his work, *Samuel Hahnemann, His Life and Work*, says, "Cinchona bark was to Hahnemann what the falling apple was to Newton and the swinging lamp was to Galileo."

Rediscovering the wheel

An interesting aspect to observe while discussing the principles of homœopathic provings, is that the clinical indications obtained by this method, over one hundred years ago, with regard to the physiological role of the various mineral salts, parallels almost identically all the more recent findings from medical research, but this time produced by the "deprivation" method. This situation amounts to a sort of "rediscovering of the wheel" by orthodox medical science. Moreover, orthodox medicine has continued to persist with it's perverse criticism of homœopathy, and as a profession, seems to suffer a sort of collective amnesia with regard to Hahnemann's work.

Homœopathic medicine enjoyed a golden era between the years of 1830 and 1940, but eventually succumbed to the allopathic school following the advent of the technological drug, antibiotics and organised, political medicine. The problem for the practising homœopathic physician at the time and interestingly one of the in-built reasons for homœopathy's decline; was that all the new drugs that had been added to the *Materia Medica* around the turn of the century, had made it virtually impossible for a practitioner to manage his armamentarium. No different to his modern high-tech counterpart, his practice eventually revolved around his thirty or so favourite drugs. The other criticism of homœopathic medicine at the time and still to this day, is that homœopathy has not produced a convincing mechanism for it's mode of action. Predictably the absence of a proven mechanism has left homœopathy wide open to attack, because its traditional principles seem to fly in the face of everything that is presently held near and dear to scientific medicine. The accusations of charlatanism, quackery and placebo effect are not uncommon. The truth is that homœopathic medicine does work and that like so many other great men, Hahnemann was about 200 years ahead of his time. Presently homœopathy is enjoying somewhat of a renaissance worldwide and undoubtedly, given time, this will finally provide the irrefutable scientific validation for it's principles; and more likely still that validation will probably come by default, from outside of the medical sciences.

Dr. Schüssler's principles

In March of 1873, Dr. Wilhelm Schüssler (1822-1898), another German Homœopathic Physician, published an article in a German homœopathic journal, entitled *An Abridged Homœopathic Therapeutics*, in which he stated:

Not Homœopathy?

> About a year ago I endeavored to discover by experiments on the sick if it were not possible to heal them, provided their diseases were curable at all, with those substances that are the natural, i.e., the physiological function remedies. These remedies must be given in small doses...whenever small doses are mentioned the reader usually at once thinks of homœopathy; my therapy however, is not homœopathy, for it is not founded on the law of similarity, but on the physiologico-chemical processes which take place in the human organism. By my method of cure the disturbances occurring in the motion of the molecules of the inorganic substances in the human body are directly equalized by means of homogeneous substances...a remedy that is selected according to the principle of similars is a homœopathic remedy, but a remedy which is homogeneous with the mineral substances of the organism, and the use of which is founded on physiological chemistry, is a biochemical remedy.

Schüssler's theory

If it were not for the fact that his article engendered criticism from a Dr. Lorbacher, of Leipzig, which prompted a reply from Schüssler and ran through six further issues, then it is quite possible that the world may never have learned of Dr. Schüssler's Twelve Tissue Remedies.

The basic hypothesis as stated by Schüssler was:

> ...the physiological fact that both the structure and the vitality of the organs of the body are dependent upon certain necessary quantities and proper apportionment of its inorganic constituents. These remain after combustion of the tissues and form the ashes. The inorganic constituents

> are, in a very real sense, the material basis of the organs and tissues of the body, and are absolutely essential to their integrity of structure and functional activity. Any disturbance in molecular motion of these cell salts in living tissues, caused by a deficiency in the requisite amount, constitutes disease, which can be rectified and the requisite equilibrium reestablished by administering the same mineral salts in small quantities...

Schüssler had built his theories on the previous work of Hahnemann, Dr. von Grauvogl of Nürnburg, Prof. Moleschott of Rome and Dr. Constantine Hering (1800-1880) of the United States, all of whom had written about the various inorganic mineral constituents of the body. It was left to Schüssler though, to develop that information into a system of medication he called "Biochemistry" (not to be confused with todays meaning of the word), which embraced the following twelve mineral salts:

The twelve salts of Schüssler

Calcium phosphate	(Calcarea phosphorica)
Calcium sulphate	(Calcarea sulphurica)
Calcium fluoride	(Calcarea fluorica)
Potassium phosphate	(Kali phosphoricum)
Potassium sulphate	(Kali sulphurica)
Potassium chloride	(Kali muriaticum)
Sodium phosphate	(Natrum phosphorica)
Sodium sulphate	(Natrum sulphurica)
Sodium chloride	(Natrum muriaticum)
Iron phosphate	(Ferrum phosphoricum)
Magnesium phosphate	(Magnesia phosphoricum)
Silicon dioxide	(Silicea)

Put simply, Schüssler's principle assumptions, can be outlined as follows:

Ashes to ashes

1. Schüssler's analysis of the inorganic mineral ash that remains after the human body is burnt, revealed that it is primarily made up of twelve mineral salts; and that therefore these minerals must play a vital role in both the physical integrity and proper functioning of the organism as a whole.

2. Further investigation predictably revealed that the different organs and parts of the body were made up of different minerals, and/or different apportionments of those minerals. He therefore concluded that those different minerals and/or different apportionments were vital for both the integrity and functioning of those individual organs and parts.

As was mentioned above, the original Schüssler method was based upon the deployment of twelve inorganic mineral salts, each made up of a cation/anion pair. With the exception of Iron phosphate (Ferrum phos.), Magnesium phosphate (Mag. phos.), and Silica (Silicea), the salts of Schüssler are made up of three cation family groups (Calcium, Potassium and Sodium).

Schüssler unfortunately brought the wrath of the homœopathic world upon himself when he stated in later editions of his *Abgekürzte Therapie* that his method was a distinct "system of cure", based upon "physiochemical" processes, not homœopathic law and therefore was not related to homœopathy in any way. Despite the fact that Schüssler claimed his method was not related to homœopathy, he none-the-less went on preparing his salts, according to the strict principles, laid down in the homœopathic pharmacopœia. The potency most favoured by Schüssler was the homœopathic 6x (that is where the salt is diluted and mixed six times on the decimal scale), or one part in one million. Although Schüssler claimed to be treating disease by correcting chemical deficiencies, the greatest weakness in his approach was to stem from his *modus operandi* - the homœopathic dose! This then became an aspect of his posthumous undoing. In the light of increased medical knowledge, no modern biochemist could be convinced that one part in one million, could correct any mineral deficiency. Regardless of the fact that Schüssler had produced so much valuable work in clinical symptomatology, orthodox medicine chose to ignore the whole lot; just because it couldn't compromise on the *deficiency* argument.

Hahnemann's weakness may have been Schüssler's strength

As mentioned previously, and notwithstanding the criticisms of Schüssler's approach from the more orthodox section of Homoeopathy, the problem still remained that the homoeopathic student or practising physician, was required to continually accommodate the new drugs that were being added to the "Materia Medica". Schüssler, with his greatly rationalised "system of cure", offered a logical and viable alternative, for those among the ranks who were finding the going a bit tough.

Allopathic criticism of homœopathy at that time was not only confined to the placebo issue either. Criticism was also focussed around one of homœopathy's other great weaknesses; that the provings contained in the *Materia Medica* often demonstrated contradictory symptomatology, within the one proving, or that similar or identical symptom indications appear for numerous provings. Rather than being a traitor to the homœopathic cause, perhaps Schüssler had unwittingly provided homœopathy with a rationale, by which this phenomenon could be explained; although it would appear that this point has never really been properly taken up to this day. As the salts of Schüssler are naturally occurring constituents of most homœopathic drugs, then the provings, and ultimately the preparation of those drugs, is also going to automatically present homœopathically the salts of Schüssler.

Can the whole Homœopathic Materia Medica be replaced by Schüssler's twelve remedies?

Professors Boericke and Dewey, in their book of 1914, *The Twelve Tissue Remedies*, made a number of comments that touched on this issue. They stated:

> Do we not when we *prove a drug* - that is, administer it to the healthy to produce symptoms - and nearly all our homœopathic provings are made, more or less, with the potentized drug, which process also potentizes the inorganic salts therein contained. ...could easily explain why the symptoms of one drug are so often found under the pathogenesis of another, why one is characteristic in one drug and only generic in another, when

> indeed, it may not rightly belong to either, but to an inorganic tissue salt, a constituent of each drug. If we compare the pathogenesis of *Phytolacca decandra* with the biochemical application of these salts, we shall see a striking and significant analogy. As the largest quantity of the inorganic salts therein contained is potash, we shall find that more symptoms of *Phytolacca* correspond to the *Kalis* (potassium salts), whilst fewer symptoms correspond to the calcium, iron and silica. ...it is a question to be decided whether we could obtain the same results by giving the inorganic salt constituents of the drug as by giving the drug itself.

In other words, maybe the entire homœopathic *Materia Medica*, made up as it is, of hundreds of individual drugs, could simply be replaced with Schüssler's twelve tissue salts. No such thing was ever done of course, and Schüssler's salts, continued to be just another part of an even more extensive *Materia Medica*; and what's more, it's remained that way to this day. Schüsslerism won many converts from the traditional homœopathic school, because of its relative simplicity, whilst others were simply content to add the salts of Schüssler to their homœopathic practice.

The end of an era

By the latter part of the nineteenth century and the early part of the twentieth century, homœopathic medicine was already losing ground to the then allopathic form of medicine. This was primarily due to a combination of two reasons; the organised opposition from allopathic medicine towards homœopathic medicine, through medical schools and governments; and the public rejection of homœopathic methods in favour of the more spectacular allopathic medicine.

Toward the later part of Schüssler's life he completely abandoned one of his original twelve tissue salts, Calcium sulphate; preferring to use in its place, Silica (Silicea), and/or Sodium phosphate (Nat. phos.).

Going public

Following the decline in the popularity of homœopathic medicine earlier this century, the survival of the Schüssler tissue remedies, was largely as a result of "going public". Pharmaceutical houses, following the decline, produced the remedies along with instruction books for home use. Mothers treated their families and in turn the children treated their own children; so much was the faith in Dr. Schüssler's tissue remedies. This *lay* acceptance of Schüssler's methods in fact still exists to this day throughout the world, but particularly in Germany and Great Britain. Throughout this time and right up to the present day, orthodox medicine predictably went about its business, prescribing minerals in greater and greater doses, but never as a *system of cure*, as was proposed by Schüssler.

The developments of Blackmore

In 1938, Dr. Maurice Blackmore (1906-1978), an Australian Naturopathic Physician, devised a method, that retained the symptomatology of Schüssler, but employed small pharmacological doses of mineral substance (ranging from 4mg in the case of Calcium fluoride, to 260mg for Sodium phosphate).

Blackmore produced his own tablets, according to a protocol that has been kept secret to this day and marketed them to other practitioners under the trade name of "Celloids®". In 1965 he established Blackmore's Laboratories, a private company that was owned and operated by himself and other members of the naturopathic profession in Australia. Following Maurice Blackmore's death, the company (now known as Blackmores Ltd.), has become a listed public company, with manufacturing plants and distributorships in various parts of the world. Although the *Celloid®* remedies now represent only a very small part of Blackmores Ltd. overall operation, they are still produced in exactly the same way as they were fifty years ago, at their plant in Sydney, Australia and supplied to thousands of practitioners worldwide. With regard to the actual nature of his remedies, Blackmore stated:

> The discovery of the Celloid micro-nutrients involving the factors of photosynthesis which converts crude mineral to colloidal states is a discovery indeed because while the biochemical indications remain constant the Celloids provide assimilable minerals in large therapeutic dosage.

Blackmore also introduced some other significant changes to the original Schüssler system of therapy and prescribing:

Small pharmacological doses and other changes to the rules

1. Blackmore believed that gross physical mineral deficiencies could be demonstrated to exist and that these deficiencies could not be replaced with the homœopathically prepared salts of Schüssler.

2. He retained the salt that Schüssler had abandoned, Calcium sulphate, but dropped Sodium chloride (Nat. mur., or common salt) instead, advocating the use of Sodium phosphate and Potassium chloride in its place. At the time, it would appear that Blackmore believed that Sodium chloride was a cell poison and for that reason significant amounts of it did not occur naturally in the food chain. Blackmore believed that the other naturally occurring salts of sodium in the food chain provided the sodium and likewise, the chloride.

3. Whereas Schüsslerism worked vaguely along the lines of the homœopathic *similimum*, Blackmore believed that in the disease state there always existed secondary deficiencies, which must be addressed simultaneously along with the primary deficiency indicators. Blackmore believed that four remedies were required in any prescription for a chronic illness, the first to correct the viscosity of the blood, the second for congestion, the third for inflammation, and the fourth for cell replacement.

4. Blackmore believed in what amounts to an exchange of ions within a prescription, an exchange that could render an incorrect prescription into a correct one.

5. Blackmore believed that the sodium salts of Sodium phosphate and Sodium sulphate, are interrelated with every other mineral. He believed that one of the sodium salts should be included in every prescription to ensure the best results. He believed that the stomach required great amounts of sodium, and that the sodium salts were catalysts, reducing acids in the blood, and balancing the viscosity of the blood by reducing food toxins.

Both Schüssler and Blackmore were victims of their time, in the sense that much of what they wrote was based upon their observations and assumptions, that in the light of more recent knowledge, have been shown to be only partly correct at the very best. There exists therefore, the temptation if not excuse, to dismiss totally, everything that these great men produced, simply on a basis of fact. This propensity of the critics, particularly from within orthodox medicine and the sciences, to dismiss the whole, because a part is found to be defective, the abandoning of the baby along with the dirty bath water, overlooks many important considerations, and amounts to a denial of natural intelligence. The fact that both the methods of Schüssler and Blackmore have survived over such an extensive period of time, is enough to demonstrate that the recipients of such treatments have found them to be effective. If there were minor errors in some of the assumptions that Schüssler and Blackmore drew in an attempt to explain their methods, then these should be forgiven, in favour of the fact that the bulk of their observations, have indeed been proven to be correct.

More changes from the author

In 1978 the author introduced a new method of prescribing, that he had established after twelve years of clinical prescribing and observation. The method was based on an hypothesis for the action of the salts, that whilst incorporating most of what Schüssler and Blackmore had established, also embraced the findings derived from the author's own clinical and hospital research, plus the more recent findings of medical research.

The author had clinically established that the low pharmacological doses of Blackmore, seemed to retain all the attributes of the homœopathically prepared salts, but in addition were capable of producing a more consistent and lasting result. They also possessed the potential to be efficacious for a far wider range of acute and chronic illnesses, thus increasing greatly their scope for application beyond that of the homœopathically prepared salts. This improvement in performance also has to do with Blackmore's principle of prescribing for secondary deficiencies along with the primary deficiency.

Twelve to Ten

The complement of minerals prescribed by the author has been reduced to ten, by incorporating Schüssler's deletion of Calcium sulphate and Blackmore's deletion of Sodium chloride.

As stated previously, Schüssler abandoned calcium sulphate, preferring to use silica and sodium phosphate; and Blackmore dropped sodium chloride, preferring to use sodium phosphate and potassium chloride. The author's experience has been congruent with both Schüssler's and Blackmore's, with regard to both calcium sulphate and sodium chloride, resulting in the use of ten salts rather than eleven or twelve

Regardless of the comparative worth of the homœopathic or the low pharmacological dose, they both unfortunately fall down when it comes to prescribing. The symptomatology in each case (because Blackmore took his symptomatology directly from Schüssler) is overly complicated, confusing and at times, contradictory. This situation has undoubtedly led to incorrect prescribing, followed by poor results, leading ultimately to incorrect conclusions being drawn regarding the worth of either method. The ambiguity of the prescribing indications and confusion generated, even for a practitioner who tries hard, is such that wrong prescriptions will be made on a regular basis. In examining just this single issue of incorrect prescribing, the author has made these observations:

1. That ascertaining precise deficiencies is difficult.
2. That there is a tendency to either under-prescribe or over-prescribe.
3. That a prescription may fail, even if the major deficiency is correctly determined, if it is accompanied by too few or too many other salts.

Prescribing attitudes; time for a rethink?

It is important to develop the last point a little further, to establish what is actually meant by over and under prescribing, otherwise why not resolve the problem, by simply administering all the salts together at the one time? The situation where a prescription is suddenly made effective, because a previously overlooked salt is added, is quite straightforward and easy to understand; but where a non-indicated salt is removed from an otherwise correct prescription and the patient begins to improve, is another matter altogether.

It has been an attitude of *alternative* practitioners in particular, to view a prescription that contains medicaments beyond those that are actually called for at the time, as being of no consequence. The principle being; that as the additional item/s are to be found naturally within the body anyway, then the body will somehow sort it out for itself. Well in practice, it doesn't seem work out like that. Perhaps there is a difference then, between the way the organism processes the countless simple and complex molecules, that occur naturally in the food we eat, and those same nutrients if they are presented in an isolated form. It is logical to assume that as the body has developed recognition and absorption mechanisms and pathways, for the various nutrients through evolution, it expects to be presented with them in the form, amount and combination that it can recognise; if on the other hand, we choose to bypass nature, then we cannot expect the body to behave in exactly the same way - regardless of whether those nutrients are naturally occurring or not. When ill, the body seems to develop, and thankfully display, a specificity for the nutrients that it needs to correct the problem. We must not overlook the fact that usually those deficiencies have arisen over a long period of time, with the body working through its natural intelligence to make do with less and less, then robbing a less important function to fuel a more important one, and then finally, and only where the opportunity exists, to cast an available nutrient into the role of one that is missing or is in short supply. Shrapnel therapy has no place in scientific medicine! The general fertilizer approach to nutrients may only have some place when taken on a daily basis as a food supplement as a form of nutritional insurance and in low dose.

With regard to the mineral salts and specificity within a prescription, the author observed that in the majority of instances the non-indicated salt fell into one of two classes: it was either a salt of a cation family that had already been accommodated in the prescription (*Potassium, Sodium*, or *Calcium* family); or, where two sulphates had been included in the prescription (Potassium *sulphate*, Calcium *sulphate*, or Sodium *sulphate*). It is not to be expected that this is a principle that need be applied, or be seen to work in every single case. There will be those patients who respond regardless of whatever errors exist in the prescription. It is necessary though, to be aware of these principles, if the practitioner is attempting to produce a consistently good result and at the same time develop a finer understanding of his therapy.

Turning negatives into positives

The author also clinically established that the physiological role of the "anion" is equal, and in some cases, more important than that of the "cation". He established that the body, in a state of deficiency, has a specificity for a particular cation/anion pair, and that therefore, even if the correct cation is administered, it will not be utilised until the correct anion is offered along with it and at the same time. He also established that even the primary deficiency symptoms, can just as easily be that of an anion, as that of a cation. The author concluded therefore, that mineral preparations catering only for the cation, often by combining ligands that are physiologically useless, not only fail to produce a lasting result, but can actually do harm due to their high cation dose and the resulting disturbance to electrical neutrality. These conditions can set the stage for toxic levels of a cation being dumped into compartments or organelles due to the forced bypassing of normal cellular controls and the rebound excretion or tying-up of other cations and anions, as the body struggles to regain neutrality.

Synergistic relationships

The author also observed that not only are the minerals synergistic with each other, as proposed by Blackmore, but they are also synergistic with many other nutrients; so much so, that deficiency symptoms that are quite often ascribed to other nutrients (such as vitamins or trace elements), are in fact brought about by a primary macro-mineral deficiency, the other nutrient deficiency being merely a secondary manifestation.

An outline of the possibilities that can arise as a result of prescribing minerals in large therapeutic doses, or in the wrong form, is as follows:

1. A deficiency may be corrected and the result maintained.
2. A deficiency may be temporarily corrected or balanced but not maintained in the longer-term.
3. A cation deficiency may be corrected at the expense of a new cation deficiency.
4. A cation deficiency may be corrected at the expense of a new anion deficiency.

It also follows that the above situation can be further complicated by any combination of these events. These events are also not only going to be determined by what can be known about the patient before the practitioner prescribes; but also the completely unknown and incalculable aspects of the individual patient's own genetically determined and acquired, biochemical imprint and the manner in which this may interact with the prescribed therapy.

The author concludes therefore that the actual salts of Schüssler and Blackmore, are in fact the only legitimate way of correcting mineral deficiencies, as they are physiologically useful forms of mineral salts, natural to the earth and natural to the food-chain.

For the most part, mineral deficiencies represent the lowest possible common-denominator to disease

Chapter three

The physiological role of minerals

Because of their ubiquitous nature, the important place that the mineral elements occupy on our earth and in the biosphere generally, is almost always taken for granted. They are just there and what's more they are expected to be there! Unfortunately, this is an assumption based upon error. When viewed from a different perspective, it is very difficult to understand how these elements, that can be shown to have played such a vital role in the creation and maintenance of life over the æons, can be so much disregarded. The truth is that even the slightest imbalance of some of these mineral elements, could bring with it pressures that could lead to an absolute catastrophe for all life on earth

Evolution has conferred priority status to the mineral nutrients

The early earth and its atmosphere

To put the importance of the mineral elements into perspective, it is necessary to briefly study the beginnings of the earth itself. The age of the earth has been estimated to be between 4.5 and 4.7 billion years. It is now generally accepted that the early earth began as a waterless mass of rock with no atmosphere, the original gasses having been blown away as the solar system and our sun settled down into some sort of order. Due to the pressure of the earth's own mass and the intense radioactivity trapped in the rock as the result of its fiery birth, the earth began to heat up, melting its interior. The heavy iron material sank to form the core, whilst the lighter silicates (silicon and oxygen) rose to the surface and formed the early crust. More than ninety percent of the molten earth consisted of the elements, iron, oxygen, silicon, magnesium and sulphur. As the earth cooled there was a geochemical separation of the elements, with elements separating according to chemical affinity. An iron sulphide core was formed with a magnesium silicate mantle. With further cooling, the crust of the earth was formed consisting of silicates and metals less easily reduced than iron. During this process dissolved materials such as nitrogen and water were extruded, leading to the formation of the atmosphere and the oceans.

The early secondary atmosphere is now thought to have been made up of carbon dioxide, hydrogen, helium, methane and ammonia, and was therefore chemically reducing, containing no free oxygen or ozone.

Intense radiation produces the building blocks for life

Through the bond-severing energy of intense unfiltered ultraviolet radiation, electrical storms, and a level of nuclear energy within the earth's crust (15% of U235) that was capable of spontaneous outbursts of nuclear fission, the first building blocks of life were formed. The non-metalic elements of hydrogen, carbon, nitrogen, oxygen, phosphorous and sulphur, with their ability to form covalent compounds, represented the basic building blocks for amino acids, porphyrins, carbohydrates, proteins, lipids and nucleic acids. This atmosphere provided the *soup* from which the first, life-potential, organic compounds were formed. It took over one billion years after the formation of the earth, for the first form of life (bacteria) to appear, 3.5 billion years ago.

The first earthly pollution crisis

Some 1.8 to 2.5 billion years ago, the atmosphere began to change, as ærobic photosynthesizers like the blue-green algæ of today, began to liberate large quantities of free oxygen. This change of atmosphere, from anoxic to oxygenic, placed a tremendous strain on anærobic life to adapt or become extinct. Primitive cells developed the enzymes, catalase and peroxidase, with hæm cofactors, to destroy peroxide, and an iron or manganese based enzyme, equivalent to today's superoxide dismutase, to convert the highly reactive superoxide to peroxide and oxygen.

The incorporation of mineral elements into the life process

During this evolutionary process metal and non-metal ions such as iron, magnesium, sodium, potassium, calcium, phosphate, sulphate and chloride, began to be incorporated into primitive cells, from the seawater and ocean sediments. These elements along with lesser amounts of the important trace elements and toxic heavy metals, were released to the environment as a result of atmospheric and chemical weathering of the rocks or were directly extruded from the earth's interior. Sea, estuary and lagoon water contained significant amounts of some minerals, due to their solubility, while high concentrations of others were to be found only in the sediment beds. Almost certainly, the most significant incorporation of inorganic metallic ions into the life process (iron, magnesium, copper and zinc), was when the appearance of the colourless porphyrin molecule established the basis for all plant and animal life as we know it. By the binding of iron into the porphyrin ring, the molecule hæm is formed, which represents the oxygen bearing portion of the more complex structure hæmoglobin, and therefore the foundation for all red blooded animal life on earth. Similarly by the incorporation of magnesium as opposed to iron, the chlorophylls are formed and thus the basis for all green photosynthetic plant life on earth.

Minerals paved the way for the development of complex organic molecules

An interesting aspect to contemplate out of all this seemingly hit and miss development of life on earth, is that it was only very much later in the evolutionary process, after fatty acids had formed lipids, hexose rings had formed carbohydrates, and the porphyrin molecule had incorporated such metals as iron and magnesium; that the first phospholipids, glycolipids, hormones and vitamins appeared.

The mineral elements can therefore be shown to have not only been involved in the very genesis of life, but to have also through their ongoing incorporation, allowed life to express itself in the ways that we have learned to recognise and expect.

Minerals allow us to think, move and grow

Minerals have allowed the development of a central nervous system, a skeleton to bear and transport our package of organs and parts across the earth, the ability to be able to replicate ourselves, as a whole or to repair damage cell by cell; and as enzyme activators, to efficiently build-up and break-down complex molecules at a pace that is nothing short of amazing.

Nutrient composition of the human body

Approximate nutrient composition of the human body in grams, based on a healthy 70Kg (154lb) male.

Nutrient	Grams
Water	41,400
Fat	12,600
Protein	12,600
Carbohydrate	300
Minerals	2,264

The criteria for essentiality

The mineral component of the human body accounts for about 2.5kg of the total weight. The mineral elements are basically divided into two groups; those that are essential for life, and those where essentiality has not been established. The essential group consists of those metal and non-metal elements that appear and are required in macro (>50ppm) amounts, and those that appear and are required in micro (<50ppm) or trace amounts. They are called *macronutrients* and *micronutrients* respectively (see page 25). Essentiality is considered to be established where:

1. There is a demonstrable improvement in the health and growth of a test subject upon the addition of the mineral to a deficient diet.

2. The removal of the element from the diet containing adequate amounts of all other dietary essentials results in clear-cut evidence of deficiency symptoms.

3. A low intake can be correlated with subnormal levels of the element which is influenced by hormones or other substances is considered evidence of a biological role. The presence of a reserve, or pool, of an element which is influenced by hormones or other substances is considered further evidence of a biological role.

The various roles

Although the essential macro and micronutrient minerals enter into thousands of individual biochemical functions, their basic roles can be categorised according to the list below. It is interesting to note that some elements fulfil many functions and therefore fall across two or more categories:

1. *The Structural Role.* As constituents of bone, tooth, connective tissue and cell membrane. As stabilisers of cell colloidal emulsions. (Eg., Calcium, Phosphate, Sulphate, Magnesium, Fluoride, Silicon, Barium and Strontium).

2. *The Electrochemical Role.* As regulators in osmotic and acid-base balance. As stabilisers of cell membrane electrical gradients.
Acid (pH<7): Phosphorus, Sulphur, Chlorine.
Base (pH>7): Magnesium, Calcium, Potassium, Sodium.

3. *The Metabolic and Catalytic Role.* As enzyme activators and stabilisers, affecting most metabolic pathways and cellular function. (Eg., Calcium, Phosphate, Potassium, Sulphate, Sodium, Chloride, Magnesium, Iron, Zinc, Manganese, Selenium, Copper, Vanadium, Molybdenum, Cobalt, Fluoride).

4. *The Miscellaneous Role.* As determinators of simple cation-anion bonding. As determinators of more complex molecules, such as complexes, chelates and hormones. (Eg., Chloride, Iron, Zinc, Selenium, Copper, Iodide, Vanadium, Bromide, Cadmium, Boron).

Schüssler and others correctly identified the major mineral nutrients and their roles, up to one hundred years before modern medical science

In chapter one we learned how, Dr. Schüssler of Oldenburg, Germany, in 1873, established that the mineral content of the human body primarily consisted of twelve salts and that the individual organs and parts of the body contained either a different complement, or a different apportionment of these salts. Although Schüssler's list of salts was incomplete, with a number of essential trace elements being discovered after his time, it is interesting to note that Schüssler correctly identified all of the macronutrient elements and attached a role and essentiality to them that does not differ greatly from the one determined by present day biochemists. Essentiality of the macronutrient magnesium was not officially established until 1950, while the micronutrients, silicon and fluorine, were not classified until 1972. It is also interesting to note that although Schüssler overlooked zinc, selenium, manganese, copper, iodine, molybdenum, cobalt and chromium, he correctly identified the presence and physiological necessity for fluorine and silicon, which occur in the body in even less amounts. Why Schüssler should have bypassed these other essential trace elements, we shall never know (although it probably had more to do with the crude methods of analysis in operation at that time than anything else), as the specificity and need for zinc for instance, is scientifically indisputable, with it entering into as many as 100 different catalytic reactions. What can be clinically demonstrated though, is that although these trace elements have been shown to be essential, in the disease state, it is still the basic salts of Schüssler that are almost always the most strongly indicated elements. Maybe part of the answer lies in the fact that where enzyme catalysis is concerned, the enzyme's specificity for a particular activator, is not quite as specific as it might first appear. The enzyme NAD kinase for instance can be activated by either the Schüssler macronutrient magnesium (Mg^{++}) or the trace element manganese (Mn^{++}). As we shall see later in this chapter, not only will magnesium activate this enzyme, but it can be demonstrated that it is a more efficient and safer activator than manganese.

Why did Schüssler overlook some essential trace elements, while identifying others?

Classification of the Mineral Elements in the Human.

Classification	Elements	Percent of body weight
Macronutrient elements essential for human nutrition (> 0.005% body weight or 50 ppm).	Calcium	1.5-2.2
	Phosphorus	0.8-1.2
	Potassium	0.35
	Sulphur	0.25
	Sodium	0.15
	Chlorine	0.15
	Magnesium	0.05
Micronutrient elements essential for human nutrition (< 0.005% body weight or 50 ppm).	Iron	0.004
	Zinc	0.002
	Selenium	0.0003
	Manganese	0.0002
	Copper	0.00015
	Iodine	0.00004
	Molybdenum	
	Cobalt	
	Chromium	
	Fluorine	
	Silicon	
	Vanadium	
	Nickel	
	Tin	
Elements for which essentiality has not yet been established, although there is evidence of their participation in certain biological reactions.	Barium	
	Arsenic	
	Bromine	
	Strontium	
	Cadmium	
Elements found in the body for which no metabolic role has been established.	Gold	
	Silver	
	Aluminium	
	Mercury	
	Bismuth	
	Gallium	
	Lead	
	Antimony	
	Boron	
	Lithium	
	+ 20 others	

The metal and nonmetal elements that go to make up the salts of Schüssler

The essential mineral elements and their corresponding salts.

Macronutrients		Salts
Sodium	Calcium	Sodium phosphate
Phosphate	Magnesium	Sodium sulphate
Sulphate	Potassium	Sodium chloride
Chloride		Potassium phosphate
		Potassium sulphate
		Potassium chloride
		Magnesium phosphate
		Calcium phosphate
		Calcium sulphate
Micronutrients		**Salts**
Iron	Fluoride	Calcium fluoride
Silicon		Iron phosphate
		Silicon dioxide

Authorities still deny that mineral deficiencies are widespread in the developed societies

That Schüssler was able to correctly identify the macronutrient mineral elements and establish their basic physiological function, is one thing, but to then extrapolate this information in support of the deficiency theory to disease, is another matter altogether. Most authorities to this day lend little support for the concept that macromineral deficiencies are widespread in our society. In spite of evidence to the contrary, the average Western diet is considered to be replete in not only the macromineral elements but also the microminerals as well. The concept then, that macromineral deficiencies *do* exist and that they exist on a wide scale; and that moreover, these deficiencies are directly or indirectly responsible for most of our ills, seems even more ridiculous. Ridiculous and all as that notion may first appear, there are compelling reasons why the aspect of widespread deficiencies should be given further consideration.

Minerals are now seen as the poorer cousins to vitamins and other nutrients

Because of their ubiquitousness, minerals have been seen as the nutritional poorer cousins to most other essential nutrients. The fact that the macro and micro mineral elements are essential to life, often orchestrating the production and utilisation of other nutrients that are in turn, given greater prominence and credence, is indicative of the myopia that pervades much of today's high-tech society. It can be demonstrated that minerals generally share an interrelationship with every other nutrient in the body, in many instances this role is dominant, while in other instances, it is cooperative. The massive daily losses of each of the macronutrient elements (an average of just over 1,500mg of each one, each day) through urine, bile, sweat and fæces as a result of normal metabolic activity, should also serve to demonstrate their physiological necessity and how easy it would be for a deficiency to occur if those losses were not made good.

Daily macromineral losses

Examples of daily macromineral losses.

Mineral	Daily losses
Calcium	800-1000mg/day
Phosphate	1400mg/day
Potassium	1955mg/day
Sulphate	850mg/day
Sodium	1724mg/day
Chloride	3600-6000mg/day
Magnesium	330mg/day

How are deficiencies established?

These total daily losses amounting to more than 7000mg, must be replaced on a daily basis, if status quo is to be maintained. Even if the diet is replete, there are still reasons which ensure that further losses will occur. Some of these reasons can be outlined as follows:

1. Genetically acquired metabolic defects, usually occurring at a cell enzyme level.

2. Kidney losses through inefficient conservation, or the use of diuretics. The use of diuretics does not have to be confined to the medically prescribed category, but also includes the social diuretics of tea, coffee and alcohol. Many herbal teas and coffee substitutes, also have a strong diuretic action.

3. Reduced absorption efficiency due to lowered gastric, autonomic, hepatic and pancreatic functions. These losses in efficiency can be caused or aggravated through the consumption of food and drink that is too cold or too hot, spices, alcohol and tobacco; resulting in reduced food breakdown, malabsorption, formation of fatty soaps and peristaltic irregularity.

4. Mineral deficiencies themselves, that create their own compounding effect, by further reducing the body's ability to efficiently absorb and utilise the mineral content of food and drink.

5. Physical and mental stress. As either a cause in themselves and/or as an aggravating or multiplying factor to another cause.

6. Dietary deficiencies due to modern agricultural practices, food storage and processing. This involves the use of chemicals (pesticides and fertilisers), cultivation (monoculture) and overcropping in agriculture, food preservation (chemicals, gases, pressure cooking, freeze drying, refrigeration and irradiation), transport over long distances and the processing of food in the factory, restaurant and home, which may incur further losses.

The last point raises the proposition that deficiencies can be established or compounded by already deficient food, a factor which is today still vehemently denied by commercial agriculturalists, the food processing industry, government health departments and most orthodox nutritionists.

Agricultural losses

Mineral losses in crops grown using standard agricultural practices during the 1970s.

U.S.A. Department of Agriculture Report
Results of four year study of 1,000 crop samples
from farms in eleven midwestern States

Declines In Food Mineral Levels With Standard
Agricultural Practices

Sodium 55%	Iron 26%	Phosphorus 8%
Potassium 28%	Copper 68%	
Calcium 41%	Zinc 10%	
Magnesium 22%	Manganese 34%	

The table above demonstrates from a reliable and conservative source (the US Department of Agriculture), the fact that food losses of macromineral elements in food can and do occur and that there is a case for supplementation. The study involved a four year survey of a group of farms, in the food-basket of the United States, employing standard agricultural practices, and growing the same crops every year. The percentage declines over the four year period, whilst dramatically illustrating the before and after situation during that isolated time, in no way provides us with an original point of reference. The correct (normal) concentrations of minerals in the crops cannot be inferred, but declines such as these, strongly suggest that mineral depletion in crops has been continuing for some time.

The US Department of Agriculture in their report #2 on human nutrition, also claimed that 10% to 90% of the health care costs as they relate to human disease, could be prevented with adequate nutrition.

In time do we all become deficient?

If mineral deficiencies can be acquired from the reasons outlined previously, then it is not difficult to imagine that every man, woman and child, is going to be subject to at least one and probably a combination of these reasons, and that given time deficiency states will occur. Obviously deficiencies are not established overnight and nor are the illnesses that those deficiencies produce.

What emerges first, are vague symptoms and signs that are usually ignored by the person concerned, or if help is sought, never recognised for what they really are. The obscure is usually sought at the expense of the obvious! The notion that these simple, easily acquired deficiencies, can result in illnesses that are not presently recognised as being a deficiency state, is difficult for some people to accept. Much better to comply with the traditional disease model, and feel safe in maintaining status quo as we know it.

The form of the mineral determines its effect

The next essential aspect deserving of consideration is the form in which the minerals should be administered in order to correct deficiencies. Schüssler, by default, automatically determined the form that the minerals should take at the time that he determined their need. It logically follows that the various elements that go to make up the body as a whole and more specifically, it's individual organs and parts, are the physiologically preferred forms. If we are going to be serious about replacing deficiencies, then commonsense dictates that we prescribe only those forms that the body has a proven predilection for. This predilection, as we shall see is for very good reason, based as it is upon the laws of physical chemistry and physiology.

The common physiological forms

The common physiological forms of the metal and nonmetal elements.

Metals

Element	Physiological form
Sodium	Na^+
Magnesium	Mg^{++}
Potassium	K^+
Calcium	Ca^{++}
Iron	Fe^{++}, Fe^{+++}

Nonmetals

Element	Physiological form
Phosphorus	PO_4^{3-}, HPO_4^{2-}, $H_2PO_4^-$ Covalent P
Sulphur	SO_4^{2-}, Covalent S
Chlorine	Cl^-
Iodine	I^-
Fluorine	F^-
Carbon	HCO_3^-, Covalent C
Nitrogen	NO_3^-, Covalent N

Mineral distribution in the body is heterogeneous

The physiological forms need to be considered in relation to their distribution throughout the body. This distribution varies considerably according to the three basic physiological compartments of, plasma, interstitial fluid. and intracellular fluid.

The existence and concentration of the various metal and non-metal ions determines that the proper function of these compartments is maintained, with function being compromised by any sudden or prolonged deviation from normal concentration.

The three basic physiological compartments.

Ion distribution in the physiological compartments of the body

1. *Plasma.* The major cation in this compartment is Na^+, and the major anion is Cl^-. Both are small, fast moving and easily dissociated ions. Their major action is to provide an osmotically active pool of electrolytes to maintain fluid balance. The less concentrated ions are not considered to exert any significant physiological effect and are generally regarded as being in transit from one organ to another. There is also a concentration of 7g per 100ml of protein in plasma

2. *Interstitial fluid* (serum and urine). This compartment is essentially the same as for plasma, except that the protein fraction is smaller due to the confinement of the plasma protein to the vascular pool. Urine is included in this compartment although conservation mechanisms in the kidney will alter the final electrolyte concentration and composition depending on body need.

3. *Intracellular fluid.* It can easily be seen that there are major changes in the concentration of the major ions when intracellular fluid is compared with extracellular fluid. The predominant cations are, K^+, Mg^{++}, and the major anions are, HPO_4^{2-}, $H_2PO_4^-$, and SO_4^{2-}.

Distribution of body water

The distribution of body water in the human.

Distribution	Volume (litres)	Percent of body water
Total body water (TBW)	42	60
Intracellular fluid (ICF)	26.5	38
Extracellular fluid (ECF)	15.5	22
Interstitial fluid	12	17
Inravascular fluid	3.5	5

As can be seen from the table above, body water is distributed heterogeneously through the various compartments of the body and so too are the various electrolytes.

Special affinities exist between ions

Special affinities have been shown to exist between specific cations and anions, so that many occur in an associated state in biological fluids (eg., Mg^{++} and PO_4^{2-}; Ca^{++} and PO_4^{2-}). The mineral distribution within cells is rarely homogeneous, as there are preferential concentrations in many organelles, such as mitochondria and the sarcoplasmic reticulum of muscle. Calcium and magnesium occur in association with phosphate in these situations in such high concentrations that it is thought that they are laid down in internal membranes in crystalline form.

Specificity for a single metal cation by an anion, or other complexing agent is rare, what occurs is a relative affinity between cations and anions, depending upon the actual groups considered. This association is not accidental, but rather to fulfil a specific physiological requirement. The Lewis acid-Lewis base association principle of inorganic chemistry, allows us to understand and predict why certain cations and anions have a predilection for each other.

Concentration of ions according to plasma, interstitial fluid and intracellular fluid

Concentrations of the principle anions and cations in plasma, interstitial fluid and intracellular fluid (mmol/l)

	Plasma	Interstitial fluid	Intracellular fluid
Cations			
Sodium	142	145	10
Potassium	4	4	160
Calcium	2	1	1
Magnesium	1	1	13
Anions			
Chloride	101	114	3
Bicarbonate	27	31	10
Phosphate (HPO_4^{2-})	1	1	50
Sulphate (SO_4^{2-})	0.5	0.5	10
Organic anions	6	7	
Protein	2	1-<0.1	8

Classification of acids and bases according to Lewis

Classification of acids and bases according to the Lewis acid-Lewis Base association concept of inorganic chemistry.

Hard	Borderline	Soft
Acids		
H^+, Li^+, Na^+, K^+	Fe^{2+}, Co^{2+}, Ni^{2+}	Cu^+, Ag^+, Au^+, Tl^+
Be^{2+}, Mg^{2+}, Ca^{2+}, Sr^{2+}	Cu^{2+}, Zn^{2+}, Pb^{2+}	Hg^{2+}, Hg_2^{2+}, Pd^{2+}
Mn^{2+}, Al^{3+}, Sc^{3+}, Ga^{3+}	Sn^{2+}, Sb^{2+}, Bi^{3+}	Pt^{4+}, Tl^{3+}, Pt^{2+}
In^{3+}, La^{3+}, Gd^{3+}, Lu^{3+}		
Cr^{3+}, Co^{3+}, Fe^{3+}, Si^{4+}		
Ti^{4+}, Sn^{4+}, WO^{4+}, Vo^{2+}		
Bases		
H_2O, OH^-, F^-, Cl^-	$C_6H_5NH_2$, C_5H_5N	R_2S, RS^-, I^-
$CH_3CO_2^-$, PO_4^{3-}, SO_4^{2-}	N_3^-, Br^-, NO_2^-	SCN^-, $S_2O_3^{2-}$
CO_3^{2-}, ClO_4^-, NO_3^-	SO_3^{2-}, N_2	R_3P, $(RO)_3P$, R_3As
ROH, R_2O, NH_3		CN^-, RNC, CO
RNH_2, N_2H_4		H^-, R^-, C_2H_4

According to the Lewis principle, ions are classified as being hard, borderline or soft. Hard acids (small cations, with a high positive charge density and usually not containing unshared pairs of electrons in their valence shell) prefer to associate with hard bases (small anions, with a high negative charge density, and difficult to oxydise). Conversely, soft acids (large cations, with a more diffuse positive charge density and still containing easily excited electrons in their valence shell) prefer to associate with soft bases (large anions, capable of donating electrons easily and much more easily polarised). Through this mechanism a simple mineral salt is formed, with an electrostatic, ionic charge providing the bonding force. The salts of Schüssler are made up of ions (with the exception of Fe^{++}, which is from the borderline class) that come from the hard classification of Lewis.

The chemical viability of the salts of Schüssler is supported by the Lewis theory

Since the ions as determined by Schüssler appear in such high concentrations in the various fluid compartments of the body, we can expect that they will associate according to that which is predicted by the Lewis theory. The Lewis theory also predicts that it is possible for associations to be established that do not represent the biologically preferred forms. When determining physiologically useful combinations there would be no purpose for instance, in the association of Ca and Cl, as although chemically acceptable according the Lewis association principle, it would not be a useful preparation, as the ions naturally distribute into different compartments.

It has been commonly thought that absorption of a mineral was dependent upon its ability to be solubilised and for this reason highly soluble forms are often employed. Minerals on the other hand that are insoluble in water, or even gastric acid, have not been considered to be very efficient and for this reason have been paid scant attention. Some of the salts of Schüssler therefore, would not be commonly seen as pharmacologic, due to their strong bonding properties.

Solubility

Solubility of the inorganic mineral salts.

Water soluble	Gastric acid Soluble	Not soluble in either Water or Gastric acid
Sodium phosphate	Calcium phosphate	Calcium fluoride
Sodium sulphate	Calcium sulphate	Silica
Sodium chloride	Magnesium phosphate	
Potassium phosphate	Iron phosphate	
Potassium sulphate		
Potassium chloride		

Solubility v safety

What the argument for solubility ignores, is other existing absorption mechanisms and the ultimate safety of the preparation. Highly soluble inorganic mineral salts cause an uncontrolled flooding of the absorption sites in the small intestine and are rarely found to be naturally occurring in the food chain. This bypassing of normal cellular controls by the presentation of non-physiological forms, results in an uncontrolled uptake of free ions, thus risking cell damage or death (eg., ferrous sulphate).

Although dissociation of some of the salts of Schüssler and Blackmore does inevitably take place, it is a controlled absorption, due to their cation-anion relationship, with a chemical affinity determined according to the principle of Lewis acid-base relationships and their low dose. Because electrical neutrality of the body must be preserved, the salts are generally absorbed as an associated cation-anion pair; in this regard, many of the salts are known to be synergistic pairs.

Other factors also govern the absorption and safety of these inorganic mineral salts; that of absorption synergists and the presence of an active transport system. While some of the salts are naturally occurring synergistic pairs, they may also, along with others, form complexes with larger molecules as the ligand. Although many free ions will form insoluble compounds, as phytates and oxalates, others form bonds of physiological usefulness, although their mode of action is unknown.

Modes of absorption

The three modes of absorption.

1. *Passive diffusion.* The process by which a substance crosses a membrane from an area of high concentration, to one of a lower concentration. Passive diffusion does not require energy or a carrier.

2. *Carrier facilitated diffusion.*

3. *Carrier facilitated active transport.* The process by which a substance is transported across a cell membrane using energy or a carrier protein specific to that nutrient.

Form v safety

Because the inorganic mineral salts of Schüssler are those that are natural to the earth and to the food chain, the body through evolution has developed mechanisms for their absorption and utilisation. One such mechanism is an active transport system, where the transport of whole molecules is possible. Not only are molecules such as glucose and hæm carried by an active transport system, but there is also an active transport system for each of the inorganic salts, either as dissociated ions, the whole molecule or bound to a transport protein. It appears that the water and gastric acid insoluble minerals of silica and calcium fluoride, can only be transported as the undissociated molecule, by active transport. The very existence of an active transport system for a substance, means that evolution has conferred to that substance, preferred nutrient status. Being a preferred nutrient, means that not only is the nutrient vital to the organism, but that the body is prepared to expend vast amounts of energy in its absorption and conservation.

Some more recent mineral preparations make use of the carrier facilitated active transport principle in order to ensure better absorption. These chelated preparations, which cater only for the cation, by forming bonds with other molecules as the ligand, set the stage for toxic levels of a cation to be dumped into compartments or organelles due to the forced bypassing of normal cellular controls and the rebound excretion or tying-up of others nutrient ions as the body struggles to regain electrical neutrality.

Dose v safety

If it can be accepted that the safety and efficacy of a preparation, has a lot to do with cation-anion relationships and form, then the next logical consideration must surely be that of dose.

The inherent danger of many mineral preparations, is not only that of form, but also that of dose. As stated before, the use of highly soluble mineral salts endangers the body through uncontrolled flooding and diffusion at the absorptive sites, but this situation is further compounded if large pharmacological doses are employed (eg., ferrous sulphate).

The safety of the mineral salts when prepared according to the homœopathic method is not in question, as the dose represents mere micrograms. What could be in question though, is the ability of the homœopathically prepared salts to correct gross deficiencies. If gross deficiencies of the macronutrient minerals can be demonstrated to exist, then the correction of those deficiencies must surely be through doses greater than micrograms. The Blackmore approach of using the salts of Schüssler but in low-dose pharmacological amounts, is perhaps the ideal synthesis. The therapeutic doses employed in the Blackmore system are for the most part, within the range of daily requirement (where established), ranging from 6xH to 260mg per dose, according to the salt concerned.

Homœopathic medicine believes that every substance on earth can be considered as being a potential drug; with each substance being capable of producing either a stimulating (healing), or inhibiting (destructive) effect, according to the form and dose in which it is presented to the body. This principle was established in 1880, and is called the Arndt-Schulz law.

The Arndt-Schulz Law.

The Arndt-Schulz Law

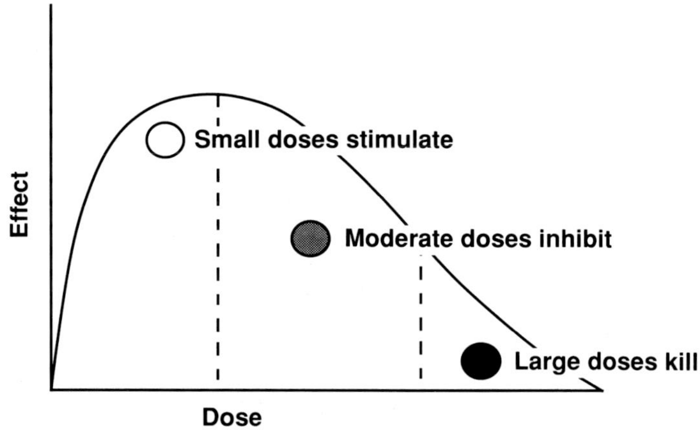

The Arndt-Schulz law of; small doses stimulate, moderate doses inhibit, and large doses kill, can be demonstrated in terms of today's biochemistry, by observing the effects of different cations (or anions) on enzyme catalysis, although the principle can be applied equally to any other substance whether it be a nutrient, or a drug.

Enzyme NAD kinase dose-response curve for activation by Mg^{++} and Mn^{++}

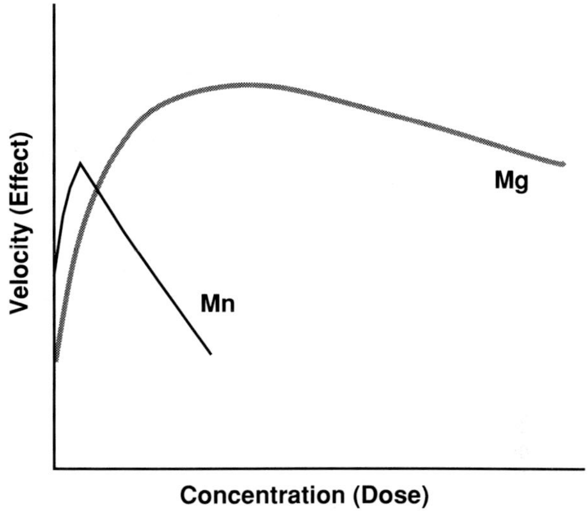

Every nutrient is a potential poison if the dose is too great

At low concentrations, both magnesium and manganese can be seen to activate the enzyme NAD kinase. Manganese however, in keeping with the chemistry of the transition elements and trace elements generally, will activate at very low concentrations, but inhibit at concentrations not substantially higher. This is in accord with nutritional experience, where a small amount of trace element will appreciably improve health, while a larger amount will, in many cases, cause a poisoning. Magnesium on the other hand, is far safer, as while it also activates at low concentrations, it shows an extended plateau over a considerable range of concentration, demonstrating that a variation in concentration will not result in an appreciable alteration of enzyme activity. In larger doses though, it will still poison the enzyme, showing that even simple ions, which are essential at low concentrations, are by no means safe in the high dose ranges.

The reason why both Mg^{++} and Mn^{++} activate the same enzyme, is because they are both approximately the same size and both carry a double positive charge. The electron orbital levels of magnesium however, are better sited for temporary electron transfer and result in magnesium being a better and safer activator for NAD kinase.

It can be seen, that beyond a certain concentration, enzyme catalysis is retarded, with the enzyme actually being poisoned, by the very same substance, that at a lesser concentration was considered to be a nutrient.

The inorganic mineral salts of Schüssler and Blackmore can therefore be considered as: *Physiologically the most preferred forms, biochemically the most active, and considering their low dose; the safest.*

Chapter four

The individual mineral salts

Introductory notes

Some helpful information before reading on

1. The minerals discussed are the original twelve of Schüssler, less Blackmore's deletion of sodium chloride (nat mur), thus a new total of eleven. As covered in chapter two, Schüssler, prior to his death, abandoned calcium sulphate, in preference for the salts of silica and sodium phosphate (see "Postscript to a salt of confusion", on page 62) and Blackmore deleted sodium chloride, but retained Schüssler's calcium sulphate. The "Getting started quickly" system of prescribing (see page 106) though, embraces both Schüssler's and Blackmore's deletions, thus reducing the original twelve salts to only ten.

2. A wide range of sources has been accessed to collate the information provided for each of the salts. The information has been sourced from old Homœopathic texts, texts on Schüssler's "Biochemistry", the most recent texts on physiology, biochemistry and nutrition; and the author's own knowledge and clinical experience.

3. As previously mentioned in both the "History" and "Physiology" chapters; Hahnemann, Hering, Grauvogl, Schüssler, Blackmore and others, dating as far back as the early 1800's, had begun to establish the physiological necessity and the pathogenetic effects of the various mineral elements. The major physiological role and deficiency indications for all the macromineral elements and the trace elements of iron, silicon and fluorine, were clearly and elegantly established well over 100 years ago. It has only been in much more recent times that modern science has *rediscovered* some of those very same indications (silicon and fluorine 1972).

4. Despite the overwhelming scientific, clinical and even epidemiological evidence for including information on some of the other essential trace and ultratrace elements that were overlooked by Schüssler, or discovered following his time, the author has chosen, at this point in time anyway, to remain true to the original salts of Schüssler.

5. the layout for each salt follows the format of:

(a) A brief overview.

(b) Biochemical notes.

(c) Clinical indications, based on body systems and parts.

6. Please do not attempt to prescribe until you have at least read the "Prescribing rules", on page 111. Preferably the entire chapters of "Getting started quickly" and "Management and prescribing procedures" should be studied in conjunction with the information that follows in this chapter.

7. For the quickest and most concise prescribing information always refer first to the "Mineral master chart" on pages 112-3.

Preparations and dosages

8. The particular preparation of mineral salts referred to in this chapter and as prescribed by the author, are the Blackmores Ltd (of 23 Roseberry Street, Balgowlah, New South Wales, Australia 2093), practitioner range of Celloid® mineral tablets.

These minerals are presented as the mono mineral (eleven in number), and also in a range of commonly occurring combinations. The use of combination formulas allows for the prescribing of fewer tablets, which is of particular benefit when treating the chronically ill, where a greater number of minerals will be taken over a greater period of time.

Unit dosages

The unit dose for each of the minerals is as follows:

Sodium phosphate	260mg
Sodium sulphate	190mg
Potassium phosphate	33mg
Potassium sulphate	33mg
Potassium chloride	65mg
Calcium phosphate	130mg
Calcium sulphate	8mg
Calcium fluoride	6xH
Magnesium phosphate	65mg
Iron phosphate	15mg
Silica	33mg

The minerals are prepared in a base of lactose, which has always been the traditional medium for medicines of this nature, and processed according to a method, that was developed by the late Dr. Maurice Blackmore in 1938 (see pages 15-16).

There are also a number of other pharmaceutical companies throughout the world who manufacture and supply practitioners with the original Schüssler tissue salt preparations. These are mixed according to traditional homœopathic law, and are usually prescribed in the 6x potency or dilution. The diluent medium in this case is usually either lactose or alcohol.

There is no reason to believe that these traditional homœopathic preparations do not work, because that certainly isn't the case, but it's been the author's experience to find that whilst at times the results achieved could be considered spectacular, they are also inconsistent. The explanation for this patchiness probably has to do with the fact that if gross mineral deficiencies can be demonstrated to exist, then in those instances, the deficiencies are not going to be remedied by dilutions in the order of one part in one million (see chapters one through four).

The prescribing information contained in this chapter is not intended to be used with any form of mineral treatment, other than the mineral salts detailed. The whole rationale for these unique cation-anion relationships with their specific physiological roles and their prescribing indications in consequence of a deficiency, will break-down if other mineral preparations are used in their place. Minerals that cater only for the cation by combining physiologically inappropriate anions, and/or in dosages that are too high are unsuitable and often unsafe.

Sodium phosphate

Role: Structural. Electrochemical. Catalytic.

Memory key: Metabolic acid remover.

Brief prescribing indications: All conditions that result from an incomplete breakdown and elimination of metabolic acid waste from the tissues (lactic and uric acid). Gastric and urinary acidity. Gout. Fibrositis. Degenerative arthritis. Fat intolerance.

Symptoms aggravated by: Changeable weather. Thunderstorms. Open air. Fatty, rich food. Afternoon or evening.

Symptoms improved by: Stable weather.

Tongue indications: Creamy or golden yellow coating at back of tongue or roof of mouth.

Exudate: Golden-yellow or honey coloured serous exudate. Leucorrhoea; scalding.

Iris indications: Acid wash. Stomach zone (hyperchlorhydria). Autonomic wreath, flared and white.

Biochemical notes: Sodium phosphate due to its solubility is not found to any extent in natural mineral deposits. Sodium and phosphate are rather distributed in the body as separate free ions, where they exert a synergistic buffering effect.

Their ability to buffer against a build-up of hydrogen ions and therefore an increase in body fluid acidity represents one of the body's most important mechanisms for maintaining physiological pH.

Sodium is a positively charged, base-forming cation, present in the body in the extracellular fluids (the intravascular fluids within the blood vessels, as well as the intercellular fluids surrounding the cells). About half of the total body sodium is found in these fluids. Under normal conditions, as little as 10% of body sodium is present within the cell, but this is only because it is constantly being pumped out of the cell to maintain its low relationship to potassium (1:10). The remaining sodium is found in the skeleton. About half of this skeletal sodium acts as a reservoir of exchangeable sodium, available to the extracellular fluids when dietary sodium intake is low, or when body losses are high.

A small amount of sodium is absorbed in the stomach, but most is absorbed rapidly from the small intestine. Sodium, as the chloride is absorbed with up to 98% efficiency, due to the chloride ion being a known synergist for the absorption of sodium. Other anions, such as sulphate and phosphate, promote lower absorption of sodium, although if chloride is absent, then these anions will be absorbed along with the sodium to maintain charge balance.

It has been estimated that 90-99% of ingested sodium as the chloride, is excess and therefore destined for excretion in the urine. This regulation of sodium metabolism by the kidney, is controlled by aldosterone.

Normally the amount of sodium in the urine parallels dietary intake, being high when intake is high and low when intake is low. When dietary intake is low, or need is high, the secretion of aldosterone is increased, stimulating the kidney to resorb more sodium. Conversely, when blood sodium level is high, the secretion of aldosterone is reduced and less sodium is retained.

Sodium phosphate

Because there is a limit to the amount of sodium that can be excreted in a certain volume of urine, sodium in the blood and in the extracellular fluid will rise if dietary intake (usually as the chloride) exceeds the kidney's ability to excrete it. When blood sodium rises, the thirst receptors in the hypothalamus react by stimulating the thirst sensation. This results in greater fluid consumption, which then allows the kidney to excrete more sodium along with an increased volume of urine. Blood sodium levels drop, followed by a lessening of thirst.

Sodium as the dominant positively charged ion in the extracellular fluids, accounts for most of the osmotic pressure that prevents water from entering the cell. This pressure balances a similar pressure caused by potassium within the cell. When the balance of sodium to potassium ions lose their normal relationship of 1:10 within the cell and 28:1 outside, water may shift in or out of cells in an endeavour to preserve their relative concentrations. The most common breakdown in this mechanism results when an excess of sodium in the ECF cannot be balanced by available potassium ions. This situation brings about raised intracellular levels of sodium and thus the attraction of water into the cell.

Most Western diets high in animal foods and refined grains and sugar, contain a surplus of the acid-forming mineral elements (chlorine, sulphur and phosphorus). For reasons of both efficiency and safety, the body must maintain pH within the very narrow range of 7.35-7.45. Any deviation from this physiological pH can bring with it cellular enzyme inactivity, cellular starvation and death.

Both sodium and phosphate act as buffers or neutralising agents and are thus capable of raising pH. Phosphate exerts only a minor role in maintaining blood pH, due to its low concentration. Hæmoglobin, plasma proteins and bicarbonate function as the primary buffering agents in the blood.

Sodium phosphate acts as a buffer in intracellular fluid and interstitial fluid (serum and urine) where there is no hæmoglobin, or plasma protein. It is capable of binding two hydrogen ions.

Absorption of sodium phosphate is by active transport and passive diffusion in the small intestine, at an efficiency of between 50-80%.

There is a reservoir of between 30-40% of the total body sodium in the skeleton, where it is bound to the surface of bone as the phosphate.

Sodium phosphate acts as a cholagogue and prevents the crystallisation of cholesterol in the gall bladder.

Sodium phosphate breaks down lactic acid in muscle due to its ability to bind hydrogen ions and prevents sodium urate crystals from precipitating into the joints and periarticular tissues.

All conditions that result from an incomplete breakdown and elimination of metabolic acids call for sodium phosphate. Although a generalised state of acidosis can be produced by a deficiency of sodium phosphate, it will be generally found that individual body systems or specific parts are affected.

Sodium phosphate

The taking of sodium phosphate does not result in a nett conservation of water and the likelihood of producing œdema and hypertension as can be the case with sodium chloride, as excreted phosphate in the urine is usually accompanied by sodium to maintain charge balance. Clinically it will be observed that in the majority of cases there will actually be a nett loss of water, rather than a nett gain.

Clinical indications

Mental/emotional: Apprehensive fear. Imagines on waking that pieces of furniture are people; hears footsteps in the next room. Great mental prostration.

Head and face: Full feeling; dull pressure headache with nausea. Patchy, florid and cyanosed appearance of face.

Eye: Golden-yellow or creamy discharge. Eyelids glued in the morning. Sclera dirty yellow.

ENT: One ear red, hot and associated with gastric acidity. Itching of nose. Offensive odour. Naso-pharyngeal mucus, thick, yellow and offensive. Thick, creamy coating over tonsils and soft palate.

Tongue: Creamy-yellow coating on back of tongue, or roof of mouth, uvula, or tonsils. Sour taste. Blisters on tip of tongue.

Teeth: Children grind teeth during sleep.

Gastrointestinal: Acidity. Sour burning gastric reflux. Pyrosis after meals. Flatulence. Fat intolerance. Stomach ache in children. Oxyuriasis. Itching, burning anus. Sour smelling stools. Cholecystitis. Cholelithiasis. Choledochitis.

Genitourinary: Sterility. Leucorrhœa, sour smelling. Scalding vaginal discharges. Gonorrhœa. Hyperemesis gravidarum. Cystitis. Scalding urine. Urethritis. Scalding of the urethra following ejaculation.

Musculoskeletal: Gout. Degenerative arthritis. Painful joints. Fibrositis of intercostal muscles. Excessive soreness in muscles following use. Burning soreness in muscles of back, neck, shoulders and chest, associated with stress.

Skin: Eczema, with scalding creamy or honey coloured serous exudate. Exudate forms golden coloured crusts. Essential pruritis. Urticaria.

Sodium sulphate

Role: Structural. Electrochemical. Catalytic.

Memory key: Problem fluid remover.

Brief prescribing indications: Conditions that arise from an abnormal distribution, concentration and elimination of body fluids. The detoxification of endogenous and exogenous compounds in the liver and the blood. Œdema; localised or general. Hydræmia. Nausea. Jaundice. Weepy eczema.

Symptoms aggravated by: Hot humid weather. Damp, wet weather. Damp living conditions. Before a storm. Seafoods. By the seaside. Lying on the left side. Tight clothing around the waist or abdomen. Afternoon, evening. Early morning, after midnight. Springtime. Lively music.

Symptoms improved by: Dry warm weather. Changing body position frequently. Open air. Day-time; once up and about. Pressure, rubbing or friction over affected part.

Tongue indications: Clear shiny, œdematous appearance, or greenish-brown. Bitter taste.

Exudate: Thick, ropy, greenish-yellow discharges. Watery vesicles. Serous exudate that forms yellow scales.

Iris indications: Check and compare with symptoms, Skin and Lymphatic zones

Biochemical notes: Although sodium sulphate is abundant in nature, it is not found to any extent in plant foods, as they contain very little sodium.

In human metabolism sodium sulphate plays an important role in maintaining cellular integrity, in the detoxification of substances within the liver and in the regulation of water passing through connective tissue.

Sodium sulphate is readily absorbed in the small intestine by passive diffusion and active transport. Small doses are almost 100% absorbed, with a synergistic action taking place between the sodium and sulphate ions. Small doses of sodium sulphate do not induce catharsis of the bowel, as do large allopathic doses when prescribed as Glauber's salts.

In contrast to sodium chloride, sodium sulphate has a diuretic effect, resulting in a nett loss of water, rather than a gain.

Water passes through capillary walls to the surrounding tissues at the arteriole end of a blood capillary. The volume of water is determined by the hydrostatic (blood) pressure, versus the tissue resistance to the flow. The fluid return at the venous end of the capillary is due primarily to the osmotic pressure of the blood proteins, drawing water back into the venule, where hydrostatic pressure is much lower. If there is any physical impediment to this orderly flow of water due to a breakdown of the capillary wall, a loss of integrity of the intercellular matrix, through which the water must pass, or a blocking of the entry pores back into the venule end of the capillary or associated lymphatic capillary; then œdema will result.

Sodium sulphate

The intercellular matrix or ground substance of connective tissue is made up primarily of sulphated mucopolysaccharide chains. While several mucopolysaccharides, such as hyaluronic acid (lubricating properties, as in synovial fluids surrounding joints) do not contain sulphate as side chains, most others do. These side chains give order, by assuming regular matrix arrays, due to the mutual repulsion of the charged side groups. Sodium, the most predominant cation in the extracellular fluid, stabilises the opposing side chains, thus also assisting in maintaining order and integrity.

Sulphate in combination with sodium, acts to reduce tissue œdema in a number of ways.

1. By maintaining the integrity of the capillary wall, thus preventing greater permeability, which would result in a greater than normal water volume being expressed into the tissue from the blood.

2. By maintaining the matrix of intercellular ground substance in a regular array, by cross-linking adjacent mucopolysaccharide chains. This facilitates the free flow of fluid between the arterial and venous circulation and the lymphatic capillaries, preventing tissue pooling of water.

3. By stabilising and anchoring mucopolysaccharide chains, which may otherwise detach and block the exit pores into the lymphatic and venous returns. Although runaway polysaccharide chains will be ultimately removed by macrophages, the ultimate solution is to sulphate the existing matrix to prevent further detachment.

4. By sufficient cross-linking in tissue to prevent enlarged spaces, or vacuolisation taking place, which can then result in a pooling of water and pitting œdema.

5. By acting as a diuretic.

The body employs a process of sulphation in the detoxification and inactivation of compounds destined for excretion in the urine or bile. Sulphate ions in the liver are used to detoxify alcohol and peptide hormones and to inactivate cholesterol and steroid hormones. Bile salts of potassium and sodium, formed from the sulphation of cholesterol are important fat emulsifiers and stimulants of bile secretion. In the blood a number of sulphur-bearing molecules, such as thiocyanate and the metallothioneins, act as detoxifiers and heavy-metal binders. Sodium sulphate in oral allopathic doses has been demonstrated to inactivate toxic doses of heavy-metals by binding to the metal, forming insoluble sulphates that are then eliminated through its laxative action.

Sodium sulphate

Clinical indications

Mental/emotional: Extreme depression; morbid thoughts, with periods of mania. Suicidal tendency. Restless desire to keep moving. Lively music saddens. Dislikes to speak or be spoken to.

Head: Headache with nausea, emesis or diarrhoea. Vomiting of bile. Headache with violent pulsations or giddiness. Bursting feeling in head with coughing. Concussion; for effects of.

Eye: Yellowness of the conjunctivæ. Burning edges of the lids. Agglutination of the lids in the morning, with photophobia and green pus. Maculæ corneæ.

ENT: Tinnitus. Lightening stitches through ears. Thick yellow mucus from nose. Stuffy dryness and burning in nose. Sore, dry throat or the hawking of salty tasting mucus. Thick, yellow post-nasal mucus.

Tongue: Clear shiny œdematous appearance or greenish-brown colour. Bitter taste.

Teeth: Toothache, better from tobacco smoke, cool air, or from holding cold water in mouth.

Respiratory: Asthma or dyspnœa, worse every change from dry to damp or humid weather. Asthma, develops from chest infection or cold. Cough, with thick ropy, greenish, mucopurulent expectoration. Rattle of mucus in chest. Must hold chest when coughing. Symptoms often worse early morning or awakes at night with attack of asthma. Pulmonary œdema. Pleurisy. Pneumonia.

Gastrointestinal: Nausea. Vomiting of bile or salty tasting water. Liver sore to touch or from jarring. Symptoms worse when lying on left side. Cholelithiasis. Obstinate constipation. Abdomen distended. Cannot bear tight clothing around abdomen. Stabbing pain through liver. Flatulent colic. Diarrhoea; yellow, watery. Dark fæces of great size.

Genitourinary: Bilirubinuria. Mucopurulent urethral discharge. Burning micturition. Polyuria. Diabetes. Greenish scalding discharge from vagina, with external parts inflamed. Prostatic hypertrophy, with mucopurulent discharge. Gonorrhœa. Menses profuse and scalding, often with colic and constipation or morning diarrhoea.

Cardiovascular: Hydræmia. Fullness feeling in chest; seeks fresh air for relief. Cardiac œdema. Dependent œdema. Pitting œdema.

Skin: Vesicular eczema, weepy, itchy and forming yellow scales. Neurodermatitis, itchy vesicles. Angioneurotic œdema. Erysipelas. Fistulous abscess, discharging watery pus. Warts and herpetic blisters on moist areas of body.

Tissues: Œdema, localised or general. Hydræmia

Potassium phosphate

Role: Electrochemical. Catalytic.

Memory key: Nerve power activator.

Brief prescribing indications: Conditions that arise from lowered nervous energy. Physical and mental enervation. Malaise/lethargy. Depression. Lack of drive and motivation. Muscles easily fatigued. Flaccid paralysis. Phobias. Insomnia. Cardiac arrhythmias. Irritability and insomnia.

Symptoms aggravated by: Worry. Stress. Mental and physical exertion. Being alone. Cold air. Cold draughts. Early morning. Nostalgia. Prolonged excitement. Glare, bright or flashing lights. Noise. Upon arising in the morning or after a rest.

Symptoms improved by: Company/excitement; initial effects of. Eating. Changing body position frequently. Covering up; against cold air or draughts. Heat, warmth. Being home. Mental distractions. Movement, gentle and slow. Rest.

Tongue: Dry tongue. (Wakes with excessively dry tongue and mouth). Mustard colour, edges red. Halitosis.

Exudate: Thick, yellow, crusty mucus from nares; often fœtid and bleeding. Salty mucus from throat.

Iris: Nerve arcs and rings (deep).

Pupil: Dilated, hypotonic.

Biochemical notes: Potassium phosphate due to its solubility is not found in nature in its mineral state. It is widely distributed through plant life but animal foods are generally poor sources.

Potassium and phosphate are the dominant intracellular ions and both suffer high daily losses which must be made good.

Potassium phosphate is well absorbed in the small intestine, with an efficiency of between 50-90%. Absorption is directly proportional to dietary intake by what is thought to be passive unregulated diffusion for the potassium ion, while the phosphate ion is absorbed by active transport. Potassium however is a known synergist for phosphate absorption, which may then allow for carrier facilitated diffusion as the whole salt (symport).

Potassium is a base-forming cation, with chemical properties similar to those of sodium. Potassium however, is physiologically unlike sodium in that it is concentrated inside the cell, rather than in the extracellular fluids. A sodium to potassium ratio of 1:10 is maintained within the cell, compared with a ratio of 28:1 outside the cell.

Most potassium exists intracellularly as the free ion, although a small amount may be found in mitochondria. Its high intracellular concentration is maintained by an active transport system that transports sodium out of the cell and potassium in, thus balancing passive leaks down concentration gradients. This active transport system, a membrane bound ATPase enzyme, activated by sodium, magnesium and potassium, is known as the sodium-potassium pump. In this way sodium which inactivates many intracellular enzymes is excluded, while potassium which activates, is ensured a high intracellular concentration.

Potassium phosphate

The kidney is less efficient in conserving or reabsorbing potassium than it is for many other nutrients. Ninety per cent of potassium excretion is regulated by the kidney. Not only is potassium filtered by the glomerulus, but it is both actively absorbed and secreted by the renal tubules. However, the ability of the kidney to correct potassium imbalance is much better in elevated blood levels than in depleted blood levels. While a healthy kidney can excrete quite large potassium excesses, it is less efficient in conservation, resulting in a normal daily loss of about 7% of the circulating blood level, even when the intake of potassium is low.

Because potassium is an intracellular ion, the body's potassium status cannot be adequately determined by assessing blood levels. The level of potassium carried in the blood will only rise; when there is a breakdown of cellular structure, releasing potassium into the blood; the kidney function becomes impaired and too much potassium is conserved; or, there is a dietary excess.

Blood levels of potassium decrease when the rate of protein synthesis or glycogen deposition within the cell increases; in alkalosis, which indicates that potassium is leaving the blood and entering the cell; with persistent diarrhoea or vomiting; some diuretics often used in treating hypertension or œdema; severe protein-kilocalorie malnutrition; surgery and dietary deficiencies.

The proper balance of potassium in both the ICF and ECF is necessary for the maintenance of the nerve cell resting potential. A fall in potassium concentration in the ECF, but not in the ICF, will cause membrane hyperpolarisation, which results in fatigue, lack of response to stimuli, muscle weakness, disturbed cardiac rhythm and flaccid paralysis. A fall of potassium in the ICF, but not in the ECF, will cause membrane depolarisation, resulting in, irritability, insomnia, over-sensitivity, hyperactivity, exaggerated reflexes, and cardiac disorders such as tachycardia and dilatation with gallop rhythm. A fall of potassium in both compartments, will maintain membrane potential, but reduce cell metabolism due to the lowered activity of some enzymes (kinases which require both K and PO) and thus depleted stores of ATP, producing again, symptoms of fatigue, apathy and depression.

In skeletal muscle activity, both potassium and phosphate are known to exert an influence. During activity, potassium ions are released from the muscle into the surrounding interstitial fluid, in order to dilate the arterioles and thus service the muscle with a greater supply of blood.

In cardiac muscle, a lowered intracellular potassium level leads to decreased glycogen synthesis, ventricular arrhythmia, fibrillation, ischæmia and the increased possibility of infarction. This situation can be further exacerbated when cardiac patients are prescribed diuretics as part of their medication.

Potassium phosphate

Potassium activates approximately fifty intracellular enzymes, most of which are inactivated by potassium's antagonist, sodium. These enzymes are required for such functions as, oxidative phosphorylation and glycolysis. Potassium and phosphate have also been implicated in cell replication and division, through their influence with phosphate polymers important for RNA conformation, and subsequent protein synthesis at the ribosomes.

Clinical indications

Mental/emotional: Depression. Poor memory. Lack of concentration. Hypersensitivity to noise and glare. Nostalgia. Weepy. Anxiety, though morbid thoughts. Hysteria. Phobias. Insomnia. Somnambulism. Nightmares. Irritability; starts easily. Unexplained weight loss, through depression. Restlessness. Dislike of being left alone. Slightest labour seems insurmountable task. Desire for pleasant company, or excitement. Globus hystericus. Bulimia. Anorexia nervosa. Lowered pain threshold. No desire to arise in the morning.

Head and face: Vertigo or giddiness when rising suddenly or looking upwards. Occipital, dull headache. Headache, with gone feeling in stomach. Pale sunken face, hollow eyes.

Eye: Excited, staring appearance. Loss of accommodation. Ptosis. Eyelids twitch. Floaters.

ENT: Nerve deafness. Tinnitus. Discharge of ichor from ear, foul smelling. Hypersensitivity to noise. Epistaxis in weak, delicate subjects. Ozæna. Sneezing from slightest exposure. Post-nasal, thick, yellow mucus. Throat dry, desire to swallow. Salty mucus raised from throat. Hoarseness and loss of voice. Fœtid breath.

Tongue: Dry. Wakes with excessively dry tongue. Mustard colour, edges red. Halitosis.

Teeth: Toothache, with gums that bleed easily. Gums spongy, receding and have bright-red seam.

Gastrointestinal: Excessive hunger. Feels better after eating. Nervous "gone" feeling in pit of stomach; feels better after eating. Indigestion or heartburn when depressed. Stomach-ache, from fright or excitement. Flatulence. Swollen, distended abdomen from build-up of gas. Diarrhoea, painless and watery, fœtid odour, from depression or anxiety. Bowel colic, better bending double. Constipation, with dark stools. Tenesmus.

Respiratory: Asthma, brought on by eating. Asthma from depression. Dyspnœa, from slightest exertion. Cough with thick, yellow, salty, fœtid expectoration.

Cardiovascular: Tachycardia. Bradycardia. Arrhythmia. Palpitation, generally following emotional upset or physical exertion.

CNS: Neuralgia from depression. Paresis. Muscles easily fatigued. Flaccid paralysis. Ptosis. Neurasthenia.

Potassium phosphate

Genitourinary: Amenorrhoea (primary or secondary), with depression. Menses irregular, late or scanty, in pale, weepy females. Dark-red, watery, fœtid smelling menstrual flow. Intense sexual desire, or complete loss of. Impotence. Dyspareunia. Enuresis, associated with depression or nervous debility. Polyuria.

Musculoskeletal: Muscles easily fatigued. Flaccid paralysis. Paresis. Muscular stiffness and weakness after rest, but improved by gentle movement.

Tissues: Toothache, with gums that bleed easily. Gums spongy, receding and have bright-red seam. Malignant tumours. Unexplained weight loss, through depression. Pale sunken appearance.

Skin: Eczema, with anxious or depressive subjects. Alopecia areata. Pruritis (essential). Premature ageing of the skin. Fœtid, malignant ulcerations. Watery blebs.

Febrile: Fevers associated with debilitating, wasting diseases.

Potassium sulphate

Role: Structural. Electrochemical. Catalytic.

Memory key: Cell oxygenator.

Brief prescribing indications: Conditions arising from hypoxia. All symptoms that demonstrate abnormal cellular respiration. All conditions that call for oxygen. Third stage of inflammation. Mucopurulent discharges. Pyogenic and fungal infections. Pyrexia. Dry flaky skin.

Symptoms aggravated by: Hot stuffy rooms. Smoky rooms. Springtime. Late afternoon, evening. Hot, humid, or changeable weather. Hot drinks. Heat. Hot air.

Symptoms improved by: Cool, fresh, open air. Stable weather. Dry weather.

Tongue: Yellow, slimy. Taste lost.

Exudate: Yellow-green, slimy, purulent and mucopurulent discharges. Nose/sinuses blocked, but clear watery drip from nares.

Iris: Check and compare with symptoms; Skin and Lymphatic zones. Arcus ischæmia.

Biochemical notes: Potassium sulphate is found in nature as the complex mineral polyhalite

Potassium and sulphate are both predominantly intracellular ions (see also potassium phosphate) that influence the structural integrity of the cell, by being involved in the production and repair of cell coats; the stabilisation of the cytoplasmic matrix; the adhesion of cells to each other; and in particular the oxidative processes in the cytochromes of mitochondria, which produce most of the cellular metabolic energy.

Inorganic sulphate is readily absorbed in small amounts from the small intestine by both active transport and passive diffusion. The potassium ion is thought to be absorbed by passive unregulated diffusion, at an efficiency of about 90%. Sulphur in the organic form is also provided by the sulphur bearing amino acids methionine and cysteine. Inorganic sulphate can also be converted into sulphur amino acids by intestinal bacteria, but only while the sulphate is in the intestine, once the sulphate is absorbed into the blood, sulphate can only be incorporated into polysaccharide and glycoprotein chains.

The combining of the anion sulphate, with the cation, potassium, rather than sodium (see sodium sulphate), changes its sphere of influence, from the extracellular compartment to the intracellular compartment.

Much of the manufacture of sulphated mucopolysaccharides and glycoproteins, takes place in the granular endoplasmic reticulum and Golgi apparatus, organelles within the cell cytoplasm. Here sulphate or carboxyl groups are incorporated into the long chains as an essential part of their structure. Small vesicles then carry the completed products to

Potassium sulphate

the cytoplasm, or to the cell membrane.

The intracellular use of mucopolysaccharides usually involves attachment or complexing with specific proteins; they are then known as glycoproteins, mucins or mucoproteins. The cytoplasmic matrix is believed to be composed of large protein molecules, possibly joined to carbohydrates, mineral salts and other absorbed substances. Potassium is known to be essential to the solubilisation of such protein and sulphate for the correct conformation. After manufacture, they are secreted into the extracellular spaces and often into the blood. These compounds are jelly-like, slippery or sticky, with some providing lubrication, some functioning as flexible intercellular cement, and others as a component of the cell membrane coat. As a component of the intercellular cement, any breakdown will result in poor cellular adhesion and mucoprotein exudations, with epithelial and mucous membranes exhibiting scaling, exudation and desquamation.

Analysis of the cell membrane indicates that it is made up of approximately 5% carbohydrate, which is present as glycolipids or glycoprotein. Most of this is present on the outer surface of the membrane, as the cell coat, or glycocalyx. Present knowledge suggests that the glycocalyx participates in the adhesion of cells, as a protective barrier against pathogenic organisms and as an antigenic determinant, marking the cell coat and serving as a means of cellular identification.

Although most of the glycocalyx is thought to be manufactured in the Golgi apparatus of the cytoplasm, some is believed to be manufactured by enzymes close to the membrane itself, again, both potassium and sulphate are necessary for its production.

The role of potassium sulphate as a cell oxygenator is to do with its involvement in oxidative phosphorylation in the cytochromes of the mitochondria. The salt is involved with the iron containing flavoprotein enzymes such as succinic dehydrogenase and NADH dehydrogenase, which contain sulphate as part of their structure and require potassium for activation. Many other enzymes involved in mitochondrial oxidative phosphorylation, also require potassium. A deficiency of potassium sulphate results in poor oxygen utilisation of the enzyme system and thus the craving for fresh air to increase oxygen concentration at the cellular level (see "Symptoms improved by").

Clinical indications

Mental/emotional: Lack of concentration. Cotton-woolly feeling in head. Confusion, irritability and anxiety of the senile.

Head and face: Headache, dull, worse afternoon/evening, or in warm, stuffy environment. Falling of hair. Dandruff. Scalp moist and sticky. Oily scalp. Painful, sticky, crusty pimples on scalp. Profuse desquamation, frontal, nasal and malar areas. Basal cell carcinoma.

Eye: Yellow-green mucopurulent discharges. Crusts on lids. Cataract.

Tongue: Yellow, slimy. Taste lost.

ENT: Thin, yellow-green discharge or thick pus. Otitis media. Colds with yellow, slimy mucus. Nose blocked with yellow-green discharge. Dry, stuffy, blocked sinuses, often with clear watery discharge. Yellow post-nasal discharge. Throat, dry or hawking of yellow-green mucus.

Potassium sulphate

Gastrointestinal: Fullness in pit of stomach, or colic. Water gathers in mouth. Dread of hot drinks. Abdomen cold to touch. Yellow, slimy, watery diarrhoea. Flatus with sulphurous odour. Itching anus.

Cardiovascular: Palpitations, worse at night or in bed. Pulse, weak or fast.

Respiratory: Bronchial asthma with yellow-green expectoration. Cough worse during evening or in heated room. Rattling of mucus in chest. Rattling of mucus when coughing. Dyspnoea from the slightest exertion. Much sighing and yawning. Bronchitis with yellow-green mucus. Bronchiectasis. Emphysema. Empyema.

Genitourinary: Gonorrhœa. Yellow discharge from vagina. Burning of genitalia. Candidiasis. Menstruation, late and scanty. Prostatic discharges, from deep-seated infection. Deranged sperm, through infection. Cystitis, chronic.

Musculoskeletal: Rheumatic pains that are of a shifting, wandering or flitting nature.

Skin: Eczema, with yellow or watery exudate; with loosely attached crust or an abundance of scales. Skin dry and flaky. Psoriasis. Ichthyosis. Erysipelas. Sycosis barbai. Face dry but hairline greasy. Hair falls. Tinea. Face and scalp oily and sticky, but skin flakes. Profuse desquamation and sloughing. Paronychia. Skin cancers.

Febrile: Pyrexia. Temperature rises late afternoon/evening, then abates by midnight. Intermittent fever.

Potassium chloride

Role: Electrochemical. Catalytic. Miscellaneous.

Memory key: Congestion remover

Brief prescribing indications: Conditions arising from faulty collagen synthesis. Second stage of inflammations, characterised by; swelling, congestion and pain. Fibromas. Herpetic ulcers. Burns. Keloids. Contusions. Hypochlorhydria.

Symptoms aggravated by: Dry heat. Fatty, rich food. Physical exertion.

Symptoms improved by: Cold applications to affected part. Keeping still.

Tongue: White or greyish-white coating.

Exudate: Thick white, viscid mucus. Clear, watery exudate from herpetic vesicles. Dry, white, powdery exudate on surface of skin.

Iris: Stomach zone (hypochlorhydria). Arcus sclerosis. Acid wash. Flared, white autonomic wreath.

Biochemical notes: Potassium chloride in the mineral state is found abundantly in nature. In most fruits and vegetables, potassium is the major inorganic cation, with phosphate, chloride and sulphate, appearing as the major inorganic anions.

Potassium chloride is readily absorbed in the stomach and the small intestine by passive diffusion, at an efficiency of about 90%.

There are very few known metabolic processes where the ions of potassium and chloride act as an associated pair. This is due to the fact that potassium primarily fulfils an intracellular role, while the action of chloride is almost entirely limited to the interstitial compartment.

The presently identified spheres of action are; the production and maintenance of hydrochloric acid in the stomach; pH regulation in the kidney; and the red blood cell function of the chloride shift, which helps to maintain plasma pH.

Some of the other major traditional roles for potassium chloride are presently not supportable from a scientific standpoint. The author feels that in keeping with all the other salts, many of the physiological and biochemical extrapolations drawn at the time, were, in the light of present-day knowledge, either totally wrong, or only half correct. What cannot be questioned though, is that the major deficiency signs and symptoms have ultimately been proven to be correct. There is no doubt that the same fate will ultimately befall the salt potassium chloride, and that those presently observed but not understood *traditional* symptoms, will in time be elucidated by science.

When scientific researcher, Paul Callinan M.Sc, was commissioned in 1983 by Blackmores Laboratories of Australia, to conduct the most extensive literature search ever undertaken, to establish where possible,

Potassium chloride

support for the traditional prescribing indications for the salts of Blackmore; he made the comment that: "If the same project had been undertaken just five or so years previous, not just potassium chloride, but also silica and calcium fluoride would have been research failures."

It is then, simply a matter of time before science catches-up on those presently missing pieces of the puzzle, not only for potassium chloride, but also for some of the more subtle indications for some of the other salts as well.

The parietal cells of the gastric mucosa secrete hydrochloric acid which is essential to hydrolyse dietary proteins; the absorption of many minerals; to kill potentially harmful bacteria; and to convert the protein digesting enzyme pepsinogen into its active form, pepsin. Gastric acid contains hydrochloric acid, potassium chloride, traces of other electrolytes and practically no organic matter. In a proposed model for hydrochloric acid production utilising both potassium and chloride, potassium is pumped from the stomach lumen into the parietal cell, in exchange for hydrogen ions, while bicarbonate is pumped into the extracellular fluid in exchange for chloride, which then accompanies hydrogen into the lumen, forming hydrochloric acid.

As carbon dioxide is produced by cellular metabolism, it diffuses into the blood plasma and then into the red blood cells. As carbon dioxide is taken up and released from the red blood cells, chloride shifts in and out from the plasma to counteract any change in the acid-base balance that might otherwise occur as vast amounts of carbon dioxide are transported to the lungs. This transfer of chloride in and out of the RBCs, is called the *chloride shift*.

In chloride deficiency, less bicarbonate will diffuse out of the red blood cell, as there is no corresponding anion from the plasma that can replace it. In such a situation, potassium will accompany bicarbonate out of the cell, maintaining the blood pH buffers, but causing a potassium depletion. Hence a loss of chloride for whatever reason results in a compensating loss of potassium.

A lack of intracellular potassium results in a replacement by hydrogen ions, with a consequent fall in cell pH. Lowered plasma levels cause a renal exchange of potassium for conserved sodium, and an excessive urinary loss of hydrogen ions, a rise in plasma pH and the onset of metabolic alkalosis. As pH is a regulator of cell metabolism, alteration in potassium levels has metabolic effects that are far-reaching. In a large number of cases, chloride depletion occurs simultaneously, and in this case, correction of the potassium status, can only be achieved by the administration of potassium as the cation and chloride as the anion.

Clinical indications

Head: Headache, with nausea and white tongue, sometimes accompanied by emesis and often after eating rich/fatty food. Dandruff. Scalp has dry white powdery exudate.

Eyes: Discharge of stringy white mucus. Feeling as if sand in eyes. Iritis. Dendritic and herpetic keratitis.

Potassium chloride

ENT: Otitis media. Chronic catarrhal congestion of the middle ear, often with earache, swelling of associated lymphatics and crackling noises on blowing nose or swallowing. Parotitis. Vertigo. Blocked eustachian tubes. Thick white mucus from the nose. White ulcers in mouth. Pharyngitis. Tonsillitis, with grey-white exudate. Hawks up offensive, hard, small cheesy lumps. Pain on swallowing. Stringy, white, tenacious mucus from throat. Buccal and lingual ulcers.

Tongue: Grey-white coating. Herpetic ulcers.

Gastrointestinal: Indigestion and dyspepsia associated with white tongue coating. Indigestion, flatulence, nausea, after eating rich, fatty food. Tender and swollen abdomen, often with nausea. Ulcerative and mucous colitis, with stools streaked with white mucus. Pale stools, for want of bile. Diarrhoea, after fatty food. Anorexia.

Cardiovascular: Hypercholesterolæmia, when intimal plaques have formed. Thrombosis. Fat embolus (especially when tendency is to form many).

Respiratory: Cough with viscid, white, often stringy mucus. Bronchiolitis. Bronchitis. Fibrinous bronchitis. Pleurisy. Dry pleurisy. Fibrinous pleurisy. Asthma, following fatty food, mucus white, difficult to raise, or rattling in bronchi.

Genitourinary: Leucorrhoea. Dark, membranous, clotted menses. Endometriosis. Pelvic inflammatory disease. Mastitis. Sterility. Cystitis. Pyelitis. Urethritis (white discharge).

Musculoskeletal: Joint pains and swelling, produced or aggravated by physical activity. Joint pains at night; aggravated by heat.

Tissues: For symptomatic relief and to heal tissue quickly following bruising, surgery or burning. Keloids. Fibrous nodules in deep fascia. Fibromas. Fibrositis.

Skin: Acne (white). Boils. Herpes simplex. Burns. Keloids. Contusions. White, powdery keratinous exudate on palms. Eczema, white fibrinous exudations.

Febrile: Second stage of all congestions and inflammations, marked by, swelling, congestion and white, fibrinous or mucus exudate. Intermittent fever.

Calcium phosphate

Role: Structural. Electrochemical. Catalytic.

Memory key: Cell builder.

Brief prescribing indications: Conditions arising from poor cell development and replacement, particularly, muscle, bone, and blood. Children are primary group affected, with irritability, cramps, poor appetite and frequent colds. Anæmia; hypochromic and microcytic (along with IP). Chilblain.

Symptoms aggravated by: Cold, wet, changeable weather. Dampness. Cold draughts. Physical exertion. Springtime. Teething.

Symptoms improved by: Warm, stable, dry weather. Summertime. Warmth. Rest. Covering-up against cold draughts.

Exudate: Tenacious mucus of an albuminous white nature, often streaked with yellow or blood.

Iris: Poor iris texture. Nerves arcs (children).

Biochemical notes: Calcium phosphate is abundant in nature and through the food chain. In humans it forms the basis of the skeleton; regulates cell division; stimulates blood clotting following injury (Ca only); enters into many biological reactions; is essential for proper nerve and muscle function; and for the proper secretion of many hormones.

Of the 1,200 grams of calcium in the body, 98% is found in the skeleton, connective tissue and teeth (1%). The remaining 12 grams is widely distributed in the blood, muscle, liver, nerves and heart.

Blood levels are maintained by the parathyroid gland, to a tolerance of ±3%. About 10% of calcium phosphate in bone serves as an exchangeable pool, if dietary supply falls short of physiological need. On average, about 500mg is exchanged or incorporated into the skeleton each day, this suggests that about 1/5 of the skeleton is resorbed and reformed each year.

Calcium phosphate is absorbed in the upper three quarters of the small intestine where the digestive mass is more acidic. Calcium is actively transported through the absorptive cells, with phosphate now recognised as being the main synergist for calcium absorption. Phosphate also appears to be a natural regulator for calcium absorption, promoting absorption at low calcium concentrations, but forming poorly absorbable polyphosphate complexes, if calcium intake is excessive.

The absorption efficiency for calcium phosphate is generally in the order of 30-50%, but may rise to 80%, depending upon the types of food ingested at the time; adequate vitamin D; parathyroid hormone (PTH); fluoride; ascorbic acid; the amino acids, lysine and arginine; acidity of digestive contents; the presence of lactose; calcium to phosphate ratios of 1:1 to 1:2; physical exercise; and the body's need for calcium.

Factors that are known to reduce calcium absorption are; oxalic acid; phytic acid; dietary fat; magnesium polyphosphate complexes; glucocorticoids; emotional stress; increased gastrointestinal motility; lack of exercise; dietary fibre; caffeine; and some medically prescribed drugs (anticonvulsants, cortisone and thyroxine).

Calcium phosphate

Once calcium has been absorbed from the small intestine, it is transported in the blood with some 1.6% being bound to phosphate as the undissociated molecule. The remaining calcium is found loosely bound to plasma proteins, albumin and globulin, (46%), bound to citrate (1.7%), bound to bicarbonate (3.2%), and as the physiologically active, free ion (47.5%)

If blood calcium levels fall, the parathyroid secretes parathormone (PTH), which has several functions. Within minutes, it stimulates the kidney to resorb calcium that would normally be excreted, and within hours it has acted on bone to cause some of the exchangeable calcium to be released by stimulating the metabolism of some of the carbohydrate of bone to citrate and lactate, in which the calcium is soluble. This calcium then enters the blood where it raises the blood and intercellular fluids to more normal levels. The parathyroid also stimulates the absorption of calcium from the gastrointestinal tract; this occurs after several days, resulting from the formation of the active form of vitamin D, that in turn leads to the synthesis of calcium-binding protein. When blood calcium levels return to normal, the secretion of parathormone also returns to normal.

When blood levels of calcium are elevated, the thyroid hormone calcitonin (TCT) is secreted. Calcitonin acts to lower both calcium and phosphate levels, by inhibiting bone resorption. The hormones parathormone and calcitonin are therefore responsible for maintaining blood calcium levels within the very narrow limits demanded by the body.

Calcium in the urine is normally about 90% reabsorbed by active transport. About 60% of the reabsorption occurs in the proximal tubules, with the remainder taking place in the ascending limb of the loop of Henle, and the distal tubule. Distal tubule reabsorption is regulated by parathyroid hormone, with elevated blood PTH levels increasing reabsorption. Vitamin D, also increases reabsorption, while elevated levels of the hormones, calcitonin and cortisol, increase urinary loss. There are also small losses with bile and pancreatic secretions, and from heavy sweating.

In bone, calcium phosphate is laid down in the crystalline form or as hydroxyapatite (calcium phosphate and calcium hydroxide). These crystals give strength and rigidity to the collagen matrix. Mature bone is made up of the minerals, calcium, phosphate, magnesium, sodium, potassium, zinc, fluoride and carbonate. The bone shaft, which is the rigid part of bone, is constantly being remodelled and reshaped throughout life, as body weight alters or shifts, putting different stresses on the bones. At the end of long bones is the epiphysis, which regulates bone growth. Beneath the epiphysis, is the more porous trabeculæ, which has constant contact with the blood supply, so that calcium can be withdrawn to meet physiological needs, if dietary intake is inadequate. Trabecular bone predominates in the vertebræ of the spine.

Calcium phosphate

In teeth, the crystals of hydroxyapatite are more dense and the water content is lower than in bone, and where fluorapatite is available, it will replace some of the crystals of hydroxyapatite, normally deposited during tooth formation. The protein matrix of tooth enamel is keratin, and in the middle dentin layer, it is collagen in common with bone. In contrast to bone though, teeth undergo only microscopic changes once they have erupted. The slow rate of exchange between the tooth calcium and that of the blood, is confines almost entirely to the dentin layer, although, it is thought that there may be some calcium and fluoride exchange between the tooth enamel and the saliva.

Calcium is essentially an extracellular ion, as high intracellular concentrations would inactivate magnesium-dependent enzymes. Regardless, mitochondria have been found to preferentially accumulate significant amounts of calcium phosphate (laid-down in the membrane in crystalline form), the two being transported together, across the mitochondrial membrane. Although their function there is presently not fully understood, it appears to be coupled to the energy producing electron transport chain.

Many hormones act at the cell membrane, via the enzyme, adenyl cyclase, which then activates cellular "messengers" to alter metabolic direction. Both calcium and phosphate are necessary for this function. Intracellular calcium movement is controlled by calmodulin, a carrier protein, which binds to calcium at the cell membrane and transports it to the enzymes, mitochondria and other cytoplasmic elements, which have a specific calcium requirement. In this way, movement is strictly controlled.

Calcium is known to play a key role in the process of mitotic division, whereby cells divide, in tissue repair and in the more specialised function of red blood cell production. Although its role is not understood in detail, it has been established as a regulator of cell division and hence is essential for growth.

Both calcium and phosphate are essential for muscle contraction. Calcium acts as a neuromuscular trigger, by a process relating to the formation of phosphate deposits, where it acts as a bridge between crosslinking phosphate groups, attached to contractile protein strands. Phosphate is also necessary to inactivate the calcium following the contractile response, concentrating with calcium in the vesicles of the sarcoplasmic reticulum.

In nerve function, calcium on one hand stabilises the electrical polarity of the nerve cell membrane, preventing electrical depolarisation, and on the other, it is necessary for the secretion of neurotransmitter at the synapse and neuromuscular junction. If blood calcium is low, the membrane is less stable and the nerve may fire more easily. Muscles

Calcium phosphate

supplied by such nerves can twitch, or produce the sustained contractions of tetany. High levels of blood calcium, produce a sedative influence on the nerve cells, by rendering the membrane highly stable.

Calcium is also necessary for the proper secretion of neurotransmitter at the nerve synapse and neuromuscular junction. When an electrical impulse, an action potential, reaches the synaptic knob, calcium floods into the nerve ending, triggering the release of neurotransmitter, the amount released being proportional to the calcium influx. The secretory process which calcium initiates, requires phosphate-bond energy from phosphorylation (ATP and cyclic AMP). In this way, both calcium and phosphate are closely linked in the efficient function of nerve tissue.

Clinical indications

Mental/emotional: Poor memory. Anxiety over trivia. Poor concentration. Children; irritable, fretful, slow comprehension.

Head and face: Cold, icy, numb, sore or crawling sensation, especially over sutures. Fontanelles remain open too long. Pallor. Waxy, sallow complexion. Dry skin, wrinkled prematurely. Acne.

Eye: Photophobia. Inflammation and dryness.

ENT: Cold, painful ears and mastoid, following exposure to cold wind. Frequent ear, nose and throat infections. Colds with dentition. Nasal polypi. Chronic enlargement of tonsils. Painful deglutition. Constant hawking, while talking. Tickling cough, worse after retiring. Sore throat in the morning upon waking but eases after breakfast.

Teeth: Slow or imperfect dentition. Febrile convulsions during teething. Frequent ENT infections during teething. Toothache, with tearing, boring pain, worse at night. Weak, chalky teeth that rot easily. Gums painful and inflamed or pale.

Gastrointestinal: Poor appetite (especially children). Complains of epigastric or umbilical ache, but usually doesn't refuse food. Abdomen tender to touch, sunken and flabby. Craves salted or smoked meats. Much flatulence and flatus. Sour and burning gastric reflux. Heartburn. Stool is hot, watery, profuse, smelly and sputtering.

Respiratory: Frequent infections. Asthma, in children. Asthma, following exposure to cold or damp air. Tuberculosis.

Cardiovascular: Cold and numb extremities. Chilblain. Sluggish circulation. Anæmia.

CNS: Neuralgia, from exposure to cold. Neuralgia at night, with tearing pains, as if in bone. Crawling, cold, numb sensations. Cramps, from exposure to cold, or at night in bed.

Genitourinary: Dysmenorrhoea, with deep cramping ache in uterus and back. Amenorrhoea. Menses of young women; early with bright-red flow, or late, with dark-red flow, with uterine colic and referred back pain. Sexual desire increased, especially before menses. Leucorrhoea, like white of egg. Painful erections. Polyuria, from exposure to cold, or from weakness; often with painful micturition. Phosphaturia. Enuresis in the young and elderly. Nephritis in the young. Phosphate stones and gravel.

Calcium phosphate

Musculoskeletal: Shifting joint pains during cold, wet weather. Joint pains with cold, numb feeling. Cramps from exposure to cold, or at night in bed. Fractures fail to unite. Bone diseases as a result of poor nutrition. Growing pains. Shins ache, sore to touch. Backache after exposure to cold. Rickets. Osteomalacia. Osteoporosis.

Skin: Pallor. Waxy, sallow complexion. Dry, wrinkled prematurely. Acne, boils in the very young. Keratinous exudate on palms.

Febrile: Cold, night sweats from emaciation.

Calcium sulphate

Role: Structural. Electrochemical. Catalytic.

Memory key: Suppuration remover.

Brief prescribing indications: Purulent and sanious discharges, after the pus has found a vent. Thick, lumpy, yellow-green, often blood streaked mucus. Abscesses. Ulcers. Boils. Fistulas. Acne. To heal long suppurating wounds.

Symptoms aggravated by: Overheated warmth. Wet, damp weather. Working with water. Physical exertion.

Symptoms improved by: Cool, open air. Dry weather.

Tongue: Flabby, with coating resembling dry clay.

Exudate: Thick, lumpy, yellow, purulent mucus, often blood streaked. Pus or sanious discharges with a vent.

Iris: Check and compare with symptoms; Skin zone, and Lymphatic zone.

Biochemical notes: Calcium sulphate is abundantly found in nature as selenite, alabaster and gypsum (plaster of Paris). It is a major constituent in most hard water sources throughout the world.

Calcium sulphate is absorbed from the upper part of the small intestine with an almost 100% efficiency for the sulphate, and between 30%-80% for the calcium ion, owing to the various factors which govern calcium absorption.

Calcium sulphate, like potassium sulphate, is involved with the production of mucopolysaccharide for connective tissue, and glycoproteins for cell coats, induction of calcification, control of water and metabolite movement, and in the healing of wounds. But, while potassium sulphate is more concerned with normal cell cement requirements, calcium sulphate is concerned with tight cell junctions. The attachment of cells to each other creates organs, provides barriers to enclose fluids and provides the tight external packaging of the skin.

Calcium sulphate has an important role in the region where the outer components of two cell membranes fuse into one, a junction known as the zonula occludens.

Central to such cellular adhesion, is the role of specialised mucopolysaccharides and of calcium. Several mucopolysaccharides act as intercellular cement; while their exact function is not clear, they are known to bind opposing cell walls, by virtue of their long-chain structures and side groups. Calcium is a known constituent of intercellular cement and assists additionally, by acting as an electrostatic bridge, between the negatively charged cell membranes, creating stability, where tight cell junctions are required.

As previously discussed in the "sodium sulphate" and "potassium sulphate" sections, the role of sulphate to act as a stabiliser of connective tissue is widespread. The mucopolysaccharides and glycoproteins contain negatively charged sulphated side groups, which repel each other, causing the molecular chains to adopt a rigid structure, which cannot be easily distorted, because of the strong forces of repulsion. Sulphated mucopolysaccharides are known to produce a more solid structure, while tissues containing non-sulphated chains are much softer. If unsulphated, the molecular chains will soften and may detach from their parent structures, resulting in cell fragmentation; the exudation of intercellular matrix components, especially mucoproteins and serum; and the congestion of intercellular, lymphatic and vascular spaces. These conditions can then easily set the stage for the traditional calcium sulphate prescribing indication of, ongoing suppuration, that becomes infected and won't heal.

Calcium sulphate

Wound healing and tissue regeneration, is generally related to adequate supplies of calcium and sulphate being available. Connective tissue has great regenerative ability, as it is one of the most important sites of cell division and new cell growth; consequently, areas destroyed by trauma or inflammation are usually easily repaired. Where there is no provision for cell division and replacement (as in cardiac muscle), the site is filled by mucopolysaccharide connective tissue, which forms a scar.

The calcium ion is intimately related to wound healing as it is essential for cell division and has known functions as an intercellular cement and membrane stabiliser. Together with sulphate, calcium promotes rapid cell replacement and healthy granulation in wound healing.

Clinical indications

Mental/emotional: Changeable mood. Irritable. Anxious; better in open air. Sleepy during day; wakeful at night. Sleepless from thoughts. Craves stimulants to overcome tremulous weakness.

Head and face: Dandruff. Hair falling. Purulent, yellow, crusty exudate on scalp. Headache from becoming cold, but made better in cool air. Acne. Boils.

Eyes: Inflammation with thick, yellow discharge. Dendritic keratitis.

ENT: Otitis media; purulent discharge, often streaked with blood. Thick, yellow mucopurulent discharge from nose, streaked with blood. Yellow post-nasal mucus. Colds, with thick mucopurulent discharge. Nose dry, crusts form. Suppurating tonsils. Ulcerated throat. Quinsy.

Tongue: Flabby, with coating resembling clay.

Gastrointestinal: Craves stimulants to overcome tremendous weakness. Desire for fruit, tea, claret and green sour vegetables. Purulent diarrhoea, mixed with blood. Anal discharge of pus. Anal fistula. Anal abscess.

Respiratory: Cough with thick, lumpy, mucopurulent or sanguinopurulent expectoration and fever. Empyema. Sanies. Tuberculosis.

Pneumonia, bacterial.

Cardiovascular: Pericarditis. Palpitation at night in bed.

Genitourinary: Vaginal itch following menses. Pelvic inflammatory disease. Prostatitis, with infection or abscess. Gonorrhœa with sanious discharge. Mastitis, with pus discharge. Cystitis, with pus. Pyelitis.

Calcium sulphate

CNS: weakness with languor, craves stimulants to overcome tremulous weakness. Twitchings.

Skin: Boils, carbuncles, abscesses, ulcers, fistulas, to control suppuration and to heal. Sanious discharges. Cuts that do not heal readily and become infected. Purulent exudations on skin that form yellow scales. Dry eczema. Herpes zoster.

Febrile: Chronic intermittent fever with chill, worse evening. Fever from septicæmia.

Postscript to a salt of confusion

Ever since Schüssler abandoned calcium sulphate to use silica in its place, there has been confusion as to whether calcium sulphate should be persisted with or not.

Many, if not most of Schüssler's followers, continued to include calcium sulphate as part of their armamentarium and most books written about Schüssler's method since his time, have also embraced all of the original twelve salts. In 1938 when Maurice Blackmore introduced his Celloid system of mineral therapy, he too included calcium sulphate. These, and other historical events, have all helped to shape present-day attitudes toward the salt and yet at the same time, have done nothing to clear up the confusion surrounding its potential uses.

As a starting-point in trying to unravel some of this confusion, the salient and generally accepted characteristics and traditional prescribing indications for a calcium sulphate deficiency should be re-examined.

The traditional Schüssler/homœopathic understanding of the physiochemical properties of calcium sulphate, was one of destroying worn-out blood corpuscles in the liver, by taking away their water and then eliminating them through biliary action. It was thought at the time, that through a deficiency of calcium sulphate, this breakdown was rendered incomplete and thus the blood was encumbered with an oversupply of useless cells. These cells, not being eliminated via the usual channels, were then said to accumulate in the mucous membranes and skin, producing catarrh and purulent eruptions.

This scenario, to explain why a calcium sulphate deficiency produces the effects that it does, is of course less than accurate, according to today's understanding of erythrocyte destruction, but, as stated elsewhere in this text; regardless that the old biochemical extrapolations are found to be wanting, the actual clinical observations of a deficiency, are as true today as they were then.

Prior to and during Schüssler's time, the sorts of diseases that manifested the so-called, classic calcium sulphate indications, were far more common-place than they are today. These illnesses originated primarily as a result of poor nutrition, poor sanitation, overcrowding and a lack personal hygiene. Today, it is only in the underprivileged societies of the world where one could observe these or similar conditions on a wide-spread scale. Tuberculosis was rife throughout Europe during the later part of the eighteenth century and the first half of the nineteenth century, so too was bubonic plague, syphilis and many other venereal diseases. Superficial wounds, ulcers and many other simple conditions commonly became septic due to a lack of hygiene and were thus likely to give rise to indications where calcium sulphate should be prescribed - or is this really the case?

Postscript to calcium sulphate

While there are many *guiding symptoms* for the prescribing of calcium sulphate, there is really only one salient *characteristic*, and that is; *the presence of pus with a vent*. Unless there is discharge that contains pus, then calcium sulphate is not the remedy. The discharge can vary in nature from straight-out pus to sanies, or mucus of a viscid, lumpy, slimy, yellow-green appearance that is often blood streaked; but it must contain pus and refuse to heal. Exudates and transudates that are of a non-infected, or purely serous nature do not call for calcium sulphate, nor do pyogenic infections that have generally speaking, not begun to discharge.

The traditional employment of calcium sulphate was only following the use of silica, or if the action of silica had not brought about a total cure. In this regard, it is interesting to note, that most of the prescribing indications for silica are exactly the same as for those of calcium sulphate where pyogenic discharges are concerned, but unlike calcium sulphate, silica can also be indicated where the discharges are of a clear, non-infected ichoroid nature.

Schüssler's preference for silica over calcium sulphate is actually quite logical, with the seemingly converse actions of the two salts, not so contradictory and somewhat artificial. Silicon is a nutritive ion for all connective tissue, where it promotes new cell growth and structural order. Silica ripens the suppurative phase, encourages drainage directly to the surface by establishing an opening, or indirectly by reabsorption; then, following these processes, silica completes the healing process by quickly restoring the diseased tissue to normal. Therefore, just as with calcium sulphate, silica possesses the ability to resolve the suppurative phase, and then to heal afterwards.

As the integrity of skin, hair, nails, bone, ligament, tendon and cartilage is dependent upon silica being available, it therefore seems logical to assume, that when structural order and new cell development in connective tissue is impaired as a consequence of a silicon deficiency, tissue breakdown with secondary suppuration is more likely to occur.

In terms of basic prescribing indications, calcium sulphate actually possesses nothing that is particularly unique and which can't be found amongst the indications for a number of the other salts, particularly, silica, potassium sulphate, potassium phosphate and sodium sulphate.

Even the so-called unique *characteristic* of, *pus with a vent*, can just as easily be an indication for silica, as it is for calcium sulphate.

Postscript to calcium sulphate

When one studies the prescribing indications for the three salts of Schüssler's original twelve, that share sulphate as the anion (sodium sulphate, potassium sulphate, and calcium sulphate), purulent or mucopurulent discharges of a yellow or green colour prevail. It is therefore almost certainly the case, that it is the sulphate ion and not the calcium ion that determines the prescribing picture for calcium sulphate, with many of the symptoms being the same or similar for each salt in the sulphate group. This example serves to demonstrate, that not only does the anion have a role to play, but that the anion can actually dominate the prescribing picture. It must also be understood, that while there are a number of salts in the Schüssler system that share the same cation, (sodium x 3, calcium x 3, and potassium x 3), it is the combining anion that confers the uniqueness and clinical prescribing indications for each salt in a group. In the case of calcium sulphate there are actually fewer symptoms that can be related specifically to calcium, but nonetheless, it is that combining of calcium with sulphate, that imparts to the salt it's distinctiveness. This ensures that the aggregate of calcium sulphate indications although similar to silica, potassium sulphate, potassium phosphate and sodium sulphate, are not exactly the same.

The clinical situation is therefore further confused by the fact that it is not only silica, as Schüssler suggested, that could possibly be utilised in lieu of calcium sulphate, but also a number of other salts as well. There are though, discriminating features pertaining to each salt, that the practitioner must learn to recognise, so that the correct salt may be differentiated before prescribing. These discriminating features are to be found in the overview contained immediately under the heading for each salt and the "clinical indications" section for each salt. If the clinical indications alone, are not sufficient to distinguish between two or more salts for a given case, then the application of the "symptom qualification" principle, with regard to the conditions which make the patient's symptoms better or worse, must be applied. Ideally, questioning or observing for symptom qualifications should be automatically applied in every case, regardless of whether the correct remedy can be chosen from the symptoms alone or not. The additional information gained from symptom qualification questioning, should never be considered superfluous, as it will most-times either confirm, further confirm, or totally deny the salt chosen from the symptoms alone.

As was mentioned previously, purulent or mucopurulent discharges of a yellow-green colour, can be an indication for not only calcium sulphate, but also silica, potassium phosphate, potassium sulphate or sodium sulphate. By way of practical example, what is it then, that allows us to discriminate for, or against calcium sulphate? The principle considerations that should be embraced are; the nature and consistency of the discharge, not just the colour, the other prevailing or peripheral symptoms, whether they are directly related to the discharge or not, and any aggravating or ameliorating influences.

Postscript to calcium sulphate

If for instance, a patient presented with asthma that is worse at night in bed, or following exposure to cold, but is improved by standing in a hot steamy shower and characterised by copious mucopurulent sputum that is thick and lumpy; how do we proceed to select the remedy? First of all we know that the colour of the sputum is yellow-green, and that this colour can be an indication for either, sodium sulphate, potassium phosphate, potassium sulphate, calcium sulphate, calcium fluoride or silica (Calcium phosphate is, albuminous, yellow streaked). The consistency of the mucus is, copious, thick and lumpy, this indication then narrows the field down to sodium sulphate, calcium sulphate, potassium phosphate, calcium fluoride and silica, as potassium sulphate is more indicated where the mucus is watery. Calcium fluoride is also probably eliminated at this point, as its indication is confined to small lumps of yellow-green mucus being raised; so too is potassium phosphate, because of the lumpishness of the mucus. The fact that the symptoms are worse following exposure to cold, is an indication for, silica and potassium phosphate, but the preference will probably be for silica, with the symptoms actually being brought-on following exposure to cold, rather than just aggravated by exposure to cold. Symptoms that are worse at night and upon lying down, are again, silica indications, with potassium phosphate and calcium fluoride merely being aggravated following rest. Finally, a further confirmation of silica as the remedy of choice in this case, comes from the fact that the patient's symptoms are relieved by steam (humidity). Silica has therefore survived the culling process unscathed, but it should be noted, that if it were not for the assistance given by *symptom qualifications,* the question could not have been resolved from a study of the *symptoms* alone.

The afore-mentioned example is in no way intended to demonstrate the redundancy of calcium sulphate as a remedy, but rather, the selective process that must be undertaken in each case where calcium sulphate, or any other salt for that matter, may seem to be indicated.

In summary then, it is the author's belief that if these stringent principles of selection were adhered to, then calcium sulphate would rarely be called for, unless in the context of an environment of poor nutrition, poor sanitation, social over-crowding and a lack of personal hygiene. Even in these circumstances, Schüssler was probably quite correct in preferring the action of silica over that of calcium sulphate. Though to mandatorily apply silica in lieu of calcium sulphate, infers that all the traditional homœopathic principles of prescribing are to be ignored. If Schüssler had conformed to these principles, he probably would have hung-on to calcium sulphate, so that it could still be used on those odd occasions where it may be indicated; but, he may also have made better use of potassium sulphate instead. The potential for the use of potassium sulphate in the same or similar circumstances around which the controversy over silica and calcium sulphate has centred, is enormous. Discussion in the old traditional textbooks with regard to the role of potassium sulphate in this context, is conspicuous by its absence.

Calcium fluoride

Role: Structural. Catalytic.

Memory key: Tissue strengthener.

Brief prescribing indications: Conditions that arise from a loss of integrity and strength of connective tissue. All weaknesses of bone, enamel, ligament and tendon. All prolapsed tissue. Hard excrescences. Nodes and nodules.

Symptoms aggravated by: Damp, cold, changeable weather. Rest (morning, upon arising). Physical motion, following rest.

Symptoms improved by: Dry, warm, stable weather. Rubbing/friction over affected part. Hot applications to affected part. Physical movement, gentle and slow. Warmth; heat.

Tongue: Cracked, mapped or fissured.

Exudate: Hard, lumpy, greenish, fœtid discharges. Hard, knotty glands, tendons or periosteum.

Iris: Check and compare with symptoms; Stomach zone and Skin zone.

Pupil: Distended.

Biochemical notes: Fluoride constitutes about 0.03% of the earth's crust, and calcium fluoride is abundant in nature as fluorspar or fluorite, which closely approximates the composition of human tooth enamel. It is a common constituent of soil and is the primary natural source of fluoride in water. Plants may absorb calcium fluoride in the particulate or colloidal form, by active transport, via the root hairs. Fluoroacetic acid is also found as a form of fluoride in several plant species.

Calcium fluoride is only slightly soluble in water at physiological temperature and is equally resistant to gastric acid. Calcium fluoride can only be dissolved in hot, concentrated, sulphuric acid.

Fluoride as an essential micronutrient is important for a variety of functions within the body, beyond its long-known value as a protector of tooth enamel. It also stimulates osteoblastic activity, prompting the formation of new bone, but at higher levels, promotes reabsorption by stimulating osteoclastic activity; appears to stimulate fibroblastic activity, for the formation of connective tissue; and stimulates chondroblastic activity for the construction of cartilage. Fluoride increases the production of the enzyme, cyclic AMP, produces anticoagulant effects in the blood, stimulates the secretion of the collagen matrix and seems to enhance the rate of wound healing.

Calcium fluoride is absorbed at an efficiency of between 62%-96%, but the absorption sites are as yet unknown. Due to its insolubility, it would appear that calcium fluoride is absorbed as the whole molecule, either by nonionic diffusion, active transport, or endocytosis.

Calcium fluoride is likely to exist in plasma undissociated and may be deposited directly into fluorapatite crystals, as the whole molecule. Much of the absorbed calcium fluoride is also probably taken up by osteoblasts, where fluoride is known to stimulate osteoblastic activity.

Calcium fluoride

Due to its insolubility, and the fact that it is absorbed, transported and deposited at the target sites as the undissociated molecule, calcium fluoride is considerably safer, even at much greater concentrations (80-150 times), than sodium fluoride, where there is an uncontrolled absorption (98%) of the free fluoride ions. Sodium fluoride, as added to some public water supplies (Australia 80%, USA 40% and Europe/UK 10%) is soluble in water and cheap, and thus ideally suited for the purpose of mass-medication. The problem is of course, that although the level of fluoride is set at 1 part per million, and it has been calculated that the average daily dose from drinking water, should be in the order of 1.5mg, there is no way to ensure that this dose will not be exceeded, when other related factors are taken into consideration. Individual habits with regard to eating and drinking vary enormously, so too does the age v need factor where fluoride is concerned, with the greatest need being virtually confined to the very young, with budding or erupting teeth, and menopausal women. Regardless though, of these and other problems associated with artificially fluoridated water, long-term epidemiological studies conducted by the US Public Health Service, based on the health records of 2 million people, found no evidence of increased deposition of fluoride in soft tissues, such as the kidneys and heart; no increase in mortality and morbidity rates; no growth depression or abnormalities; no increase in cancer or nephritis; and no increase in the births of mentally retarded children.

When calcium fluoride is available, crystals of fluorapatite replace the crystals of hydroxyapatite, normally deposited in the enamel during tooth formation. Fluorapatite in tooth enamel is virtually insoluble in acid and therefore more resistant to caries. The enamel is still able to take-up fluoride shortly after the teeth erupt and fluoride in the saliva is presumed to be the means by which this is achieved. It is presently not generally believed that there is an exchange of fluorapatite once the enamel has matured, as there is in bone, as tooth enamel has no cellular activity. This view is not shared by all scientists, some of whom believe that a mechanism exists which provides for an ongoing deposition of fluoride into the enamel throughout life.

Fluoride, when incorporated into bone is found as the calcium salt. It displaces hydroxide from hydroxyapatite and forms fluorapatite. Fluorapatite then becomes the main storage form of fluoride in bone, and contributes markedly to the hardness and strength of the crystal lattice. This pool of fluoride can be mobilised at any time by resorption, when required to replenish plasma levels, and is primarily found at the bone surface.

In low doses, fluoride stimulates osteoblastic (raised alkaline phosphatase levels) activity for new bone formation, especially at the periosteum and endosteum. Fluoride also improves the crystal size and quality of bone, resulting in slower reabsorption by osteoclasts. If the concentration of fluoride is too high, an irregular matrix formation results and osteoclastic activity is stimulated (raised acid phosphatase levels), which promotes the reabsorption of calcified tissue. Hence, the action of the fluoride ion seems to be directly related to local concentrations.

Calcium fluoride

Fluoride is widely distributed in soft tissue, both intra and extracellularly, at concentrations comparable to those of plasma. Intracellularly in osteoblasts, it is known to stimulate the secretion of the collagen matrix, and hence plays an important role in the integrity of cartilage fibrous capsules, vascular walls and suspensory ligaments.

While normal plasma levels of fluoride have been found to stimulate bone and tooth calcification and the deposition of phosphatic complexes, the reverse seems to be the case in soft tissues, with normal levels reducing calcification in the protein matrix. High levels of fluoride however, increase calcification of soft tissue and are probably responsible for the pathological conditions seen at these concentrations. The major enzymes concerned in deposition and resorption processes, are intracellular alkaline phosphatase and acid phosphatase. Fluoride at normal plasma levels has been found to activate acid phosphatase, whereas at higher concentrations it inhibits its action. Alkaline phosphatase has been found to react similarly, but is less sensitive.

In common with all trace elements it can be seen that fluoride activates enzymes at low concentrations but inhibits them at higher concentrations.

Clinical indications

Mental/emotional: Depression, arising out of groundless fears. Fear of financial ruin. Disposition to place higher importance on money matters than situation deserves. Decreased elasticity of thought. Reduced tenacity of thought.

Head: Bony overgrowths, hard and benign. Exostoses. Osteomas. Creaking noises in head.

Eye: Cataract. Flickering and sparks before eyes. Blurred vision, ache after use; better from closing and light pressure. Subcutaneous palpebral cysts.

ENT: Otosclerosis. Tinnitus, from ossicular degeneration. Stuffy, dry, head cold with ineffectual desire to sneeze. Copious, fœtid, thick, greenish, lumpy discharge from nares. Chronic sinusitis, with mucopurulent discharge. Indurated tonsils. Irritated, tickling, dryness in throat, better from warm drink.

Teeth: Imperfect, or defective enamel. Caries. Teeth loose in gums. Hypersensitivity to hot, cold or acidic foods and drinks. Receding gums.

Tongue: Cracked and mapped appearance.

Gastrointestinal: Vomiting of undigested food. Fæces difficult to expel, motions recede. Anal fissures. Hæmorrhoids. Prolapsed anus.

Respiratory: Asthma, where small lumps of yellow mucus are raised after much effort. Tickling cough, or irritation when lying down. Emphysema. Croup.

Calcium fluoride

Cardiovascular: Dilated blood vessels. Aneurisms. Varicose veins. Cardiac hypertrophy. Capillary fragility.

Musculoskeletal: Ganglia, wrist. Cystic or calcified nodules anywhere sited in connective tissue. Osteophytes. Articular or periarticular degeneration. Tenosynovitis. Repetitive strain injury. Necrosis of bone (aseptic or septic). Prolapsed or strained intervertebral disc. Cracking and crepitation of joints. Weak bones. Fractures fail to heal. Osteomalacia. Osteoporosis. Nodes on dorsal aspect of finger joints.

Genitourinary: Uterine prolapse with dragging in pelvis and thighs. Cracked nipples. Polyuria, frequent urging. Incontinence. Encopresis. Indurated or benign nodular testes. Prostatic hypertrophy. Hydrocele.

Tissues: Indurated lymphatic glands. Painful nodular fascia. Ganglion cysts of the wrist. Knotty breasts. Cystic or hard calcified nodules anywhere sited in connective tissue

Skin: Skin hard and thickened, with tendency to fissure. Varicose ulcers. Keratosis. Cracking behind ears in children. Perléche. Cheilosis.

Magnesium phosphate

Role: Structural. Electrochemical. Catalytic.

Memory key: Neuromuscular coordinator

Brief prescribing indications: Conditions that demonstrate a loss of integrity at the myoneural junction. Spasms. Neuralgias. Anxiety, tension and depression. Confusion. Disorientation. Hyperexcitability.

Symptoms aggravated by: Cold; air, water, or weather. Physical exertion. Noise. Glare. Alcohol; prolonged effects of. Cold draughts. Flatus, difficult to expel. Night. Touch. Symptoms are usually worse on right side of body.

Symptoms improved by: Bending double. Covering up against the cold or draughts. Alcohol; initial effects of. Eating, refined carbohydrates. Heat, warmth. Friction over affected part. Hot applications to affected part. Keeping still (in the short term). Pressure or rubbing of affected part.

Iris: Nerve arcs and rings (superficial). Acid wash. Flared autonomic wreath.

Pupil: Constricted and/or out of round.

Biochemical notes: Magnesium phosphate in the mineral state is not found to any extent in nature. Since magnesium is an essential structural element of chlorophyll, the green pigment in plants, green leafy vegetables, grains, nuts and legumes are major contributors to dietary magnesium. Vegetables, cereals and beans contribute just on 50% of the recommended daily requirement of magnesium.

Magnesium and phosphate share a close relationship as they are both important intracellular ions, with phosphate being the most abundant anion and magnesium, the second most abundant cation, after potassium.

In the adult, the total magnesium content is a little less than 30 grams, 60% of which is concentrated in bone. About one third of this magnesium is closely bound with phosphate; the remainder adheres to the bone surface from which it is readily mobilised to maintain normal blood and tissue levels. When blood levels fall, parathyroid hormone secretion is increased, causing increased magnesium reabsorption in the renal tubules. If blood levels rise, there is an increased deposition of magnesium into bone and an increased urinary loss, due to a fall in parathyroid hormone levels. Most magnesium in the blood is bound to red blood cells rather than in the plasma, where its concentration is low.

Magnesium acts as a catalyst in over 300 biological reactions, most of which take place within the mitochondria of cells. Magnesium and phosphate are necessary in all reactions involving the expenditure or release of energy; in almost all reactions involving, carbohydrate, lipid, protein, and nucleic acid metabolism; and in those reactions related to the synthesis, degradation and stability of DNA. In order to maintain this high level of metabolic activity, the concentration of magnesium within the cell is seven times that of the blood.

Magnesium phosphate

Magnesium acts to stabilise the nerve membrane potential, and regulates secretion of the neurotransmitter acetylcholine at the myoneural junction by functioning as a calcium antagonist and enzyme activator.

Magnesium is absorbed throughout the length of the small intestine at an average efficiency of 35% to 40%. The rate of absorption is directly related to the level of dietary intake, rather than being regulated by body magnesium status. If dietary intake of magnesium is high, then absorption efficiency will be lower, and conversely, if dietary intake is low, absorption will be greater.

The presence of phosphate also exerts a regulatory role in magnesium absorption, with it increasing absorption if magnesium intake is low, and decreasing absorption when the intake is high. This relationship with phosphate as an absorption regulator, provides an inbuilt safety factor when magnesium is prescribed as the phosphate; and one that is not present in other magnesium preparations. This unique and natural relationship with phosphate is also true for iron and calcium. Magnesium levels in the blood appear to be primarily controlled by excretion, with parathyroid hormone being the main regulating factor.

The kidney is the major regulator of magnesium concentrations, with the degree of excretion being directly proportional to the serum level. Although there appears to be no direct controls for kidney magnesium excretion, parathyroid hormone exerts the most direct effect, with raised levels of the hormone increasing reabsorption in both the proximal and distal tubules of the nephron. Urinary losses are increased by the use of diuretic substances and the consumption of alcohol. Some magnesium is lost in the liver, pancreas and intestinal secretions, but these are usually reabsorbed further along the intestinal tract, except in conditions such as, prolonged diarrhoea, when magnesium losses may be high. There are also small losses of magnesium in sweat.

Magnesium and phosphate are required in all reactions involving energy production such as the synthesis of metabolically important compounds, absorption and transport of nutrients and any nerve or muscle activity. Magnesium is a known activator of phosphate in nucleic acids, intracellular molecules and phospholipids.

Magnesium is required by over 300 enzymes for activation. These enzymes are required in such metabolically varied functions as energy production by phosphate transfer and glycolysis, lipid metabolism, and protein digestion.

As a vital constituent of cell membrane, it activates the enzyme adenyl cyclase, which is responsible for the transmission of hormonal action. Magnesium is also involved in the membrane active transport systems Na-K-ATPase, and Ca-Mg-ATPase, and in the formation of stable membrane phospholipid complexes of considerable importance in membrane permeability. Magnesium is essential for DNA and RNA replication in the cell nucleus and for protein synthesis at the ribosomes.

Magnesium acts as a stabiliser of nerve function, by increasing the threshold of nerve membrane depolarisation.

Magnesium phosphate

Magnesium regulates excessive secretion of the neurotransmitter acetylcholine, probably by blocking the uptake of calcium at the neuromuscular junction. At low magnesium levels, there is an increased influx of calcium into the nerve end plate, resulting in an increased secretion of transmitter, and an increased rate of muscle contraction. This situation can result in tetany. Magnesium and phosphate also reduce the duration of the muscular contraction, by two mechanisms; they are involved in the repackaging and withdrawal of transmitter after release, and, in the activation of such enzymes as acetylcholine esterase, responsible for the rapid breakdown of remaining molecules.

In skeletal, smooth and cardiac muscle, the energy for contraction is dependent on magnesium and phosphate. Although the binding mechanism is not clear, magnesium is considered to be involved in the removal of calcium, vital for the contractile response, back into the sarcoplasmic reticulum. Thus, while calcium is necessary for muscle contraction, magnesium is necessary for muscle relaxation. Magnesium is also essential for proper cardiovascular function, with research indicating that both intracellular and extracellular magnesium losses are implicated in myocardial lesions of diverse ætiology. Magnesium phosphate is also necessary for the activation of most vitamins.

Clinical indications

Mental/emotional: Anxiety. Forgetful. Neuroses. Depression. Insomnia, can't quieten mind, wakes during the night and can't get back to sleep, wakes tired. Wakes with clenched teeth or fists. Hypersensitivity to pain. Irritability. Hyperexcitability. Loss of motivation. Confusion. Illusions. Talks to himself.

Head: Tension headache, worse with jarring movement, rising quickly or bending forward. Sharp shooting pains through head or scalp. Feeling of tight band around head. Acutely painful scalp to the touch. Teeth sensitive to touch and cold.

Eye: Twitching eyelids. Photophobia. Blurred vision after use of eyes or from stress. Sparks or floaters before eyes. Ptosis. Orbital neuralgia.

ENT: Otalgia (from purely functional reasons). Neuralgia. Tinnitus, from stress. Loss of smell. Post-nasal mucus, and/or sore, hoarse throat, and/or hawking of usually clear, gelatinous mucus; from stress.

Teeth: Very sensitive to touch or cold air, cannot brush with cold water. Spasmodic toothache, better from pressure on face or heat. Nervous, non-febrile spasms during teething.

Gastrointestinal: Flatulent colic; pains anywhere in the stomach or abdomen. Emesis from stress. Spasmodic pain, relieved by heat, drinking hot water, bending double, rubbing, pressure or lying down. Much flatulence or flatus; temporary relief only from release of. Feeling of tight band around abdomen. Hiccough. Bloated sensation of abdomen; must loosen clothing. Diarrhoea, watery from stress. Constipation, from stress.

Magnesium phosphate

Respiratory: Asthma, tight chest, wheezing, no expectoration, or clear gelatinous; from stress. Persistent paroxysmal coughing with no expectoration, worse lying down. Sharp, shooting pains through chest. Pleurodynia

Cardiovascular: Sharp, shooting pains or cramping through heart. Tachycardia. Arrhythmia. Angina pectoris. Hypertension. Atherosclerosis. Myocardial infarct.

CNS: Neuralgias, wherever sited. Muscular spasms, twitchings or fasciculations. Paræsthesias. Raynaud's phenomenon. Epilepsy. Tetanic spasms. Alcoholism. Delirium tremens.

Genitourinary: Uterine colic, often with referred back pain, better from, heat, pressure or bending double. Premenstrual tension (PMT/PMS). Dyspareunia. Vaginismus. Sterility, with no organic cause. Irregular menses. Polyuria. Diuresis.

Musculoskeletal: (See also CNS). Fasciitis. Myofascial pain syndrome. Repetitive strain injury (RSI). Sharp articular or periarticular pain, for whatever reason.

Iron phosphate

Role: Catalytic. Miscellaneous.

Memory key: Inflammation remover.

Brief prescribing indications: Acute localised inflammations and infections, resulting in heat and pain. First stage of all inflammations and infections. In chronic conditions, pallor, tiredness and weakness. Anæmia; hypochromic and microcytic (along with CP).

Symptoms aggravated by: Heat. Jarring movements. Excitement. Physical exertion. Night. Touch.

Symptoms improved by: Cold applications. Rest. Keeping still in the short-term. Movement, slow and gentle.

Tongue: Beefy red.

Exudate: Mucous membranes dry, irritated and inflamed; before discharges begin.

Iris: Acid wash. Flared autonomic wreath.

Biochemical notes: Iron phosphate occurs in nature as the mineral vivianite, and is widely distributed in foods. Grains, vegetables and beans are the richest non-animal sources, while meat, fish and poultry being the richest animal sources.

The major role of iron is to permit the transfer of oxygen and carbon dioxide from one tissue to another, through its involvement with the complex molecules of hæmoglobin and myoglobin. Iron also acts as an anti-infective agent, limiting the growth of microorganisms; is responsible in the cytochromes of mitochondria for the energy producing processes of oxidative phosphorylation and electron transport; for activating enzymes such as, catalases, peroxidases and several hydrogenases; catalysing the conversion of beta-carotene to vitamin A; the synthesis of purines, which form an integral part of nucleic acid; the synthesis of carnitine, a vitamin-like substance needed to transport fatty acids; the synthesis of collagen, the structural protein surrounding cells; in antibody production and in the detoxification of substances in the liver.

Iron phosphate is insoluble in water, but is soluble in gastric acid. Both iron and phosphate are well absorbed in the upper duodenum, where conditions are still acid, but poorly absorbed where conditions are more alkaline due to bile and pancreatic secretions. The efficiency of iron absorption varies between 5% to 15%, depending upon the dietary form and the relative need of the body for iron.

Before iron can be absorbed, it must first be separated from any organic material such as protein and any ferric iron must be reduced to the ferrous state. This change is accomplished in the presence of acid, either gastric (hydrochloric) acid or acids such as ascorbic acid, which is provided by many fruits and vegetables.

If the body has an immediate call for iron, transferrin, a protein in the blood with the specific function of transporting iron, comes in contact with the intestinal mucosal cell. The iron that was taken in by the cell from the intestine, will be carried across the cell and immediately released on the other side to combine with transferrin, which can bind two atoms of iron per molecule. This iron-transferrin complex in turn carries iron to the cells or to a storage site. Iron uptake can be rapid, with studies using radioactive iron demonstrating that significant amounts can be absorbed within four hours of ingestion, and incorporated into red blood cells within a day. If transferrin is about 33% saturated with iron, it does not pick-up any more. In this case, ferrous iron is released from the amino acid chelate and changed to the ferric form within the mucosal cell. In this form it combines with another protein, apoferritin, to form ferritin. It stays in this combination until transferrin calls for more iron. The iron is then given up from ferritin, changed to ferrous iron while it is still in the cells lining the intestine, and released into the blood to transferrin. If however, there is no requirement for iron, the young mucosal cell, still containing the stored iron, migrates up the villi and after 3 to 4 days, the cell, along with its iron will be lost to the fæces.

Iron phosphate

In normal health, a slow introduction of iron is physiologically preferable, as it favours the maximum formation of ferritin, the best utilised storage form. Rapid introduction of iron in water soluble forms, such as ferrous sulphate (the most common iron salt medically prescribed), not only favours the formation of the much less utilisable storage form, hæmosiderin, but in excess may poison the mucosal cells, by binding to the cytoplasmic protein and disrupting cell metabolism. The use of iron phosphate, which is insoluble in water but soluble in gastric acid, appears to be immune from inducing an uncontrolled uptake and the risk of mucosal cell poisoning.

Phosphate seems to be a natural regulator of iron absorption, as it also is for calcium and magnesium. In high doses, phosphate inhibits iron absorption by the formation of polyphosphate complexes, but in its absence, iron absorption becomes uncontrolled. In food, phosphate is the usual iron complexing agent and in its absence, severe iron loading occurs.

Over two-thirds of the iron in the body is functional iron, most of which is present in the hæmoglobin. A small portion (3%) of functional iron exists as part of myoglobin, an iron-containing protein similar to hæmoglobin, but found in muscle and designed to provide the increased store of oxygen required for intense muscular activity. The rest of the functional iron is in the tissue enzymes (5%-15%), which are present in every living cell and are essential for cellular respiration, involving the exchange of oxygen and carbon dioxide. A very small amount (4%) of iron is at any given time, present in the blood tightly bound to transferrin, free of hæmoglobin, and in transport to the cells. About 40mg of this transport iron is turned over in the blood each day. Ferritin is also in the blood serum in amounts paralleling storage iron (1,000mg, men; 400mg, women); the remaining one third of body iron is stored in the liver, spleen and bone marrow. Iron is stored as the soluble iron complex ferritin, which is one-fifth iron, or hæmosiderin, an insoluble iron-protein complex that is one-third iron.

Iron phosphate

Iron phosphate from a traditional Homœopathic standpoint, has been seen as an anti-infection and anti-inflammatory agent for over one hundred years. Very little scientific evidence is presently available to support this view, with recent studies of iron as an anti-infective agent suggest two conflicting roles. On one hand, since iron is essential for the growth of microorganisms, it means that potentially harmful bacteria will be able thrive if iron is available. On the other hand, if iron is not available, there is a decrease in iron-containing enzymes and other immune factors needed to destroy infectious organisms. In this instance, iron-deficient people are less able to fight infection. Lactoferrin in human milk is an iron-containing substance that is especially effective against E coli organisms in the gastrointestinal tract of infants. In this case, lactoferrin binds iron so that it is not available for bacterial growth. Bacterial requirements for iron increase not only with their growth, but also with temperature; hence the combined action of fever and a reduced availability of iron, acts to limit bacterial growth and depress cellular activity. The process of lowering serum iron levels in combination with fever, has been shown to be beneficial in combating infection. Animals allowed to develop fever in response to infection, had a lower mortality rate than those where fever was suppressed. In addition, the animals allowed to develop fever had low serum iron levels, suggesting that this combination is an adaptive response, conferring greater survival. Fever also increases the motility of white cells, resulting in increased bacterial destruction.

An alternative approach, could be to raise iron levels in order to saturate the bacterial environment, reducing toxin synthesis in many microorganisms and at the same time, providing white blood cells, especially neutrophils, with plentiful supplies of iron dependent enzymes, such as peroxidase.

While iron saturation during infection and fever has its merits, it does not seem to be a naturally induced mechanism; thus support for the traditional and empirical use of iron phosphate for infection and inflammation, cannot presently be explained or supported from the literature.

Clinical indications

Mental/emotional: Loss of courage and hope; better for sleep. Dizziness from anger. Can't find correct words to express himself. Desire for stimulants.

Head and face: Dull, congestive, throbbing headache; relieved by cold applications. Head sore to touch; cannot bear to have hair touched. Epistaxis. Epistaxis, relieves symptoms. Florid or pallid complexion. Florid appearance as precursor to headache or infection. Any injury to head. Sick headache, or nausea with vomiting of undigested food. Dizziness.

Eye: Inflammation, redness, irritation, dryness, or soreness, but without exudation.

ENT: Inflammatory earache, with burning or throbbing. First stage of infective process. Redness of the external meatus. First stage of head cold. Coryza, after exposure to cold. Rhinitis. Epistaxis. Inflamed, sore or dry throat, without exudation. Ulcerated, sore throat.

Iron phosphate

Teeth: Toothache, with red cheek. Toothache, worse from hot drinks or food, better from cold. Pressure on tooth increases pain. Feverishness during teething.

Gastrointestinal: Vomiting of undigested food or bright red blood. Flatulence, with taste of food eaten long before. Epigastrium tender to touch. Dyspepsia, with flushed face. Diarrhoea, with watery, undigested or bloody contents. Bleeding hæmorrhoids.

Cardiovascular: Weak, quick or thready pulse, worse following exertion. Anæmia (hypochromic and microcytic). Aneurisms. Phlebitis. Dilatations.

Respiratory: Dyspnœa, shortness of breath through anæmia. All inflammations of the respiratory tract. Hard, dry cough. Loss of voice and hoarseness. Hæmoptysis.

CNS: Malaise, weariness, feels the need for a stimulant.

Musculoskeletal: Any inflammation of muscle, tendon or joint.

Genitourinary: Frequent menses. Profuse flow of bright red blood. Vagina dry and hot. Vaginismus. Any inflammation of the kidney, bladder or urinary tract. Ischuria. Diurnal enuresis.

Febrile: All localised inflammations. First stage of all fevers. Feverishness at the beginning of any disease or ailment, before exudation. Night sweats through anæmia.

Skin and Tissues: Pallor of skin and mucous membranes with anæmia. Pain and inflammation associated with any skin disorder. Flushed, burning with cold sweat. Following lacerations or contusions. All sprains and strains. Pre-exudative stage of all inflammations. All hæmorrhages.

Silica

Role: Structural

Memory key: Calcium reorganiser.

Brief prescribing indications: Abnormal nutrition and calcification of bone, tendon, ligament or cartilage. Articular or periarticular degenerative changes. Osteophytes. Nodes. Avascular necrosis. Silica facilitates the removal of pathogenic and foreign waste from the body.

Symptoms aggravated by: Cold weather. Chilling of the feet. Before a storm. Cold draughts. Exposure to cold or becoming uncovered. Night, early morning. Lying down. Rest. Full or new moon. Touch. Physical movement. Upon arising in the morning or after rest.

Symptoms improved by: Hot, humid or wet weather. Summertime. Warm room. Pressure on, or rubbing of affected part. Covering-up of affected part (with bedclothes etc.).

Exudate: Chronic purulent and mucopurulent discharges, that won't heal. In acute abscess; to ripen.

Iris: Check and compare with symptoms; Skin zone. Arcus sclerosis.

Biochemical notes: Silicon dioxide is found in nature as sand, quartz and flint and is the most abundant mineral in the earth's crust. Silica is now proven to be an essential structural trace element for all life forms. As a nutrient, it is found in all plant foods, particularly unrefined grains, in both the inorganic and the organic form as hydrated silica in acids and bound to polysaccharides. Beer also has a high concentration of silica.

Despite the fact that Hahnemann's research into the physiological role of silica was published as far back as 1828, it was not until 1972 that silica was actually classified as an essential trace nutrient. More recently, silica, along with manganese, copper, molybdenum, chromium, nickel, vanadium, tin, arsenic, boron and cobalt, have been re-defined as *ultratrace* elements; representing those elements that are required by the body in less than *trace* amounts.

It is now scientifically recognised, that silica plays a role in stimulating growth, initiating calcification of bone, and promoting the synthesis of connective tissue. It is interesting to note that the basic role of silica, as understood today, was also accurately determined by Hahnemann in 1828, without access to today's sophisticated and precise analytical instrumentation; without animal studies; without withdrawing the element from the diet of test subjects to note the effect; and without the benefit of a massive database of scientific and medical knowledge from which to draw and relate. Hahnemann achieved this seemingly impossible feat by putting healthy human volunteers through the homœopathic procedure of *proving* (see page 11), the results of which must seriously challenge the efficiency of our modern techniques and criteria for determining physiological need (see page 23).

Silica appears to be efficiently absorbed in the small intestine, but apart from this, very little else is presently known. Silica can also be absorbed into the blood from the lungs as silicic acid, by the inhalation of the dust of stone, sand or flint, containing silica. This situation can in time lead to generalised nodular fibrotic changes to the lung tissue, and the condition, silicosis. The kidney appears to be the main excretory organ, with daily urinary loss of about 10mg. Between 5%-10% of ingested silica os excreted in the urine, with losses being more or less equal to intake. Presently there is no data as to what represents an optimum daily intake, but it is estimated that the average intake is in the order of about 200mg a day.

Silica

Silica is primarily found in connective tissue, with particularly high concentrations in cartilage, ligament, skin, hair and nails. The blood serum has a low concentration of silica (0.5mg/l), consistent with that of other trace elements. The function of silica is primarily structural, where it contributes to the rigidity of larger molecules, and assists in the laying-down of intercellular matrix. It appears to confer chemical resistance to keratinous tissue, alters the permeability of cell membranes, and may also act as a barrier to absorption and exudation. All cells of the body contain silica in small amounts, especially cells of the liver, heart, muscle and arterial walls.

Because of silica's property of forming rings, chains and sheets, in common with carbon, another group five element, silica acts primarily as a cross-linking agent in connective tissue. In the manufacture of new bone, silica and calcium levels both rise congruently. For some time it has been observed that new bone crystals will not form, until a trigger occurs, even it the major bone constituents of calcium and phosphate are present in saturated solutions. It now appears that silica provides the seed crystal that calcium phosphate builds upon. This argument is supported by the observation that the silica content of new bone is much higher than that of mature bone.

Intercellular material is composed of collagen, elastin and reticular fibres, immersed in an amorphous ground substance of mucopolysaccharides of glucosaminoglycans. These not only provide support for cellular structures, but also bind significant quantities of water. It appears that silica is necessary for the synthesis of this material. It also acts as a cross-linking agent, by forming bridges between adjacent polysaccharide chains, aiding the stability and rigidity of the tissue and significantly affecting permeability. A loss of silica from connective tissue is accompanied by losses of water and polysaccharide chains.

Hence it can be seen from the preceding information, that the traditional use of silica as a nutrient and regenerator of bone and connective tissue generally, for conditions such as degenerative arthritis, seem vindicated by more recent discoveries.

Clinical indications

Mental/emotional: Thought difficult. Many thoughts rush through mind simultaneously. Difficulty in constructing thoughts due to lack of concentration. Fixed ideas. Exaggerated fear of pins or needles. Anxious dreams. Somnambulism. Tires quickly from mental activity.

Silica

Head and Face: Hair falling, ends split. Nodules and pustules on scalp. Pain in occiput that spreads over head and settles above eyes. Neuralgia; tearing, throbbing, worse from exposure to damp cold. Lips crack. Gumboil. Root abscess. Pyorrhoea. Teeth sensitive to cold water.

Eye: Cataract. Dullness of vision. Styes. Dendritic ulcers. Orbital neuralgia.

ENT: Sensitivity to noise. Otorrhoea, purulent or ichoroid discharges, or dullness of hearing from same. Mastoiditis. Fœtid discharge from nares. Chronic coryza, with swelling of mucous membranes, dryness, crusts, bleeding, and loss of smell. Herpetic ulcers around nares. Tonsillitis, when suppuration won't stop. Parotitis. Colds settle into throat infection. Stinging pain on swallowing. Hard, painless swelling of cervical glands.

Teeth: Root abscess. Gumboil. Teeth loose and gums painful to pressure. Toothache brought on by a chill, not relieved by either hot or cold applications, worse at night.

Gastrointestinal: Motions recede and are difficult to expel. Hard, bloated abdomen. Colic with cutting pain. Constipation, fæces gather in rectum. Diarrhoea, fœtid. Hæmorrhoids. Anal fistula.

Respiratory: Asthma, worse after midnight. Tickling cough, worse when lying down at night and from cold drinks. Colds quickly settle into chest infection, with slow recovery. Cough during day, purulent and bloody. Violent cough at night or when lying down, with muco-purulent sputum, thick and lumpy. Sore throat and cough with expectoration containing small, hard, smelly lumps.

Cardiovascular: Silica is indicated for any chronic degenerative condition of the cardiovascular system.

CNS: Silica is indicated in all chronic degenerative diseases of the nervous system.

Genitourinary: Menses associated with icy-coldness over entire body, fœtid perspiration. Breasts, hard, knotty and painful. Cracked nipples. Ulcerations and fistulas. Mastitis with suppuration. Itchy, sensitive vulva and vagina. Mid-cycle bleeding, with paroxysms of icy coldness over entire body. Hydrocele. Itching and sweating of scrotum. Seminal emissions, nocturnal. Increased sexual urge, with feelings of weakness following coitus. Chronic gonorrhœa, with thick fœtid, purulent discharge. Chronic cystitis, with suppuration and bleeding. Uraturia.

Musculoskeletal: All degenerative conditions affecting, tendon, cartilage, connective tissue and bone. Degenerative joint disease. Herniated or ruptured discs. Sciatica. Osteomalacia. Osteoporosis. Gout. To callus fractures. Bone pain, growing pains, shin pains. Caries and necrosis of bone. Keloid growths. Nodes, nodules, exostoses and cysts on tendon or bone.

Silica

Tissues: All conditions that result from a breakdown or poor nutrition of connective tissue. Keloids. Nails, fragile or distorted. White spots on nails. Ingrowing toe-nails. Hair falls and/or ends split. Wounds won't heal; purulent and ichorous discharges. Indurated glands. Mastitis with suppuration. Breasts, hard and painful. Nipples crack and become infected. Delayed and imperfect dentition. Skin heals imperfectly. Sensitive gums. Gumboil. Root abscess. Icy cold, sweaty feet. Sweat has fœtid odour. Parts lain on go to sleep. Painless, hard glandular swellings. Ends of fingers dry and crack.

Skin: Boils, ulcers, carbuncles, nodules, acne, abscesses, pustules. Wounds won't heal and become infected easily. Skin heals with difficulty and suppurates easily. Ulcers, with proud flesh, elevated bluish edges and fœtid, ichorous discharge. Keloids. Old scars suddenly become painful. To promote expulsion of foreign material from body. Profuse and often fœtid smelling perspiration. Discoid lupus. Skin fissures. Premature wrinkling.

Febrile: Night sweats, worse toward morning. Malnourished, æsthetic types, sensitive to cold air - must be kept warm and covered.

Chapter five

Symptom qualification

Conditions which modify a symptom are called: Symptom Qualifications

Symptom Qualification (the homœopathic principle of "Modalities"), is one of the means by which a prescription can be tailored to suit an individual patient's needs. Symptom qualification questioning reinforces symptoms by understanding the conditions which modify those symptoms. The technique helps to remove the disadvantages of either prescribing for the name of the patient's illness, the symptoms alone, or a combination of both. The justifiable criticism often made of orthodox medical treatment, is that it is treatment for the "disease" and not the "patient". Unfortunately the same criticism can also be directed at many alternative medical approaches, because they too, concentrate only on the disease or the symptoms.

Before developing the very simple principles of questioning for symptom qualifications, it is worthwhile considering further the philosophical aspects of, *treating the patient, not the disease and treating the cause, not the symptoms*. These points were touched on in the introduction on pages 5-6, and perhaps a good starting point, regardless of our present discipline, is to ask ourselves two basic questions:

1. Where do we recognise the root cause of disease to be? And...At what level will our treatment method take effect?

2. Should we address the treatment towards the patient or the disease? And...What's the difference anyway?

Question one puts the proposition that orthodox medicine with its approaches of drugs and surgery, addresses only the *effects* and not the. *cause* of disease; and similarly, just because a modality is labelled as *alternative* or *naturopathic*, is no guarantee that it will get any closer to removing the *cause* either. The claim often associated with a natural modality, that of treating the *cause and not just the symptoms*, becomes an empty cliché, rather than a statement pregnant with practical benefits for the patient. Orthodox medicine cannot be criticised in this regard, because for the most part there is none of this pretence associated with its approach to healing. Justifiable criticism of orthodox medicine though, stems from the effect that the treatment of symptoms rather than causes has on the long-term interests of the patient; and by default, what the patient might erroneously assume as a result of his experiences, thus being lured into a false security.

Mineral therapy applied according to the principles of Schüssler, Blackmore and the author, can be demonstrated to be in complete conformity with true naturopathic principles; and If the patient remains well after the withdrawal of the treatment, it can be assumed that the root cause of the illness has been addressed as well as the symptoms (that is, so long as the cause is at all treatable in the first place).

Question two focuses on the practical reality as to whether alternative methods always conform to the principle of treating the patient rather than the disease, and whether in fact many alternative methods lend themselves to that approach anyway. Orthodox medicine is often criticised for treating *disease labels*, rather than the patient's *uniqueness*, but many alternative methods offer no greater scope in this regard than the standard medical approach.

To be able to treat the patient as an individual, first of all supposes that it is necessary to differentiate between different people suffering from the same disease. This distinction needs to be drawn, because it can easily be demonstrated that not all patients suffering the same illness will necessarily be affected in exactly the same way; and also, that the treatment modality requires the scope to be able to accommodate that situation. But is that always so?

Mineral therapy accommodates the principles of Symptom Qualification

Mineral therapy again conforms to true naturopathic principles, in that there exists within it, the means to accommodate both the obvious and subtle differences between patients, even when suffering from the same disease. This important but most times overlooked aspect of treatment is made possible because mineral therapy has taken its symptomatology directly from the homœopathic system. This procedure allows the practitioner to interpret those subtle symptoms and signs, in the belief that not only do they represent vital information that should not be ignored, but that they can be used to prescribe more accurately.

There is also a further extension of the above principles. What happens if the patient responds to treatment? Do we congratulate ourselves, rest on our laurels, and see only the need to continue with more of the same treatment? Why should we even consider tampering with a treatment that is proving to be successful? Well maybe we should! Logic dictates that the patient sitting before us on subsequent visits (regardless of improvement or not), is not necessarily the patient who sat before us at the time of the first consultation. The healing process, along with the disease process, and along with everything else in life, is a dynamic entity. This dynamic, ever changing situation, demands that reassessment of the case be made from time to time, adjusting the treatment if indicated, even if the patient *is* improving. Again, the remaining unanswered question, is whether our modality can accommodate this situation. If not, this aspect might help to explain the experience, of being able to initially help a patient, only to find that soon after a brick wall is hit and healing comes to a sudden stop!

When a patient's history is taken, it is obviously important to gather as many symptoms and signs as possible, so that a diagnosis can be made and treatment prescribed. There will be occasions though, where there is insufficient information to make a proper diagnosis, or where there are confusing or even conflicting indicators in the patient's symptom picture. This is where the process of understanding, collecting and interpreting symptom qualifications, can make the difference between whether treatment can even be offered to the patient or not, whether that treatment is going to be specifically tailored to the patient's needs and whether through greater accuracy the treatment will prove to be more successful.

A patient may at times only have a couple of actual symptoms but with skilful questioning (or observing) for qualifications, a diagnosis may still be made. This line of questioning also helps to open up the patient, often leading him off into new areas of helpful information. Questioning for qualifications should not be thought of as a last resort technique but blended in with the general probing for symptoms. Naturally though, it really comes into its own as a last resort when all else has failed.

Symptom Qualification represents a time and motion study of the patient

Qualifications could humorously be called a *time and motion* study of the patient. In fact qualifications cover a number of general factors which may affect the patient's condition. Some of the most important influences, are those of:

> Time of day, body positioning and movement, various atmospheric and seasonal weather patterns, items of food and drink, and emotional and experiential influences, insofar as these conditions either make the patient's symptoms worse or better.

The practical benefits for the practitioner can be expressed in the following way:

1. To eliminate errors in prescribing.

2. To eliminate over-prescribing.

3. To eliminate under-prescribing.

Qualifications, refer to the whole patient as an individual, not just the symptoms, or the purely somatic nature of the patient's complaint. For this reason an ear should be tuned, when listening to the patient relating his history (or when answering questions) as to whether he precedes a remark by referring to "I" or "My". "I" usually refers to a "qualification" and "My" to a symptom. An example being, "My head aches" (symptom), and "I feel worse when I'm cold -I hate the cold weather" (qualification). Now this can also mean that the patient's headache will be worse in the cold, but then because this is not a symptom but a qualification, so too will probably everything else that's wrong with the person. Not that a patient can always be expected to express himself exactly in this way, but once the practitioner is aware of the principles, he can train his mind to decode information into symptoms and qualifications as the patient is talking. In this way the practitioner systematises his approach, having a little box, as it were, for each category.

At the conclusion of most consultations, the practitioner should have quite a lot of information. A critical time for the practitioner, for no matter how well the interview has been handled, an error in prescribing based on hasty judgement, may negate the lot. Quite often two or even three minerals are indicated for the same symptoms or are very close. One carefully worded question will most times provide the differentiation necessary to prescribe accurately.

The process of Symptom Qualification illustrated

Each stroke (——) represents a symptom gathered

Symptom Qualification demonstrated

Determining the dominant mineral deficiency from symptoms alone

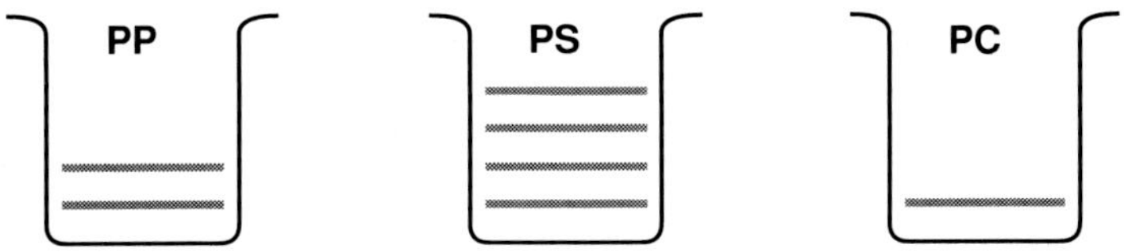

Difficult situation where the symptom indications are equally weighted

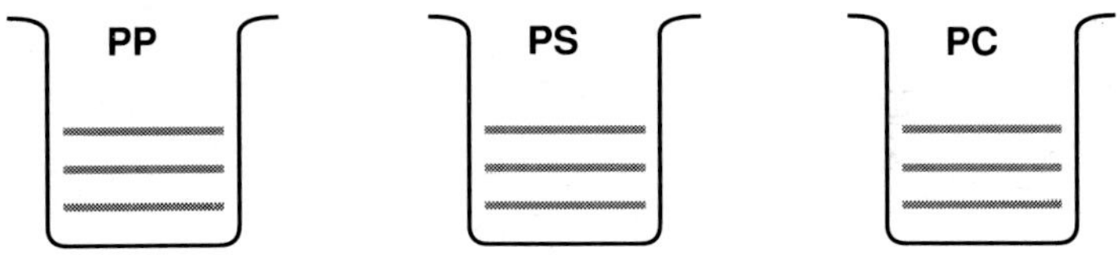

Qualifications highlight the differing physiological role of salts that share the same cation

Situation resolved by Symptom Qualification questioning: PS is the only salt where the symptoms are worse in a *Warm, stuffy room**

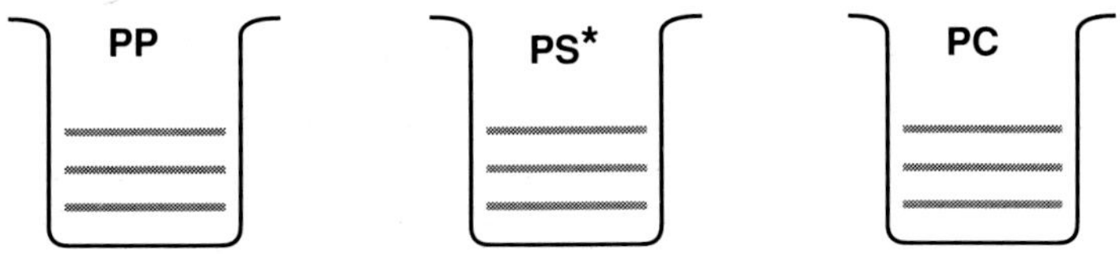

The beakers represent imaginary receptacles for all the potassium symptoms that have been gathered from a patient. If we look at the top row of beakers, it would appear, and perhaps rightly so, that the dominant and most indicated deficiency is potassium sulphate; because a greater number of potassium sulphate symptoms have been gathered. If we were to prescribe according to the symptoms alone, then potassium sulphate is strongly indicated, but, if it was also determined from questioning, that the patient's symptoms are worse *in a warm, stuffy room,* then our knowledge of symptom qualifications tells us that potassium sulphate is in fact the remedy. Neither potassium phosphate nor potassium chloride symptoms are aggravated by, *warm, stuffy rooms.*

The deficiency state of the patient is not likely to stop at potassium sulphate, due to secondary and synergistic deficiencies, so further questioning will be required to determine the remaining deficiencies. The illustration given is of course an oversimplification and represents the situation where one salt is to be chosen from a possibility of three. In actual fact, the practitioner will be faced with this process of elimination on at least two and possibly three occasions, when interviewing the average chronic case. The technique then serves as a viable means to honour one of our major objectives; to increase the accuracy of prescribing and thus make for more effective prescribing.

The qualifications are listed under each category in alphabetical order and where a number of salts are ascribed to a single qualification (eg., "Improved By", *Warmth*), not all are to be prescribed, but rather a choice has to be made by further questioning, or by collating the information already obtained. This is not to say though, that the practitioner cannot end up with more than one of the salts ascribed to that qualification, but the other salt/s, will come from the reinforcement of other symptoms or qualifications. The "Prescribing rules" as outlined on page 111, should also be considered when applying the principle of symptom qualification.

The extensive list of qualifications contained in this chapter has been compiled from numerous reference books on the subject and also the authors own findings.

To begin with, the list of qualifications provided on the "Mineral Master Chart" (page 112) should be committed to memory, as they represent the most likely conditions that the practitioner will encounter during the early stages of practice. The more extensive list that follows can then be referred to and memorised as the need arises.

Aggravated by:

Aggravated by:

Afternoon, evening PS, SP, SS
Air; cold draughts PP, MP, S, CP
  hot PS, IP, PC
  open S, SP
Alcohol; prolonged effects of MP
Away from home PP
Before a storm S, SS
Being alone PP
Being uncovered; bedclothes at night S, PP
Changeable weather SP, CP, CF, PS
Chilling of feet S
Clothing, tight around abdomen or waist SS

Aggravated by:

Cold; any form of CP, MP, S, PP
Cold air; draughts CP, MP, S, PP
Cold water; application of MP
Cold; weather CP, S, CF, MP
Company; the prolonged effects of PP
Damp SS, CP, CF, S, CS
  weather SS
  living conditions SS
Draughts; cold CP, MP, S, PP
Drinks; hot PS
Dry heat PC
Early morning; after midnight PP, SS
  before midnight S
Eating; fatty, rich food SP, PC
  cold food or drink S
  fish, seafoods SS
  fruit & vegetables CP
  meat, milk, eggs IP
Evening; afternoon PS, SP, SS
Excitement; prolonged PP, IP
Exertion; physical MP, PP, SS, IP, S, CP, CF, CS
  mental PP (children CP)
Fatty, rich food SP, PC
Fish; eating of SS
Flashing, bright lights PP, MP
Flatus; inability to expel MP, CP
Fruit & vegetables; eating of CP
Full or new moon S
Glare; bright light PP, MP
Heat; IP, PC, PS
Heights PP
Homesickness PP
Hot; air PS, IP, PC
  drinks PS
  humid weather SS, PS
Jarring movement IP
Left side; lying on SS
Light; bright PP, MP
Lively music saddens SS
Lying down S, SS, CF
Meat, milk, eggs; eating of IP
Mental; exertion PP (children CP)
  stimuli S
Midnight; after SS
Milk, meat, eggs; eating of IP
Moon; full or new S
Morning; early, after midnight PP, SS
Morning; early, before midnight S

Aggravated by:

Morning; upon arising S, CF
Motion; (strenuous movement of body) IP, MP, PC, SS, CP, S
after rest PP, S, CF
Music; lively, saddens SS
New, or full moon S
Night S, IP, MP
Noise PP, MP
Nostalgia PP
Open air SP, S
Overheated warmth CS
Physical exertion MP, PP, SS, IP, S, CP, CF, CS
Prolonged excitement PP
Rest CF, S
Rich, fatty foods SP, PC
Rooms; warm, stuffy or smoky PS
Seafood; eating SS
Seaside; by the SS
Sitting; rising from PP
Springtime PS, CP
Storm; before S, SS
Stress, worry PP
Stuffy, warm rooms PS
Teething CP
Thunderstorms SP
Tight clothing around waist or abdomen SS
Touch MP, IP, S
Uncovered; bedclothes at night S
Upon arising, in the morning , or after rest S, CF, PP
Warmth, overheated CS
Washing or working in water SS
Water; cold application of MP
working with CS
Weather; changeable, unstable SP, CF, CP, PS
cold CP, S, CF, MP
damp SS, CP, S, CF, CS
hot, humid SS, PS
Worry PP

Improved by:

Improved by:

Air; open and fresh PS, SS
Alcohol; initial effects of MP
Applications of cold to affected part IP, PC
Being home PP
Bending double MP
Body position; to change frequently SS, PP
Cold applications to affected part IP, PC
Cool, fresh, open air PS, CS

Improved by:

Company; the initial effects of PP
Covering up; affected part (with bedclothes etc.) S, PP
  against draughts S, CP, MP, PP
Day-time; once up and about S, SS
Dry warmth SS
Eating; PP
  carbohydrate (sweets & biscuits etc.) MP
  salted and smoked meats CP
Excitement; initial effects of PP, (children CP)
Flatus; expulsion of MP, CP
Fresh open air PS
Friction; over affected area MP, S, CF, SS
Heat, warmth MP, CP, PP, S, CF, SS
Home; being PP
Hot applications to affected part MP, S, CF
Humid, hot weather S
Keeping still (in the short term) IP, MP, PC, S, CP
Loosening clothing from around abdomen SS
Lying down CP
Mental diversion PP
Movement; slow and gentle PP, IP, S, CF
Open fresh air PS, CS
Pressure or rubbing of affected part MP, S, CF, SS
Rest PP, CP, IP
Rubbing or pressure over affected part MP, S, CF, SS
Standing erect PP
Summertime S, CP
Sweets; eating of MP
Urination S
Warmth, heat MP, CP, PP, S, CF, SS
Warm applications to affected part MP, S, CF
Weather; dry and warm SS, CF, CP, CS
  humid, warm or hot S
  Stable, SP, PS, CP, CF

Chapter six

Iris, pupil and tongue indications

This chapter discusses how the various markings that appear in the iris and the shape of the pupil correspond to mineral deficiencies and the sorts of symptoms that those deficiencies are capable of producing. For the most part the information is empirical, representing the accumulated experience of the author and others and cannot generally be supported by accepted scientific criteria. The principles put forward primarily stem from observation, coupled with the ability to be able to replicate conditions in a way that would suggest that there is a direct and actual correlation between iris markings and deficiencies; albeit at this stage unproven. For all these reasons, the use of the iris as a diagnostic and prognostic tool, should only be encouraged when it is used in conjunction with other, more traditional methods of diagnosis, such as patient questioning, observation, examination and testing.

It is common for a patient assessed by *iris diagnosis* methods, to be shown to possess markings in his irides that may be interpreted as indicating some kind of pathology, yet the patient is asymptomatic, and remains, asymptomatic. On the other hand, a patient may possess no obvious destructive iris markings whatsoever, and yet be demonstrated by other means, to be suffering from a life-threatening illness. Unfortunately, the *diagnosis* of iris diagnosis, is very ambiguous indeed, resting to a large extent, in the *eyes* of the beholder. Lay people, caught-up in much of the hype about iris diagnosis as purveyed by the media or the influence of some well intentioned but over-zealous practitioners, could easily be excused for believing that the human eye came equipped from the factory with a liquid crystal display. The patient ensnared in this trap, may then be obliged to carry the burden of a false-positive or false-negative diagnosis for the rest of his life; such are the vagaries and dangers of iris diagnosis per se.

Factory fitted liquid crystal displays

This particular technique utilises the circular concentric system zones of the iris only (with slight modification), and not the individual radial division into the hundreds of organs and parts of the more traditional form of *iris diagnosis*, thus the chart is greatly rationalised and is the same for both the left and right eye. The technique is easily learned and quickly performed and requires no specialised or expensive equipment.

Qualitative assessment rather than quantitative

Assessing mineral deficiencies, should be seen as *qualitative*, and not *quantitative*. This means that iris indicators, can neither be used to accurately estimate the degree of the deficiency, or the precise nature or extent of the disease; but rather that certain deficiencies exist, and that they are influencing body function adversely, in a way that the iris findings and the patient's symptom picture should correlate.

Iris markings may change over a period of time, but not commensurate with the patient's awareness to change

The technique relies on the iris findings established on the first consultation, and not comparisons made on subsequent visits. Future assessments of the patient and any changes to treatment, are made on the basis of what is happening with the patient at that time, not changes in the iris markings. *Iris markings may change over a period of time, but not commensurate with the patient's awareness to change.*

The procedure should be conducted only after interviewing and examining the patient; not before. The value of leaving the examination of the irides until after the case history taking, is that the information gained from the iris, will either provide confirmation and/or reinforcement of the details already gained from the case history; or, will provide additional information, that will enable the practitioner to go back and ask further questions. If there is any conflict or confusion between the information gained from questioning the patient and that observed in the iris, then the practitioner should always prescribe according to the patient's symptom picture alone.

Iris findings can reinforce other diagnostic indicators

The whole purpose of gaining information from the iris, is to reinforce existing information, or provide new information and thus open avenues for further investigation. If this process provides the practitioner with greater confidence in his deliberations, then it is worthwhile; otherwise if confusion creeps into the process, then it becomes counter-productive and the practitioner should therefore go back to basics and prescribe on the basis of the symptoms alone.

The actual technique of examining the iris is very simple and straight forward. The patient should be seated, at a height that makes it easy for the practitioner to look straight into the patient's eyes without stooping. If this position, such as the height of an examination couch, cannot easily be arranged then it is best to have the patient stand. Whatever position is adopted, it is important that reflections be avoided, by having the patient face away from any bright extraneous light. A bright medical torch should be held in one hand and a magnifying glass of about 5x, in the other, with the practitioner aligning himself in such a way as to be directly in front of the patient. The light source should never be applied directly into the patient's eyes, but rather from the oblique. If the light is directed straight at the eye, not only will it be distressing to the patient, but it will render a flat, one dimensional image of the iris that is difficult to assess. If on the other hand the light is directed from the side, moving the position of the light back and forth so as to obtain the optimum image, then the patient will not be distressed, evidenced by an absence of any pupillary response, and the practitioner will have an image to work with, that displays all the subtle markings lost by front-lighting.

30 seconds well spent

The examination time is obviously going to vary according to the individual case and the practitioner's experience, but generally it can be completed in about thirty seconds.

If the procedure is conducted at the conclusion of taking the case history, along with any other tests that need to be performed, then the patient's attention will not usually be drawn to the purpose of the examination, thus avoiding the task of having to answer time-consuming questions.

Key chart to iris

Key chart to zones for both left and right eyes.

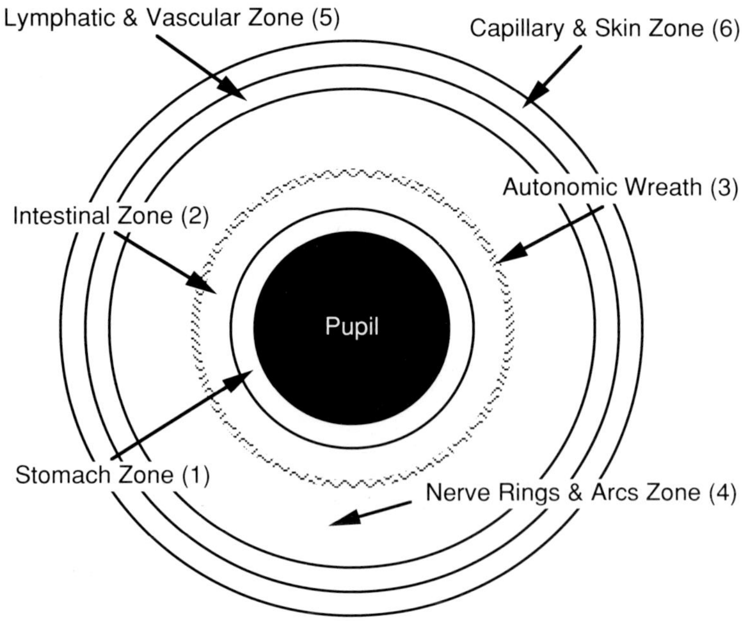

1. Stomach zone. (First concentric zone out from the pupil).

2. Intestinal zone.

3. Autonomic wreath. (Present in health).

4. Nerve ring zone.

5. Lymphatic and vascular zone. (Second last zone, displaying markings that appear in both the iris and the cornea).

6. Capillary and skin zone. (Last zone bordering the sclera and displaying markings that appear in both the iris and the cornea).

Now let's take a look at each zone in detail, study the markings with the aid of the photos provided and interpret them on the basis of indicating specific mineral deficiencies.

The exact position where the practitioner can expect to find the various zones of the iris will vary slightly from person to person; and in some cases may vary greatly. The position of each individual zone displayed on the *Key Chart*, is offered as a general guide to their placement and will be found to be quite accurate for the majority of cases.

Typical iris

Example of a typical iris.

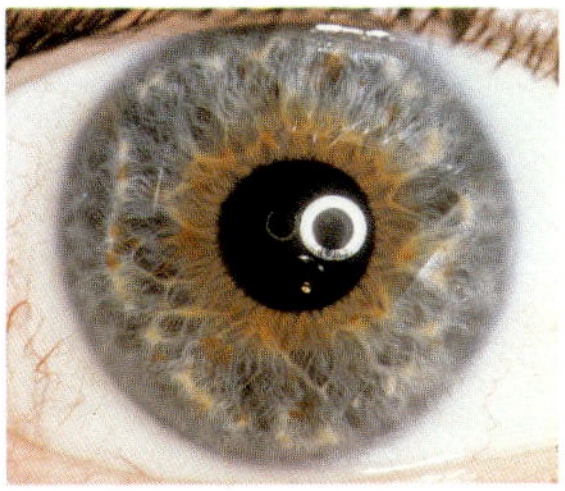

Iris colour

Colour. The actual colour of the iris is academic for the purpose of this examination. For practical reasons though, the dark brown, almost black iris, is very difficult to read.

Iris texture

Texture. The texture of the iris gives some guide to the individual's ability to recover from an illness. Initially determined by the genes, it can then be influenced by acquired weaknesses, mostly through faulty lifestyle. It is demonstrated by observing the way the anterior fibres of the iris relate to each other. A good ability to resist disease and recover quickly is demonstrated by the fibres being virtually invisible because they are so fine and even; whilst a poor ability to resist and recover, is demonstrated by the fibres being coarse, raised, twisted and opening to form holes. When examining for texture, all other markings should be ignored; only the general impression as to the underlying texture is of importance.

To possess a fine textured iris is no guarantee that the individual will never suffer an illness, but it does seem to indicate, that if ill, the person stands a better chance of making a quick and full recovery. Therefore, *texture* is the first observation and assessment that should be made.

For recording purposes, patients need to be graded in some sort of way that allows for a meaningful retrieval of information on some future occasion. A grading-scale should be introduced, that allows for a grading of iris texture, on a scale of 0 to 10 (or 0-100%), covering the range of possibilities from "Bad", through "Poor", "Average", "Good", to "Excellent".

The appropriate value for that patient is then selected from the scale and entered on the patient's card, along with any further comments that may need to be made. In this way, the practitioner, immediately upon observing the original grading, will have an instant mental image of what he observed on the patient's first visit.

The danger for inexperienced practitioners when rating patients, is that initially, patients will be rated either too high, or too low on the scale, thus leaving no room for those patients who may genuinely require that position. It's only after a few hundred patients have been observed, or the opportunity to be coached by an experienced practitioner, that the student will be in a position to rate a patient accurately.

Iris rating scales

Iris texture rating scale

Bad	Poor	Average	Good	Excellent
0	2.5	5	7.5	10

All other listings

Not at all	A little	Moderate	Very much so	Severe
0	2.5	5	7.5	10

The *Rating Scales* above are offered as an example of how a practitioner could rate his iris observations. The practitioner is also free to choose values between those offered.

Examples of Good and Bad Texture.

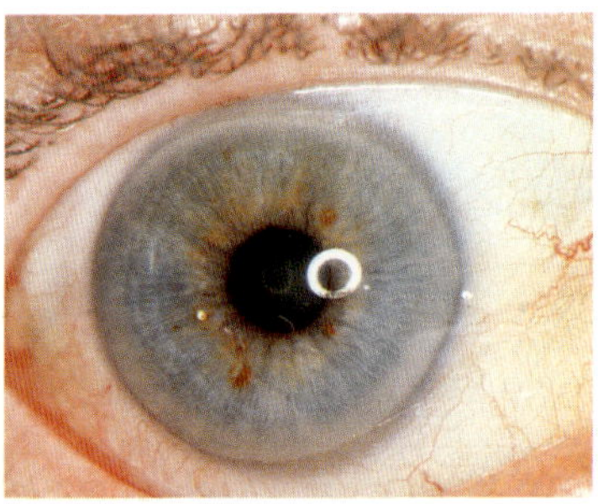

Good texture

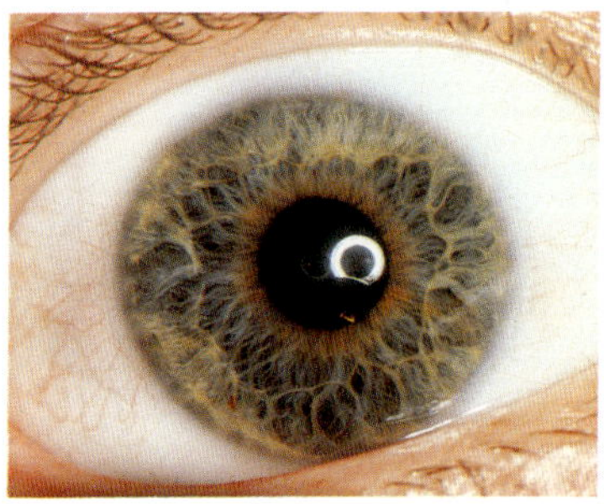

Poor texture

Stomach zone

Stomach zone. The Stomach zone is easy to locate, as it's the first zone out from the pupil, and along with the Intestinal zone, it covers the region from the pupillary border, to the Autonomic wreath.

The Stomach zone (and intestinal zone) usually has an overall darker appearance than the area of the iris between the Autonomic wreath and the sclera. This observation is perhaps in keeping with naturopathic philosophy, which states that many pathological changes have their beginning in the alimentary system, due to our disregard for the laws of diet.

There are a few major indications for mineral deficiencies that can be observed in this area of the iris:

Example of stomach signs.

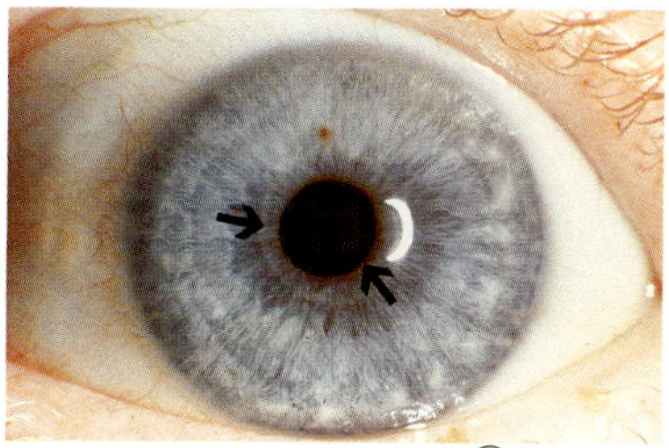

1. An overall whitish or milky discolouration, indicating an over-production of gastric acid (hyperchlorhydria), and a need for SP. There may be symptoms of gastric discomfort after meals, heartburn, indigestion, burning or sour gastric reflux, or flatulence, with this sign. Although SP is the major salt indicated, the immediate acute symptoms usually call for the addition of MP, PC and IP.

2. An orange-brown colour around the pupillary edge of the iris, indicating an under-production of gastric acid (hypochlorhydria), and a need for PC. There may be symptoms of nausea, indigestion, flatulence, vomiting, or anorexia, associated with this sign. As chronicity sets in, there is often seen (with magnification) to be a dark pitting or erosion of the inner edge of the iris, giving a serrated appearance. This sign indicates that degenerative changes have occurred within the glands and mucosa of the stomach, producing symptoms such as inflammation, ulceration or induration and conditions such as, atrophic gastritis. Although PC is again the dominant deficiency, there will be accompanying symptoms calling for salts such as, MP, IP, SP or CF to be included along with the PC.

Note. Because of the obvious relationship that the tongue has to the stomach and intestinal system as a whole, always check and compare tongue indications with those of the iris before prescribing. Most times there will be a correlation between the signs of the tongue and the iris.

Intestinal zone

Intestinal zone. The Intestinal zone is the next concentric band, situated in the iris between the Stomach zone and the Autonomic wreath. As with the Stomach zone, the Intestinal zone generally appears to be darker than the area outside of the Autonomic wreath. This again occurs for the reasons mentioned previously, and generally can be interpreted as indicating a dysfunction of the gut, resulting in poor absorption and/or elimination.

Note. Markings observed in the Intestinal zone do not in themselves give a guide to any specific mineral deficiencies that may exist. Other indicators, such as the tongue and the patient's symptom picture must be considered in conjunction with any iris findings.

Intestinal markings.

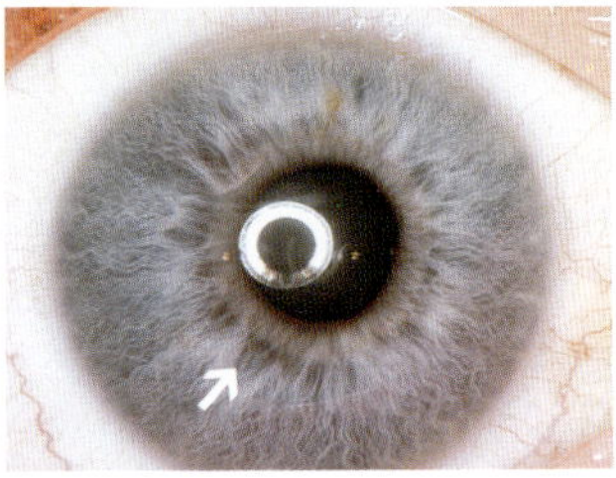

Dark markings, that may encompass the whole zone or appear in isolated pockets, indicating intestinal stasis in those areas relating to where the markings appear. Functionally these states result in increased putrefaction and absorbed toxins. Often associated with these markings, the intestinal area will be seen to extend beyond the bounds of the zone, pushing the Autonomic wreath outwards, or dip into the Stomach zone and almost touch the pupil. This sort of appearance often suggests a gross change in shape, symmetry and anatomical position of the intestines, as in a condition such as diverticular disease. Again the interpretation and significance of these markings, from both a disease and deficiency standpoint, must be made with the assistance of other diagnostic indicators.

Autonomic wreath

Autonomic wreath. The Autonomic wreath, is a fine jagged discrete circle, situated about one third of the radius from the border of the pupil and the periphery of the iris and should maintain an equidistant relationship to these landmarks. It is present in both health and disease, and represents the sympathetic and parasympathetic systems. Changes in the wreath indicate an altered state of the autonomic system that can affect the body in a variety of ways.

Autonomic wreath markings.

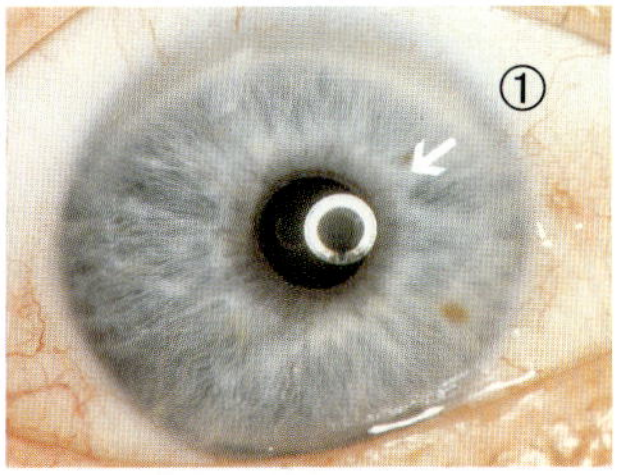

Flared wreath

②

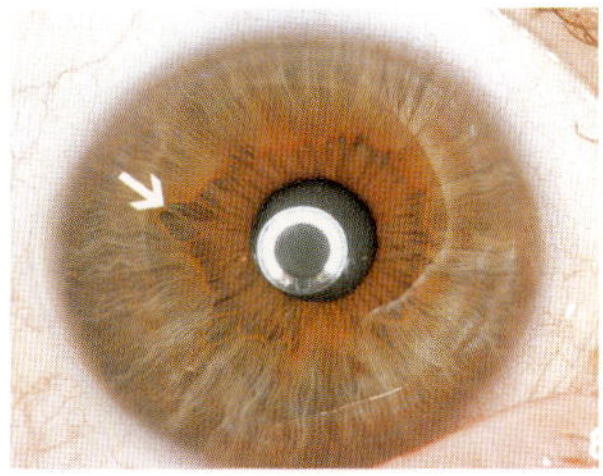

Jutting wreath

③

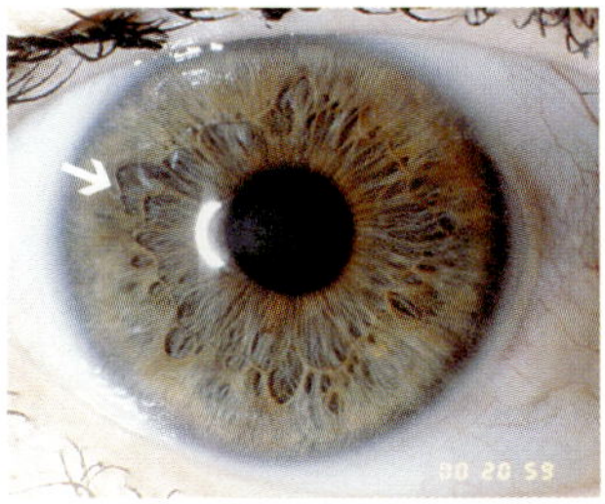

Hypotonic wreath

④

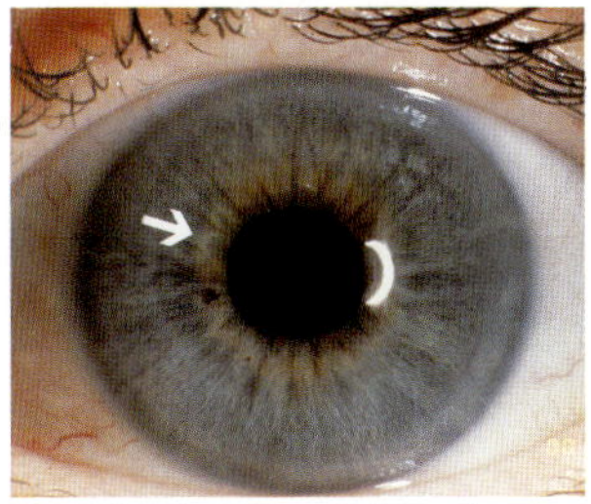

Hypertonic wreath

1. A flared, fuzzy wreath, with an overall whitish appearance, indicating irritation of the nerves due to the infiltration of acidic metabolic wastes. The minerals that are indicated by such an appearance are SP, MP, PC, and IP.

2. A marked or sudden divergence of the wreath, inwards or outwards from its normal position. This sign may be seen to be associated with a wreath that otherwise has a normal appearance, or it may be flared as in the previous example. The interpretation of this sign from both a disease and a deficiency standpoint is difficult to assess without the consideration of many other factors. There exists the belief in iris diagnosis, that as the wreath juts around a lesion, it points to the specific organs or parts, where one may expect a problem to exist.

3. Hypotonic or dilated appearance of the wreath, causing it to appear further from the pupil than is normal. The indication is for PP.

4. Hypertonic or constricted appearance of the wreath, causing it to appear closer to the pupillary border than is usual. The indication is for MP.

Note. Allowance should be made for dual indications, such as a wreath that is hypertonic and flared.

Nerve arcs and rings

Nerve arcs and rings. Represented by circular concentric lines that can appear anywhere in the iris between the Autonomic wreath and the Skin & Capillary zone. The lines are furrows in the surface of the iris, caused by muscular contraction. They are present where there is mental and emotional stress, and also give a guide to the individual's ability to cope with those pressures.

The colour of the Arcs and Rings is totally dependent upon their depth. If they are superficial, then they appear to be light in colour, whereas if they are deep, then they appear to be darker.

Sidelighting is essential to elicit the superficial furrows, as it will cause them to appear much darker than would be the case if frontlighting were used. If the light is directed from the lateral side, the Arcs on the lateral side of the iris will appear darker, whilst those on the medial side will appear lighter. If the direction of the light is reversed, then so too will be the colour of the Arcs.

Examples of Nerve Arcs and Rings.

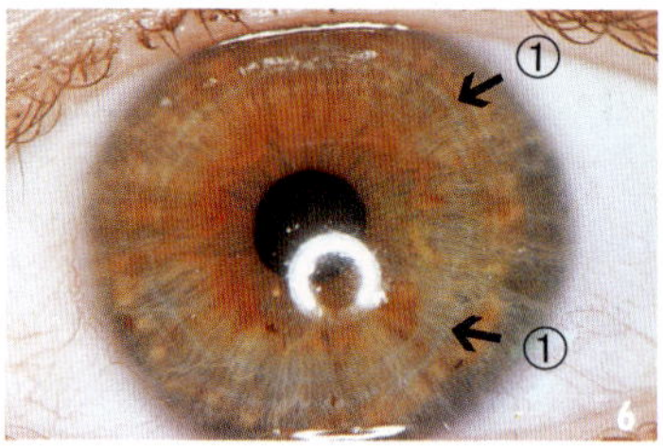

Superficial rings

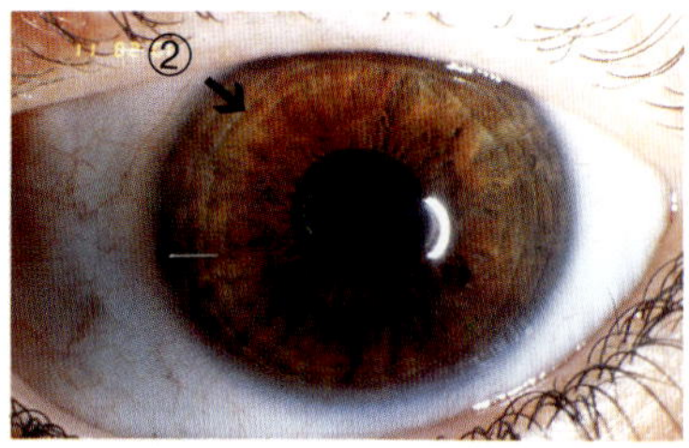

Deeper rings

1. If the Arcs and/or Rings are few in number and superficial, it indicates neuromuscular tension and anxiety. The minerals that are indicated, are MP with adults, and MP and CP with children.

2. If the Arcs and Rings are greater in number and deeper, giving a darker appearance, then there is nervous enervation and depression (capable of manifesting itself in a multitude of ways), and an indication for PP and MP.

Lymphatic and vascular zone

Lymphatic and Vascular zone. In this zone we see changes that lead to cardiovascular disease and lymphatic congestion and adenopathy.

Arcus sclerosis. This sign indicates that the arterial walls may have thickened and hardened and that intimal atheromatous plaques may have formed. The sign usually presents itself in the eye long before any clinical manifestation can be observed, and is largely confined to patients who are middle-aged and over. Although the sign will be seen to encompass the entire zone, it is generally more intense and opaque in the upper and lower quadrants; corresponding anatomically to the head and legs respectively.

Arcus sclerosis

Examples of the Arcus sclerosis.

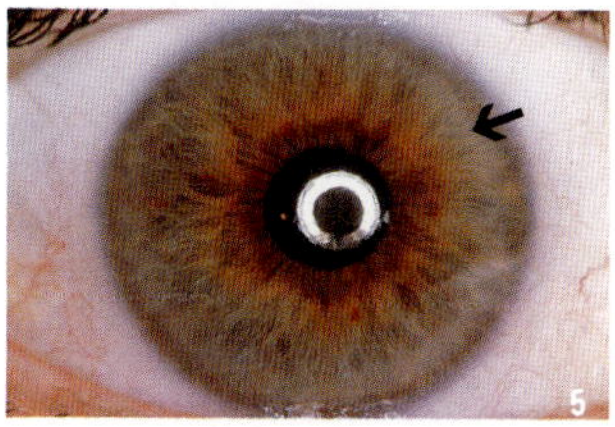

Early sign

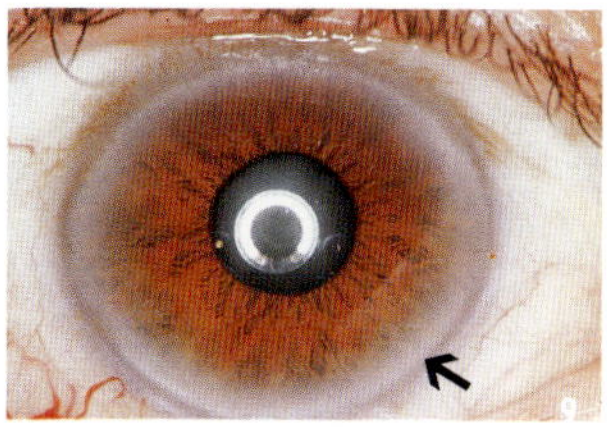

Advanced sign

The sign which appears as an iridescent opacity of a white or creamy-white colour is actually not to be seen in the iris, but in the epithelium of the cornea; it just happens to correspond with the second last zone of the iris, when viewed straight on. When observed in the very early stages, it is iridescent and translucent, rather than opaque and can only be demonstrated by directing the light obliquely to the plane of the cornea.

In older patients, with more advanced markings, the upper quadrant often combines and merges with the *Arcus ischaemia* (to be discussed in the next and last zone), to form one continuous creamy-white opacity that encroaches upon the sclera itself.

The appearance of the Arcus sclerosis gives rise to such symptoms as, poor memory, lack of concentration, lack of motivation, confusion, depression and often, senility. The same sign in the lower quadrant often indicates poor circulation in the lower extremities, cold feet, indolent or intractable leg ulcers, thromboses, etc.

The minerals indicated by the appearance of the Arcus sclerosis could be any of the potassium salts, i.e., PC, PP, or PS, plus usually MP. The appropriate potassium salt must be made on the basis of a correlation of all information pertaining to the patient.

Lymphatic rosary

Lymphatic rosary. The sign appears as small irregular shaped beads, of a white, creamy-white or yellowish-brown colour, usually in small groups, but often seen to encompass the whole iris (as beads of a rosary). The sign is in the iris, not the cornea, and is generally more evident on the lateral and medial aspects of the iris. The appearance of this sign may suggest conditions of a catarrhal nature, that can affect any of the body's mucous membranes (sinusitis, postnasal drip, tonsillitis, leucorrhoea, etc.). The mineral salts that may be indicated by this sign are primarily, PC or PS, but other secondary deficiencies of CP, SP and/or MP are often involved. Indications for other minerals, must again be derived from the patient's presenting symptoms.

Lymphatic rosary example.

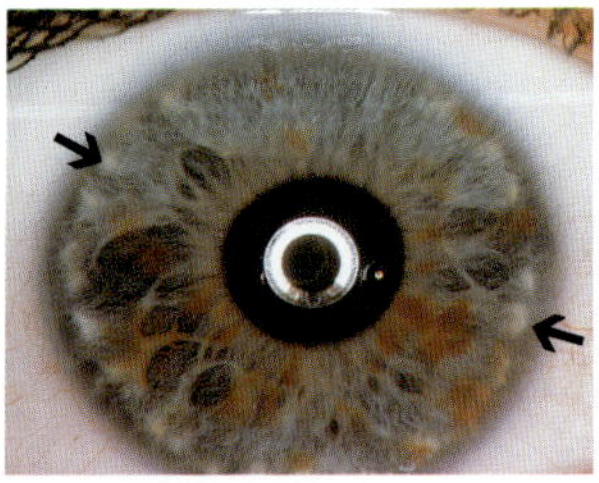

Capillary and Skin zone. This is the last zone, situated between the Lymphatic and Vascular zone, and the sclera. Signs that appear in this zone indicate changes that affect the capillary and peripheral circulation, and the function of the skin.

Arcus ischaemia

Viewing the Arcus ischaemia

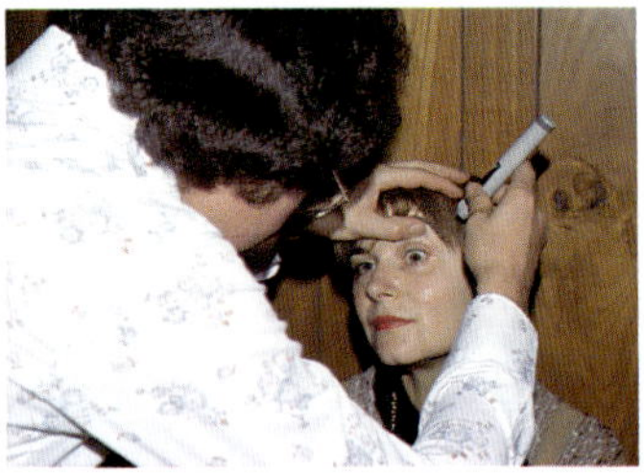

Examples of the Arcus ischaemia

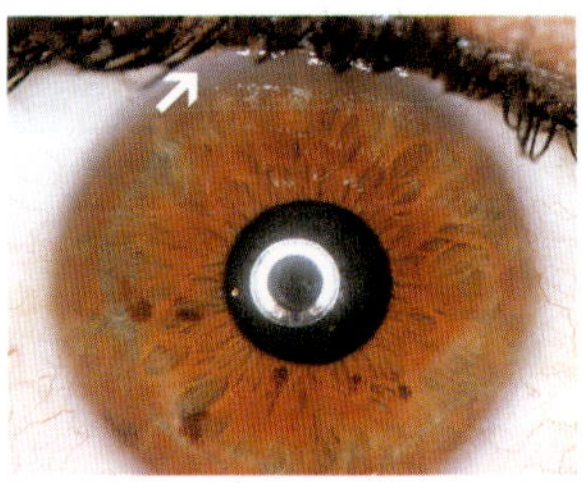

Early sign

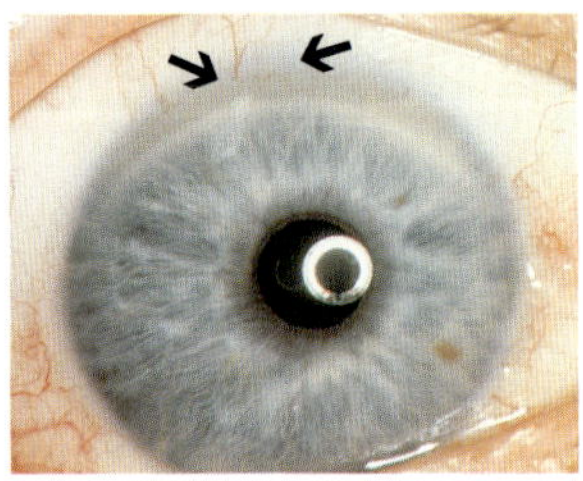

Advanced sign

Arcus ischaemia. This sign which appears as the sclerotic coat is drawn up over the edge of the cornea, may be seen anywhere around the periphery of the iris, but usually most noticeable in the upper quadrant. In its early manifestation it has a translucent, iridescent appearance over the edge of the cornea, with a bluish-white appearance encroaching onto the sclera. Unlike the *Arcus sclerosis*, this sign can often be observed in patients as young as early teens. In its more advanced manifestation it has a slimy, creamy-white appearance, is totally opaque and in this form is limited to much older adults.

The sign seems to indicate that there is an impediment to the passage of nutrients to the cell, particularly oxygen. Brain cells, being the most sensitive to this deprivation, suffer the earliest, giving rise to symptoms of poor concentration and memory, easy distractibility, mild depression and lack of motivation, due to the mild state of hypoxia. Ultimately the condition goes on to produce symptoms of severe states of anxiety and depression, confusion and senility in older subjects.

In the cutaneous epithelium there will often be signs of increased desquamation and sloughing of the cells, most apparent on the face, upper arms, and lower legs.

The appearance of the Arcus ischaemia indicates a need for PS, and probably MP, with other minerals being prescribed according to the individual patient's needs.

Example of Skin sign.

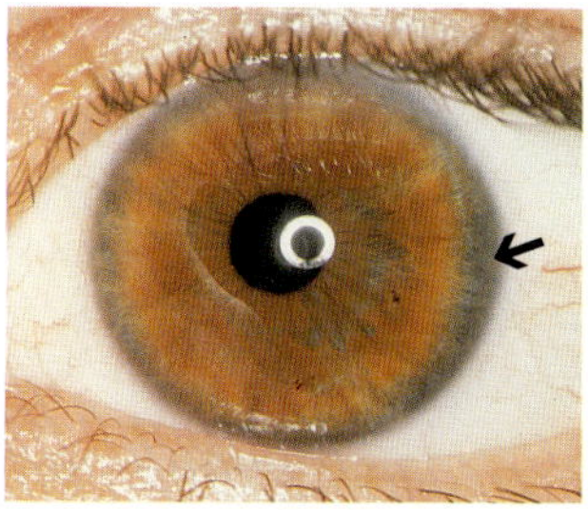

Skin zone

Skin sign. This sign, which appears in the iris itself, just before the border with the sclera, indicates that the acidic wastes of metabolism have infiltrated the skin from the tissues. The sign has a dark, muddy appearance, where the definition of the individual iris fibres is lost. The sign is most times seen as a complete ring with very little deviation in intensity and has quite well defined borders. It can indicate that waste removal systems, such as the lungs or kidneys, are insufficient in their function and that the skin has been placed under an extra load. Apart from any pathological reasons, this sign can be induced functionally, by simply interfering with the normal action of the skin, i.e., by overcovering, insufficient physical activity, or the use of antiperspirants and baby oils.

The minerals that may be indicated by the appearance of this sign, are usually, PS, SP and S. Commonsense advice should also be given with regard to proper skin care and lifestyle.

Acid wash

Acid wash. This is a sign that may be seen over the entire iris or only a section, and appears only between the Autonomic wreath and the Skin zone.

Example of Acid wash sign.

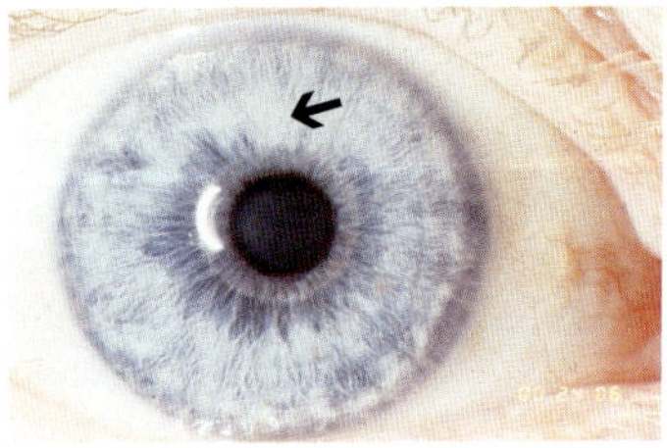

The sign appears as if the normal (or abnormal) iris texture, were to be covered by a watercolour artist's wash; a sort of milky overlay.

The sign is very easy to read in the blue eye, where the wash appears as a true white colour, but more difficult to see in a brown eye, where it can take on a yellowish tinge.

The sign indicates that the tissues are being *washed* with acidic catabolic waste products, that the normal channels of elimination for whatever reason, have not been able to remove. These infiltrated wastes cause immediate irritation and in time, pathological changes, to the tissues concerned.

The sign is most frequently seen in middle-aged and over patients, who have a diet rich in animal fats, and younger patients who consume, apart from excesses of animal fat, large amounts of refined carbohydrate.

The minerals that may be indicated by such an appearance are, SP, PC, IP, and MP.

Diagnosing deficiencies from Pupillary shapes

Pupillary signs

As the practitioner becomes familiar and accustomed to looking for iris indications, he should not miss the opportunity to assess the patient's pupils, as the indications observed will further help to reinforce the symptom picture.

The five shapes illustrated on the next page, represent the individual possibilities, but allowance should be made, just as with the tongue, for dual indicators. As there are also a number of medical reasons (stroke, influence of certain drugs, fear, pain, etc.) that could give rise to a pupillary abnormality, these should not be disregarded when making an assessment. The diagnosis will quite often reveal a composite of two mineral salt deficiencies, e.g., pupil out of round and too large, MP, and PP; or pupil out of round and too small, MP, and MP.

1. Normal size and shaped pupil.

2. Out of round pupil. This sign usually indicates an altered state of tone in the muscular coat of the stomach due to stress. It can also indicate external pressure from other parts, onto the stomach, producing an altered anatomical position and shape. The mineral salt indicated is MP.

3. Contracted, myotic pupil. This sign, excluding the influence of certain drugs, etc., results from states of anxiety and tension. The mineral salt indicated is MP.

4. Dilated pupil. This sign, excluding the influence of certain drugs, etc., is a sign of fatigue and enervation. The mineral salt indicated is PP.

5. Distended pupil. This sign which looks like an inverted tear-drop, indicates a downward shift anatomically of organs and parts (stomach, intestines, uterus, bladder). The mineral salt indicated is CF.

Pupillary shapes.

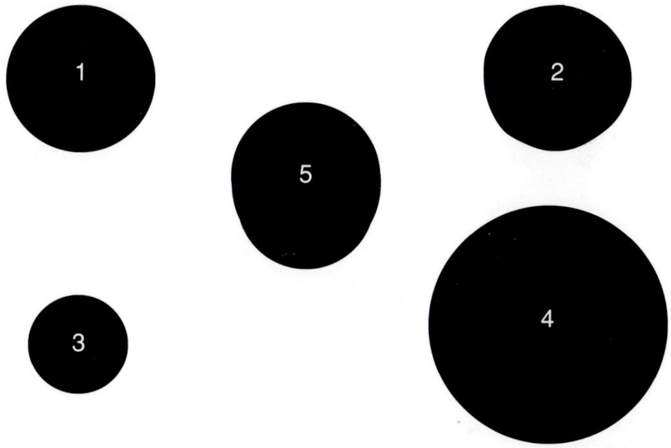

Examples of pupillary shapes

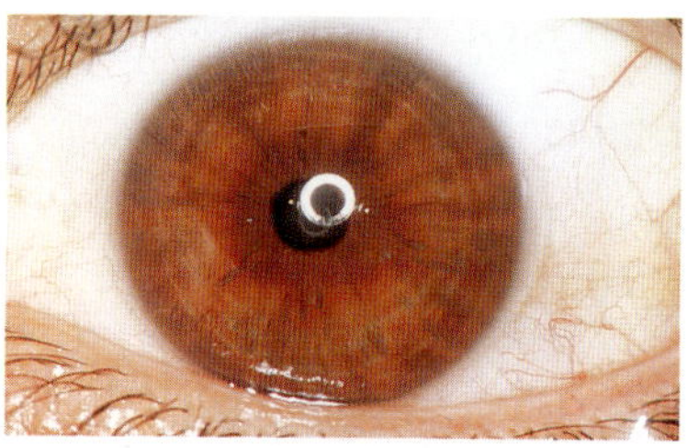

Constricted and out of round

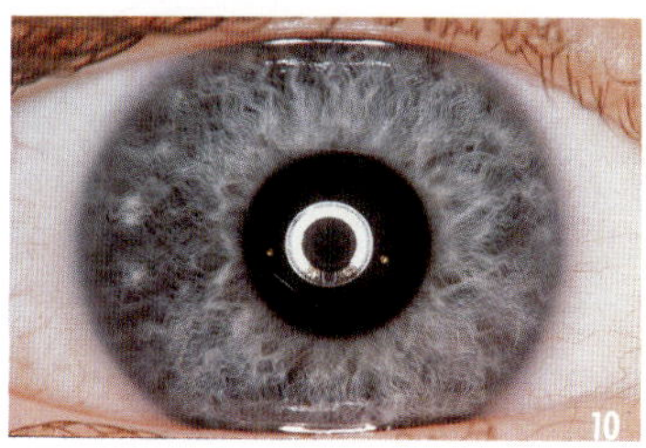

Dilated/hypotonic

What do you see?

Test yourself. What do you see in these iris photographs and how would you rate your observations? Answers upside down on this page.

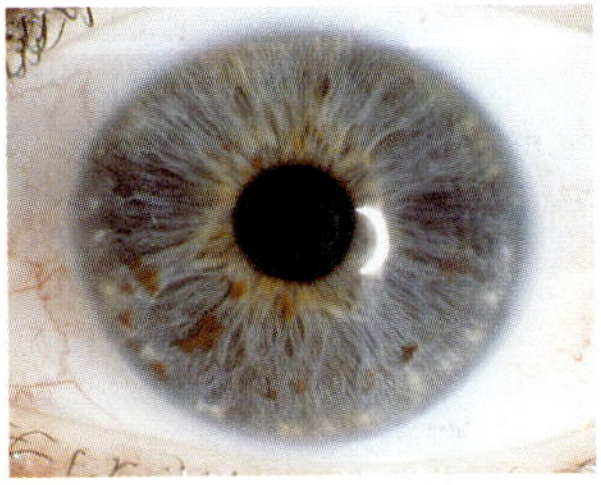

Test one

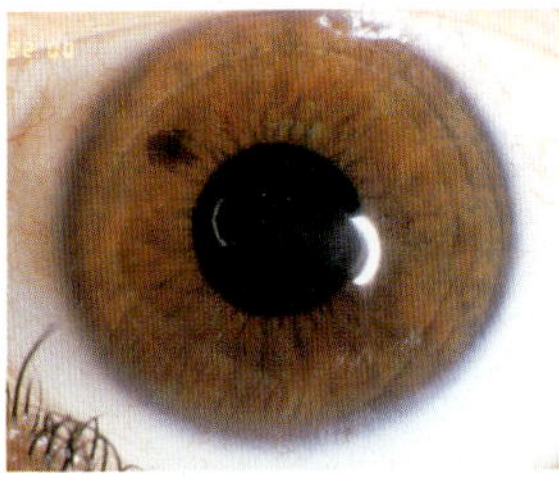

Test two

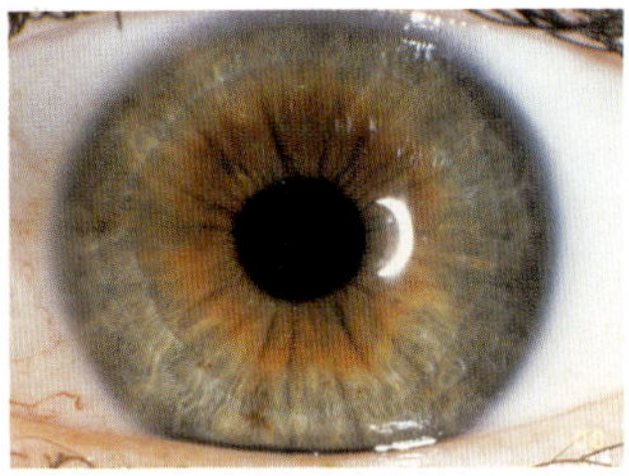

Test three

Test one

Texture 6
Stomach, hypo 6
Autonomic, hyper 9
Nerve arcs 1
Lymphatics 6
Arcus ischaemia 3

Test two

Texture 6
Pupil, dilated
Stomach, hypo 6
Nerve arcs 7.5
Skin 5
Arcus ischaemia 6

Test three

Texture 7
Pupil, out of round 5
Stomach, hypo 5
Nerve arcs 6
Lymphatics 1
Skin 6
Arcus ischaemia 7

Tongue indications

Diagnosing deficiencies from the tongue

The tongue represents a quick, easily accessible and non-invasive aid to diagnosis. In itself, the tongue does not provide for a reliable sole means of determining mineral deficiencies and should always be combined with other indicators and the patient's overall symptom picture. Apart from any value that the tongue may have as an indicator of mineral deficiencies, the various coatings also serve as a window into the functioning of the gastrointestinal system.

To observe; the patient should be asked to open his mouth wide and fully extend the tongue. The practitioner should conduct the inspection with the aid of a bright light or medical torch.

Not only specific single indications, but also dual indications are possible due to the fact that the tip of the tongue may display one sign, while the back of the tongue may display another; or there may be two signs superimposed upon each other. This situation then means that two minerals may be indicated, rather than one. Some common examples of dual indications are; a cream coating at the back of the tongue (SP), with a white coating towards the tip (PC), and; a coating of any colour combined with a cracked/mapped appearance (CF).

The practitioner's ability to be able to recognise and interpret tongue signs has more to do with experience than it does with anything else. It is essential therefore, that the practitioner take the opportunity to observe every patient's tongue, so as to establish as quickly as possible, a mental image of the various coatings, colours and markings.

S P Cream coloured coating at the back of the tongue and/or the roof of the mouth; often associated with an acid taste.

S S Clear, shiny, œdematous appearance, or greenish-brown with a bitter taste.

P P Dry tongue. Wakes with an excessively dry tongue and mouth. Tongue sticks to roof of mouth. Mustard colour, edges red. Halitosis.

P S Yellow, slimy. Taste lost.

P C White or greyish-white coating.

C S Flabby, with coating resembling dry clay.

C F Cracked, mapped or fissured.

I P Bright red or raw beefy appearance.

The various tongue indications are also given in the "Overview" to each of the individual mineral salts (pages 36-81), and in the "Tongue" column of the "Mineral master chart" on page 113.

Chapter seven

Getting started quickly

Prescribing quickly and easily

Six steps to easy prescribing

The very caption of "Getting started quickly" implies that the principles of prescribing have been simplified. The problems associated with simplifying anything that is inherently complex, are that during the process of rationalisation, aspects that are integral to the proper functioning of the operation are discarded or diminished to the point where the whole process becomes valueless.

The procedures outlined here for prescribing quickly and easily, although rationalised, have been carefully thought-out and time-tested. This will ensure that the objectives of being able to ease a practitioner into the system and at the same time retain the capacity to produce a consistently good result, are maintained.

Here then is the basic step-by-step procedure for prescribing - the easy way.

Step 1. Learn at least the basic prescribing indications for each salt outlined on the "Mineral master chart" on pages 112-3.

Step 2. Have the patient fill out the questionnaire on pages 108-9.

Step 3. Analyse the questionnaire as instructed on page 110.

Step 4. Talk to the patient.

Step 5. Refer to the "Repertory" on page 144, for additional help.

Step 6. Put all the information together and prescribe according to the "Prescribing rules" on page 111.

Preparations and dosages

The particular preparation of mineral salts referred to and as prescribed by the author, are the Blackmores Ltd (of 23 Roseberry Street, Balgowlah, New South Wales, Australia 2093), practitioner range of Celloid® mineral tablets.

These minerals are presented as the mono mineral (eleven in number), and also in a range of commonly occurring combinations. The use of combination formulas allows for the prescribing of fewer tablets, which is of particular benefit when treating the chronically ill, where a greater number of minerals will be taken over a greater period of time.

The unit dose for each of the minerals is as follows:

Sodium phosphate	260mg
Sodium sulphate	190mg
Potassium phosphate	33mg
Potassium sulphate	33mg
Potassium chloride	65mg
Calcium phosphate	130mg
Calcium sulphate	8mg
Calcium fluoride	6xH
Magnesium phosphate	65mg
Iron phosphate	15mg
Silica	33mg

Mineral deficiency profile questionnaire

Never	In the past	Sometimes	Often	
☐	☐	☐	☐	**Instructions.** Read each question carefully before placing a tick in the box that you think most applies to you. Please feel free to make any additional comments.
☐	☐	☐	☐	1. Do you find it difficult to sustain concentration for any time, and/or forget things easily?
☐	☐	☐	☐	2. Do you ever get weepy, depressed or find it hard to motivate yourself?
☐	☐	☐	☐	3. Are you over-sensitive to certain noises or bright light?
☐	☐	☐	☐	4. Do you ever panic if away from home, even for a short time, or dislike being left alone?
☐	☐	☐	☐	5. Do you ever feel anxious, panicky, or shaky inside, often when there may be no reason to?
☐	☐	☐	☐	6. Do you become impatient, irritable or aggressive too easily?
☐	☐	☐	☐	7. Do you feel better in yourself when you eat, or are in company?
☐	☐	☐	☐	8. Do you crave carbohydratates (biscuits, sweets, etc.), or pick at food between meals?
☐	☐	☐	☐	9. Do you sigh or yawn a lot?
☐	☐	☐	☐	10. Does a drink of alcohol settle you down and make you feel better?
☐	☐	☐	☐	11. Do you suffer sharp shooting pains in the body, or twitching of the face or eye muscles?
☐	☐	☐	☐	12. Do you experience any palpitation or hot flushes soon after going to bed?
☐	☐	☐	☐	13. Do you have difficulty getting to sleep or wake during the night?
☐	☐	☐	☐	14. Do you wake up feeling tired?
☐	☐	☐	☐	15. Do you wake in the morning, or are woken during the night with stiff and painful joints?
☐	☐	☐	☐	16. Do you suffer from headaches at work, after work, or at weekends?
☐	☐	☐	☐	17. Do you suffer from dandruff, or dry flaky skin on your face arms or legs?
☐	☐	☐	☐	18. Does your scalp get oily, or moist and sticky if not washed every 2-3 days?
☐	☐	☐	☐	19. Does your head ever feel fuzzy, as if it's full of cotton-wool?
☐	☐	☐	☐	20. Does your hair fall or do the ends split?
☐	☐	☐	☐	21. Are your fingernails soft, or do they flake or crack?
☐	☐	☐	☐	22. Do you catch colds and other infections too easily?
☐	☐	☐	☐	23. Do you suffer from tinea or thrush (candida)?
☐	☐	☐	☐	24. Do you suffer from blocked sinuses or sinus headaches?
☐	☐	☐	☐	25. Do you have any post-nasal, throat or chest mucus that is yellow-green in colour?
☐	☐	☐	☐	26. Do you have any post-nasal, throat or chest mucus that is white in colour?

27. Does the skin on your lips, hands or feet crack?
28. Do you have acne that has pure white heads or is blind and sore under the skin?
29. Do you have acne that heals very slowly and tends to leave scars?
30. Do you have acne that has yellow pussy heads?
31. Is your skin too oily with a tendency to form blackheads?
32. Do you suffer indigestion, gastric reflux and/or flatulence after meals?
33. Do rich, fatty foods or chocolate disagree with you?
34. Do you ever feel as if you have a tight band around your chest, head, throat or abdomen?
35. Do you pass a lot of gas or become bloated with gas?
36. Do you suffer from haemorrhoids (piles)?
37. Do you suffer from haemorrhoids that itch or bleed?
38. Do you ever suffer from cystitis or urethritis?
39. If you are a male, do you ever experience difficulty urinating, with a reduction in flow?
40. Do you bruise easily, or do cuts take a long time to heal?
41. Do you suffer any weakness of tendons, cartilages, ligaments, discs or bones?
42. If you are a female, do you suffer cramps on the first day of your period?
43. If you are a female, do you lose large clots of blood during your period?
44. If you are a female, do you retain fluid in your breasts, belly, face or fingers, etc?
45. Do you suffer from mouth ulcers or any form of herpes?
46. Are you more sensitive to the cold than other people that you know?
47. Are any of your symptoms worse during cold weather?
48. Are any of your symptoms worse during changeable weather?
49. Are any of your symptoms worse during damp weather?
50. Are any of your symptoms worse during hot humid weather?
51. Are any of your symptoms worse in hot, stuffy rooms or buildings?
52. Are any of your symptoms made worse if you are under stress?
53. Are any of your symptoms improved by hot humid weather?
54. Are any of your symptoms improved by hot applications to the affected area?
55. Are any of your symptoms improved by cold applications to the affected area?
56. Are any of your symptoms improved by pressure to the affected area?

Mineral deficiency profile analysis

Instructions for the practitioner in analysing the questionnaire

1. The following values are ascribed to the check boxes on the questionnaire:

Never = 0
In the past = 1
Sometimes = 2
Often = 4

2. Draw up a grid as illustrated, allocating a column for each mineral (10 columns, as there is no provision for calcium sulphate indications on the questionnaire). There is no particular order that need be adopted, columns can just be assigned to a mineral as the need arises from the information given on the questionnaire by the patient.

Minerals										
Total score										

3. Each time minerals are indicated from the analysis below, arbitrarily enter their patient-assigned value in the appropriate column of the grid (In the past = 1, Sometimes = 2, Often = 4). When the analysis is completed, add up the columns and enter the score totals at the bottom. The prescription is then arived at by processing the scores according to the "prescribing rules" on the next page.

Analysis information

1. PP, MP
2. PP
3. PP, MP
4. PP
5. MP
6. PP, MP
7. PP
8. MP
9. PS
10. MP
11. MP
12. PS
13. PP, MP
14. PP
15. S, CF
16. PP, MP
17. PS
18. PS
19. PS
20. S, PS
21. S, CF
22. PS, CP
23. PS
24. PS
25. PS
26. PC
27. CF, S
28. PC
29. PS, S, CF
30. PS
31. PS
32. SP, PC, IP, MP
33. SP, PC
34. MP
35. MP
36. CF, S
37. PC, IP
38. SP, PC, IP
39. PC
40. PC, IP, CP
41. S, CF
42. MP, CP
43. PC
44. SS
45. PC
46. CP, IP
47. CP, S, CF
48. SP, CF, CP, PS
49. SS, CP, CF, S
50. SS, PS
51. PS
52. PP, MP
53. S
54. MP, S, CF
55. PC, IP
56. MP, SS, S, CF

See examples of analysis on page 114

Prescribing rules

Chronic symptoms

1. The prescription should contain not fewer than three and not more than six mineral salts.
2. The prescription should contain only one salt from each cation family group (Na., Ca., K.). This means that only one ot the salts of sodium, one of the salts of potassium and one of the salts of calcium, should be used at the one time. Where more than one salt in a cation family is strongly indicated from the patient's symptom picture or "profile questionnaire", then a choice is made according to the sheer weight of evidence, or by seeking further information.
3. The prescription should contain only one salt from the sulphate anion group (PS, SS, or CS). Where more than one of the sulphates is strongly indicated from the patient's symptom picture or "profile questionnaire", then a choice is made according to the weight of evidence, or by seeking further information.
4. Mandatorily include a sodium salt (either SP or SS), and MP in every prescription for chronic symptoms. If the patient's symptom picture does not clearly indicate a sodium salt, or if the indications for SP and SS are equally weighted; then always prescribe SP.
5. Doses are to be given three or four times a day (with each meal, or with each meal and at bedtime), according to the individual need.

Acute symptoms

1. The prescription should employ between one and four salts, and doses should be given every 15 minutes to every two hours according to the need.
2. Faster and better results can be gained by advising the patient to chew the tablets before swallowing with a few mouthfuls of hot water.
3. The doses should be maintained for a time beyond the point where the symptoms have ceased.

Children and babies

1. Babies; quarter to half dose.
2. Children, two years and over; full adult dose. (A growing child's need for all the basic minerals is as great or greater than for that of an adult).

Acute reactions to treatment

1. An acute reaction to treatment is characterised by an induction of symptoms that the patient didn't have previously, or an exacerbation of the actual condition under treatment.
2. Reactions affect only about 10% of patients and occur within the first few days of treatment. The symptoms generally last for about three days and once settled do not usually return.
3. Reactions seem to be confined to the treatment of chronic disease only and apart from perhaps a temporary exacerbation of the existing condition, usually take the form of; flatus or flatulence, indigestion, nausea, headache, tiredness, aches and pains, skin rashes or pruritis.
4. Abandon the whole treatment for three days, then reintroduce it at half dose for a further three days, then restore it to full dose if no further reaction occurs.

Mineral Master Chart

Mineral Salt	Memory Key	Prescribing Indications
Sodium phosphate	Metabolic acid remover	All conditions that result from an incomplete breakdown and elimination of metabolic acid waste. (Lactic and uric acid). Gastric and urinary acidity. Gout. Fibrositis. Degenerative arthritis. Fat intolerance (along with PC).
Sodium sulphate	Problem fluid remover	Conditions that arise from an abnormal distribution, concentration, and elimination of body fluids. Liver and blood detoxification. Oedema; localised and general. Hydraemia. Nausea. Jaundice. Weepy eczema.
Potassium phosphate	Nerve power activator	Conditions arising from lowered nervous energy. Physical and mental enervation. Malaise/lethargy. Depression. Lack of drive and motivation. Muscles easily fatigued. All phobias. Irritability and insomnia (along with MP).
Potassium sulphate	Cell oxygenator	Conditions arising from hypoxia. All symptoms that demonstrate abnormal cellular respiration. All conditions that call for oxygen. Third stage of inflammation. Mucopus. Pyogenic and fungal infections. Pyrexia. Dry flaky skin.
Potassium chloride	Congestion remover	Conditions arising from faulty collagen synthesis. Second stage of inflammations, characterised by; swelling, congestion and pain (usually along with IP). Fibromas. Herpetic ulcers. Burns. Keloids. Contusions. Hypochlorhydria.
Calcium phosphate	Cell builder	Conditions arising from poor cell development and replacement, particularly, muscle, bone, and blood. Children are primary group affected, with irritability, cramps, poor appetite and frequent colds. Anaemia (along with IP). Chilblain.
Calcium sulphate	Suppuration remover	Purulent and sanious discharges, after pus has found a vent. Thick, lumpy, yellow-green, often blood streaked mucus. Abscesses. Ulcers. Boils. Fistulas. Acne. To heal long suppurating wounds.
Calcium fluoride	Tissue strengthener	Conditions that arise from a loss of integrity and strength of connective tissue. All weaknesses of bone, enamel, ligament and tendon. All prolapsed tissue. Hard excrescences. Nodes and nodules.
Magnesium phosphate	Neuromuscular coordinator	Conditions that demonstrate a loss of integrity at the myoneural junction. Spasms. Neuralgias. Anxiety, tension and depression (along with PP). Confusion. Disorientation. Hyperexcitability. Angina.
Iron phosphate	Inflammation remover	Acute, localised inflammations and infections, resulting in heat and pain. First stage of all inflammations and infections. In chronic conditions, pallor, tiredness and weaknes. Anaemia (always with CP).
Silica	Calcium reorganiser	Abnormal nutrition and calcification of bone, tendon, ligament or cartilage. Articular or periarticular degenerative changes. Osteophytes. Nodes. Avascular necrosis. Silica facilitates the removal of pathogenic waste from the body.

Aggravated By	Improved By	Exudates	Tongue	Pupil	Iris
Changeable weather. Thunderstorms. Open air. Fatty, rich food.	Stable weather	Golden-yellow or honey coloured serous exudate. Leucorrhoea; scalding.	Cream (worse at back of tongue or roof of mouth).		Acid wash. Stomach zone. Autonomic wreath flared white.
Hot, humid weather. Damp, wet weather. Seaside. Sea foods. Tight clothing	Dry, warmth. Changing body position frequently. Open, fresh air.	Thick, yellow mucus. Watery vesicles. Serous exudate that forms yellow scales.	Clear, shiny, or greenish-brown		Lymphatic, skin & vascular zones, but compare with PS & CS indications.
Worry. Stress. Mental & physical exertion. Cold air. Being alone.	Company. Eating. Warmth. Rest.	Thick yellow, crusty mucus or foetid bleeding from nares. Salty tasting mucus.	Dry tongue. Mustard colour, edges red.	Dilated, hypotonic.	Nerve arcs and rings (deep).
Hot, stuffy rooms. Late afternoon, evening. Hot, humid, changeable weather.	Cool, fresh, open air. Stable weather. Dry weather.	Thin, slimy, yellow-green, purulent and mucopurulent discharges. Nose dry.	Yellow slimy. Taste lost.		Skin & lymphatic zones. Arcus ischaemia.
Dry heat. Fatty, rich food. Physical exertion.	Cold applications. Keeping still.	Thick white, viscid mucus. Clear & watery from herpes. Dry, white exudate on skin.	White or greyish white.		Stomach, lymphatic zones. Arcus sclerosis. Acid wash. Auto-wreath.
Cold, wet, changeable weather. Dampness. Cold draughts. Exertion. Teething.	Warm, dry, stable weather. Warmth. Rest.	Tenacious mucus of an albuminous white nature, often streaked with yellow or blood.			Nerve arcs (children). Poor iris texture.
Overheated warmth. Wet, damp weather. Working with water. Physical exertion.	Cool, open air. Dry weather.	Thick, lumpy, yellow purulent mucus. Pus or sanious discharges with a vent	Flabby, clay coloured.		Skin & lymphatic zones. Compare PS & SS findings.
Damp, cold changeable weather. Rest. Upon arising in the morning.	Dry, warm, stable weather. Rubbing. Hot applications. Physical movement.	Hard, lumpy, greenish, foetid discharges. Hard knotty glands, tendons and surface of bones.	Cracked and mapped.	Distended	Stomach & skin zones.
Cold; air, water, or weather. Noise. Glare. Alcohol; the prolonged effects of.	Warmth. Pressure and rubbing. Eating carbohydrates. Alcohol; initial effects of.			Constricted and/or out of round.	Nerve arcs (superficial). Acid wash. Flared autonomic wreath.
Heat. Jarring motion. Excitement. Physical exertion.	Cold applications. Rest. Keeping still.	Mucous membranes dry, irritated and inflammed. Before discharges begin.	Bright red or raw beefy appearance.		Acid wash. Flared autonomic wreath.
Cold weather. Cold draughts. Night. Rest. Morning upon arising.	Hot, humid or wet weather. Summertime. Covering-up. Daytime.	Chronic purulent and mucopurulent discharges that won't heal. In abscesses, etc., to ripen.			Skin zone. Arcus sclerosis. (Compare with symptoms).

Analysis and prescribing examples

Example 1.

This example is a case, where the prescription has been made solely on the basis of the information supplied by the questionnaire. No further questions need have been asked of the patient.

In the cation family groups, PP has been chosen arbitrarily by the weight of PP symptoms over PS and PC (PP = 20; PS = 16; and PC = 4). SP has been chosen over SS, (SP = 2; SS = 2) by simply adhering to the "Prescribing rules" (mandatorily prescribe a sodium salt in all chronic cases and choose SP if SP and SS indications are equally weighted). CF is chosen over CP, again simply from the way the symptoms are weighted.

MP, apart from being heavily indicated is to be mandatorily included in a chronic case. S is included due to the number of indications, but IP is discarded for what is seen to be insignificant indications.

PP	MP	PS	S	CF	CP	PC	SP	IP	SS
2 2 2 2 2 2 2 2 4	2 2 2 2 2 2 2 2 2 1 1 2 4 2 2	1 2 1 2 1 1 1 2 1 1 1 2	2 2 2 1 1 2 2	2 2 1 1 2 2	1 1 1	1 1 1 1	1 1	1 1	2
20	30	16	12	10	3	4	2	2	2

Prescription: SP, PP, MP, S, CF

Example 2.

In this case the PP and PS indications are evenly weighted, which, apart from anything else, is a clue to seek more information from the patient. That SS seems to be clearly indicated over SP, also means that if PS was to be chosen over PP, we would be required to prescribe SP rather than SS, in order to remain in conformity with the "Prescribing rules" (no two sulphates).

In actual fact, this case was resolved by first prescribing as the profile analysis seemed to suggest (SS, PP, MP, S, CF), and then later changing the prescription (as the symptom profile changed), to SP, PS, MP, S, CF.

The mental and emotional symptoms were given priority and remedied first before the somatic symptoms, thus PP was chosen to begin the treatment rather than PS.

The PP and MP were also prescribed every two hours for the first two weeks of the treatment.

PP	MP	PS	S	CF	CP	PC	SS	IP	SP
2 2 2 1 2 2 2 4	2 2 2 2 2 2 2 2 1 2 4 2 2	2 2 1 1 1 4 4 1 1	2 2 4 1 1 1 2 2	2 2 4 1 1 1 2 2	1 2 1 1 1 1	1 4 2	2 1 2	1	1
17	27	17	15	15	7	7	5	1	1

Prescription for first eight weeks: SS, PP, MP, S, CF
then changed to: SP, PS, MP, S, CF

Prescribing for chronic symptoms

Prescribing rules

Simple rules that take the guess-work out of prescribing, enabling you to prescribe fewer salts and produce a better and more consistent result

1. The prescription should contain not fewer than three and not greater than six mineral salts.

2. The prescription should contain only one salt from each cation family group (Na., Ca., K.). This means that only one of the salts of sodium, one of the salts of potassium and one of the salts of calcium, should be used at the one time. Where more than one salt in a cation family is strongly indicated from the patient's symptom picture or "profile questionnaire", then a choice is made according to the sheer weight of evidence, or by seeking further information.

3. The prescription should contain only one salt from the sulphate anion group (PS, SS, or CS). Where more than one of the sulphates is strongly indicated from the patient's symptom picture or "profile questionnaire", then a choice is made according to the weight of evidence, or by seeking further information.

4. Mandatorily include a sodium salt (either SP or SS), and MP in every prescription for chronic symptoms. If the patient's symptom picture does not clearly indicate a sodium salt, or if the indications for SP and SS are equally weighted; then always prescribe SP.

5. Doses are to be given three or four times a day (with each meal, or with each meal and at bedtime), according to the individual need.

General prescribing hints

Some quick and helpful hints for learning to prescribe and manage the chronic case quickly

* The art of prescribing is inextricably linked to patient management and visa versa. Therefore this chapter and the chapter, "Management and prescribing procedures" are complementary and should be read and applied in conjunction with each other. If good management is not combined with correct prescribing, then it will be difficult to maintain a consistently good result.

* When prescribing for the usual chronic case, there is nothing to be gained from increasing the medication beyond three to four doses a day. It is time rather than dose, that will emerge as the most important factor.

But, don't neglect to study these matters in detail - when all else fails; read the book!

* Depending upon the nature of the chronic illness under treatment, future appointments should be arranged no less than one month apart. There must be sufficient time between visits, for both the patient and the practitioner to assess change. During the initial stage of treatment, the practitioner will be more reliant on the patient's assessment of change, than he will be upon his own observations.

* Once the treatment is successfully under-way, the appointments should be arranged every two or three months.

* The commonly treated forms of chronic illness can be expected to respond within the first three to four months of treatment.

* More than fifty per cent of patients will show benefit within the first month of treatment

* About twenty per cent of patients will show a response to treatment during the first week.

* About ten per cent of patients will not respond to treatment at all.

* The patient's cooperation should be sought to comply as faithfully as possible with the prescribed dose regimen. Try to get the patient to understand that no chronic illness occurs overnight and that most chronic illnesses are many years in the making. Encourage the patient to see his treatment as a project, not only to conquering the illness concerned, but also to attaining a level of health and efficiency that he may not have not experienced before.

* If the patient were to forget a dose of his treatment, then he may catch-up, so long as there is still about two hours separation between that dose and the next. There is nothing to be gained from taking double doses in order to catch-up on doses forgotten.

* If the prescription requires the use of five or six salts as permitted by the "Prescribing rules", the practitioner should lessen the treatment load for the patient by working as many salt combinations as possible. It will be found that there will be psychological resistance, and a decrease in treatment compliance if the patient is asked to take too many tablets or doses.

* When considering combinations, the practitioner should endeavour to retain as much flexibility as possible, by not combining a salt that may need to be prescribed at extra dose with one that will not. When deciding upon combinations, the practitioner should choose salts that have a natural affinity for each other such as, S and CF, PP and MP, PC and IP, etc., and ones where there is little likelihood that anything would occur between the patient's visits that would call for a change in those combinations.

* It may be a help to explain to the patient that his mineral prescription has had to be determined from a multiplicity of possible combinations, hence it is not possible to prescribe a simple pre-prepared formulation. It should also be pointed out, that it is because of this reason that he has the opportunity to be treated as an individual. From the practitioner's standpoint, it is this flexibility of being able to assemble the prescription from individual components that allows for creative prescribing, and this should definitely be seen as an advantage, not a disadvantage. The alternative is to be locked-in to a limited range of formulas, arbitrarily determined by pharmaceutical company boffins, and based more on unit sales potential and profitability than anything else. This method of treatment represents one of the last bastions, where the doctor can retain full control over his prescribing, unfettered by any consideration other than the patient's welfare.

* The patient should be encouraged to communicate any difficulties that may arise between visits. He should be discouraged from interpreting any changes himself, or seeking advice from other health care professionals in a way that would effectively undermine the practitioner's control of the case.

* If the patient's condition has had a history of passing through periods of exacerbation, or if from the practitioner's experience these events are thought likely to occur, then the patient can be equipped with treatment or advice to cover those times. The situation can be approached in a number of ways:

1. At the time of an exacerbation the treatment and dose are left unchanged and the patient advised that this is just a passing phase. The danger with this approach is that the patient may not be prepared to suffer the extra pain and inconvenience.
2. To equip the patient on the first visit with treatment that will cover the times of exacerbation should they occur. The patient's regular treatment is probably better suspended through these times to avoid creating confusion for the inexperienced practitioner.
3. To wait until the need arises and prescribe accordingly at the time. This can often simply mean increasing the dose of certain components of the patient's regular treatment.
4. Any treatment given at the time should be prescribed on the basis of the prevailing symptoms and given at an increased dose (at least every two hours) as would be the case for the treatment of any acute symptoms.

Whichever approach is adopted, the patient should be encouraged to communicate events, but once experienced, to immediately initiate these changes in his own treatment as required.

* An example of how to deal with an exacerbation using the regular treatment that the patient has on-hand:

A patient under treatment for primary osteoarthritis has regular treatment consisting of: SP, PC, IP, MP, S, CF. The PC and the IP are being prescribed as a combination formula, so too is the S and CF. The patient's exacerbation consists of; a combination of steady pain, throbbing pain, sharp stabbing pain, heat and swelling. The prime indicated salts of MP, PC and IP are already being prescribed for the patient, albeit at normal dose. The suggested advice is to tell the patient to simply increase the dose of these formulas to, one every two hours (about six doses a day). This increased dose may need to be persisted with for periods of two weeks or more.

* When the patient's illness has been remedied for a period of not less than two months, then the opportunity exists to begin experimenting with a reduced dose of the treatment. Do not discontinue the treatment at this stage.

* The patient should be instructed to take the treatment at half dose for at least a further two months before cutting it out altogether. If the symptoms begin to return once the treatment has been reduced to half dose, it should be quickly restored to full dose for at least another two months before attempting to reduce it again. If the symptoms continue to return each time the treatment is abandoned, then an ongoing maintenance dose should be suggested.

Prescribing for acute symptoms

Prescribing rules

Simple rules to ensure a better result

1. The prescription should employ between one and four salts, and doses should be given every 15 minutes to every two hours according to the need.

2. Faster and better results can be gained by advising the patient to chew the tablets before swallowing with a few mouthfuls of hot water.

3. The doses should be maintained for a time beyond the point where the symptoms have ceased.

General prescribing hints

Some quick and helpful hints for learning to manage the acute case quickly

But, don't neglect to study the subject properly - when all else fails; read the book!

* With the treatment of acute symptoms, the practitioner will not possess the luxury of time, as with chronic disease. He must assess the condition quickly and accurately, prescribe correctly and the results must come swiftly, otherwise the patient will not persist with the treatment. There is also the added danger that further complications may develop, consequential to a wrong diagnosis and/or treatment.

* The practitioner's clinical diagnostic skills will be put to the test, so the first and perhaps most important decision will be whether to accept the case or not.

* The conditions that lend themselves to this approach and the precise nature of the appropriate treatment will very much depend upon the diagnostic and prescribing skills of the practitioner. In this regard the treatment of acute disease is a something akin to stepping into a minefield for the inexperienced practitioner.

* According to naturopathic philosophy we understand that in many instances the acute illness has resulted from some underlying and predisposing weakness in the person's general state of health. In the immediacy of the situation though, this factor will be of little importance to the practitioner or the patient.

* The acute symptoms must be dealt with first and they must be dealt with efficiently. This means that consideration and investigation of any underlying cause must be left until later.

* If the practitioner does not understand the nature of the patient's symptoms, then he should seek a second opinion from a colleague, or refer the patient on.

* It is common for a patient who is already under treatment for a chronic condition, to suffer an unrelated acute illness. The practitioner should be forever mindful of this possibility and not fall into the trap of associating all symptoms with the original chronic illness, such as an exacerbation. Do not try and offer a diagnosis and treatment over the telephone.

* The practitioner should endeavour to keep abreast of the symptoms when treating an acute illness, by organising lines of communication such as telephone reports or visits.

* If the acute symptoms are as a result of an exacerbation of a chronic

condition, then the symptoms are interpreted and treated in exactly the same way as with an acute illness.

* The number of mineral salts used in the treatment of acute symptoms can range from one to four salts.

* In the treatment of acute symptoms it is important that only those minerals that are indicated are actually prescribed. Do not clutter the prescription with unnecessary treatment as this can actually forfeit results

* Doses should be administered every ten minutes to two hours according to the symptoms and the need. It is the frequency of the dose that matters, not the actual amount of the dose.

* The tablets should be chewed or crushed and sloshed around the mouth with some hot water before swallowing.

* Once the acute or distressing symptoms have been arrested, the treatment should not be immediately abandoned, but rather the frequency of the dose reduced.

* As the symptoms associated with most acute illnesses are labile, the practitioner should instruct the patient to immediately increase the frequency of the dose again if the symptoms should return.

* Once the symptoms are under control, the practitioner should conduct a full assessment of the patient so as to determine and treat the underlying deficiencies.

Prescribing for greater effectiveness

Steps to prescribing with greater precision, skill and effectiveness

The full potential of mineral therapy cannot be challenged until the practitioner's knowledge and prescribing ability has passed beyond the easy prescribing technique outlined above. For this reason it would pay the practitioner not to come to rely on the questionnaire, but rather to see it merely as a stepping-stone to gaining experience, confidence and the promise of better things to come.

Step 1. Study the much more detailed prescribing information in chapter 4, "The individual mineral salts".

Step 2. Study and apply the "Symptom qualification" technique as detailed in chapter 5.

Step 3. Study all the pages of this chapter and apply the information in conjunction with chapter 8, "Management and prescribing procedures".

Step 4. Spend sufficient time with the patient. Listen and observe carefully, and most of all remember; that you are treating the patient not the disease.

Step 5. Continue to apply the "Prescribing rules" on page 111, and any other steps from "Prescribing quickly and easily" on page 107, that you feel are a help.

Here are five actual case histories that will help you understand how to prescribe

They will also demonstrate to you how important it is to get all the information from the patient, because after all, we are treating the patient, not the disease

You will also see what to do to control the acute distressing symptoms, while the under lying cause is being corrected

Prescribing examples without the questionnaire

Primary osteoarthritis (case number one)

Presenting symptoms: Middle aged woman, complaining of, pain (varies between a dull nagging ache, to throbbing, **(IP, PC)**, or at times sharp shooting, **(MP)** and stiffness of the right thumb (carpometacarpal), left shoulder (acromioclavicular), neck, lower spine and some finger joints (distal interphalangeal), **(SP, S, CF)**. There are hard nodular swellings on the dorsal aspects of the distal interphalangeal joints (Heberden's nodes), **(S, CF)**. There is at times a slight swelling and redness over the affected joints, **(PC, IP)**.

Symptom qualifications: The joints ache during night or with rest, **S, CF.** Are stiff and painful upon arising, **(S, CF)**, Are worse during cold weather, **(S, CF, CP, MP)**. Shoulder is worse if uncovered at night, **(S, PP)**. Pain and stiffness, worse with movement following rest, **(S, CF, PP)**. The symptoms are better during warm, stable weather, **(SP, PS, CP, CF)**, and from warm applications to the joints, **(MP, S, CF)**.

Tongue: Heavy cream coating, **(SP)**.

Iris: Acid wash, **(SP, IP, PC, MP)**. Flared autonomic wreath, **(SP, IP, PC, MP)**.

Pupil: Hypertonic and out of round, **(MP)**.

X-ray: There are marked degenerative changes with osteophytic lipping of the lower cervical and lower lumbar spine, **(S, CF)**. There is subchondral cyst formation in the right hip joint. **(S, CF)**.

Prescription: SP, PC, IP, MP, S, CF.

The PC, IP, and MP were prescribed, with meals, between meals and at bedtime (6 a day), for the first two weeks of treatment for pain control. The SP, S, and CF were prescribed with each meal (3 a day). Following the first two weeks, all minerals were prescribed three times a day.

Primary osteoarthritis (case number two)

Presenting symptoms: Same basic symptom picture as for the case above, but with the salient differences that there is œdematous swelling of the knees and ankles, **(SS)**, the finger joints are generally puffy, with difficulty in getting rings off at night, **(SS)**. The symptoms are aggravated during hot, humid weather, **(SS, PS)**, and damp weather, **(SS, CP, S, CF, CS)**, rather than the cold weather aggravation of case 1., and the tongue is puffy, clear, and shiny, **(SS)**, rather than cream.

Prescription: SS instead of SP.

All the other minerals and dosages remain the same as for case history number one.

Sinusitis (case number one)

Presenting symptoms: The patient has suffered from sinusitis for many years. Most episodes stem from an infected throat or the common cold. There is copious post-nasal mucus that has a yellow-green, slimy appearance, **(PS)**. At other times when there is no infection, the nose is stuffy and blocked **(PS)**, there can also be a clear, watery drip from the nares **(PS)**. Frontal headaches are common with orbital, malar and ethmoidal pain. There is a concomitant hearing loss at these times.

The patient also complains of poor concentration and memory **(PP, PS, MP)**, and a fuzzy, cotton-woolly feeling in the head **(PS)**.

Symptom qualification: The symptoms are worse during the cold, changeable months **(SP, PS, CP, CF)**, and warm stuffy, overheated rooms **(PS, CS)**. The symptoms are better during stable weather **(SP, PS, CP, CF)**, and in the cool, fresh open air **(PS, CS)**.

Tongue: Cream at the back **(SP)**.

Iris: Lymphatic rosary **(PC, PS)**. Arcus ischæmia **(PS, MP)**. Nerve rings **(PP, MP)**.

Prescription: SP, PS, MP, S, CF.

The PS and MP were given every two hours at times of exacerbation. S and CF were also prescribed as part of the patient's regular treatment, due to the chronicity of the complaint and the influence that silica and calcium fluoride have over these tissues (see chapter four), rather than any direct and specific prescribing indications. Although the relating of this case history deliberately focuses on the specifics of the patient's illness, do not forget to treat the patient as a whole by obtaining a total symptom picture. With regard to the silica and calcium fluoride, if a full case history is taken, it will often be found that supporting clues will come from problems arising in other seemingly unrelated areas, such as joint, tendon or cartilage.

Sinusitis (case number two)

Presenting symptoms: With this case there are no seasonal weather influences as with the one above. Episodes occur during or following periods of stress **(PP, MP)**, and post-nasal mucus is thick, yellow, with a bad taste from mucus hawked and fœtid breath **(PP)**. Yellow crusts form in the nostrils and there is some bleeding **(PP)**.

Symptom qualifications: Symptoms are worse with stress **(PP, MP)**, and cold air **(PP, MP, CP, S)**. The symptoms are improved by rest **(PP, CP, IP)**, and warmth **(PP, MP, CP, S, CF, SS)**.

Tongue: Cream **(SP)**. Bad breath **(PP)**.

Iris: Deep nerve rings **(PP, MP)**.

Pupil: Hypotonic and out of round **(PP, MP)**.

Prescription: SP, PP, MP.

The PP and MP were prescribed every two hours for exacerbations.

Frequent ENT and URT infections

Presenting symptoms: Six year old child with long history of frequent ear, nose, throat and upper respiratory infections **(CP)**. The infections have generally been more often during the winter months and when coming into contact with other children who carry infections to school. The episodes are now more frequent and severe, regardless of long courses of antibiotic therapy. Symptoms usually begin as a sore throat or coryza **(PC, IP)**, then quickly change to, yellow-green runny mucus from nose **(PS)**, and ear ache **(PC, IP)**. There is a raised temperature during the late afternoon/evening, which abates around midnight **(PS)**. About two to three days into the infection it is usual for the child to develop bronchitis with profuse mucopurulent expectoration **(PS)**, and a nagging cough when lying down at night or if he becomes uncovered during the night **(S)**.

The child also has patches of dry, itchy, flaky eczema, often with a crusty serous exudate **(PS)**.

Symptom qualifications: Condition is worse during, cold, damp, changeable weather **(SP, SS, CP, PS, S, CF, CS, MP)**, evening **(PS, SP, SS)** and the cough is worse at night when lying down or if he becomes uncovered **(S)**.

Tongue: Creamy-white **(SP, PC)**.

Iris: Poor texture **(CP)**. Superficial nerve rings **(CP, MP)**. Lymphatic rosary **(PC, PS)**.

Prescription: SP, CP, PS, MP.

For times of infection the child was prescribed a two hourly dose of PC, IP, PS and MP, and the regular treatment was suspended. During the early stages of treatment if the two hourly doses were unsuccessful in stopping the infection before the night cough set-in, then evening/night-time doses of silica were also added.

Chapter eight

Management and prescribing procedures

Patient management, is an aspect of the practitioner-patient relationship, about which every practitioner seems to have his own individual point of view. Personal preference has thus ensured that there are many methods in use, because in reality there is no single approach, that can be employed with all modalities and in all situations. Regardless of personal preferences though, how well the patient is managed, will often determine the outcome of the treatment more than any other single factor. This principle affects all modalities, but in particular it affects the alternative modalities, where the chronically ill patient may be under treatment for a considerable period of time. The principles offered in this chapter are therefore subjective and represent merely one point of view, but they are particularly tailored to the needs of the mineral therapist and have been proven to be most effective and efficient.

Proper management may emerge as the single most important factor in the patient's treatment

Regardless of the potential efficacy of a modality, the practitioner may still enjoy less than satisfactory results, due to an inadequate patient management programme. In fact many alternative modalities do not lend themselves to good patient management, particularly when viewed according to proper naturopathic principles.

These shortcomings need not apply to this particular form of mineral therapy, as it lends itself well to good patient management and is in direct accordance with true naturopathic philosophy. This means that its tremendous healing potential can be better unleashed, working to the advantage of both the patient and the practitioner.

The late Maurice Blackmore, stated that, "Mineral therapy sells itself by result." This blunt but nonetheless true statement represents perhaps the first plank in building a successful patient management procedure. As most patients being treated will be suffering from some form of chronic illness, there are two things that should be immediately apparent. The first is that they will probably be under treatment for some time, and second; that there is no way to predict, when they should expect to see benefit, or how long they will be under treatment in total.

The most important consideration in the practitioner's mind during the first consultation, should be to prescribe accurately, for that is where the future lies. It is counter-productive to spend undue time (and perhaps credibility), labouring the virtues of either himself or the treatment, if that time is spent at the expense of proper patient care. This method of mineral prescribing lends itself to a "no fuss" approach to patient management right from the first consultation, which indirectly actually adds credibility to both the practitioner and the treatment. Put yourself in the patient's position. You have suffered from your chronic illness for probably many years. You are fed up with the palliative measures offered thus far (probably with side-effects), but most of all you are fed up with the promises, promises that may have been real or inferred, but nonetheless, promises. The last thing you need, is another promise, but what you do need, is informed and constructive information.

This informed and constructive help is obviously going to vary according to all the known tangibles, the nature of the disease, the severity, the length of time that the patient has suffered the illness, the age of the patient, his past medical history, what treatments have been tried previously, and probably most of all, the practitioner's own experience in treating the particular complaint. Regardless of all that, the most vital piece of information is going to remain lost to the practitioner for the time-being, and that is; what is going to be this particular patient's response, even if the prescription is correct?

What the practitioner can do though and what mineral prescribing allows for, is to lay out for the patient (as required), some necessary information, information that in turn will help to build patient confidence and compliance.

There are certain "response patterns" and other associated events to do with patient management, that can be used to offer necessary advice to the patient on the first visit, or help to explain future events as required. If the patient's condition is at all treatable, and the prescribing has been accurate, then the first results should be seen during the first few months of treatment. In actual fact, most of the common chronic illnesses can begin to show response within the first few weeks, and quite often even within the first few days.

At what point should we expect to see results?

The first thing then, that the practitioner can rely on with reasonable confidence; is that the patient can be expected to improve within three to four months of treatment. If results have not been realised by that time, when prescribing has been accurate and the patient has dutifully taken every single dose expected, then any further perseverance with that treatment needs to be seriously questioned.

The degree of result obtained within the first few months of treatment is also obviously going to vary from patient to patient, and may not always be to either the patient's or the practitioner's satisfaction. It is when, and only when, the patient fails to respond in any way at all, that the practitioner should become concerned. Results, no matter how insignificant, should be seen as the "thin edge of the wedge", and sufficient encouragement for the treatment to be continued. Any "change" in the nature of the patient's condition, even a worsening, can also perhaps represent a positive indication for continuation of the treatment.

Getting results is only the first hurdle

After considering all these possibilities, there will only be about 10% of patients who will reach the point where defeat has to be admitted. That doesn't mean that the remaining 90% of patients are going to stick it out and be cured either, as there are further considerations beyond just getting the initial response. To the newcomer practising mineral therapy, there will be much sweating and gnashing of teeth over the first results, but in time this will come to be seen as only the first hurdle, and believe it or not; the most predictable of a number yet to come.

When the total symptom picture of chronically ill patients attending for the first time is analysed, the practitioner will discover, that apart from any unique aspects pertaining to the illness that brought them along, patients most times suffer from other symptoms or illnesses as well. Hence the importance of taking a "total" symptom picture from the patient, regardless of whether all the symptoms pertain to the illness in question or not, or whether any particular relevance can be made of the symptoms at that time either.

The importance of this detailed, and to some practitioners, laborious task of note-taking on the first visit, is not, as would be imagined, to ensure accuracy of prescribing alone. The immediate details of the case can easily be collated from memory on the first visit regardless of whether notes are taken at the time or not, but the importance of detailed notes, comes into play on future visits. It's during future visits, particularly if the patient does not seem to be responding to treatment, that the notes of the first visit may save the day for both the practitioner and the patient.

Having discussed from a general standpoint some of the relevant aspects of patient management, let's now look more specifically at these issues to see how they can directly influence the outcome of the treatment.

Problem patient one: "I think I'm no better."

Patients suffer short memories once they begin to improve:

Patients have a nasty habit of suffering short memories once they begin to improve. They somehow even completely overlook aspects of their condition that they emphasised on the first visit as being important. Maybe this is akin to the natural response of blotting-out or forgetting unpleasant experiences, but for whatever reason, the phenomenon is not at all uncommon.

If it were not for the detailed note taking of the first visit, offering the opportunity to walk the patient back through his symptoms, the initiative may be well and truly lost at that point. It is necessary therefore to actually read back to the patient from the notes taken, every single symptom (not disease), that he mentioned on his first visit, until hopefully a point is reached where the patient will say something like, "Oh, gee, you know I haven't had *that* since I saw you last!" "I'd completely forgotten I even mentioned *that* !"

Problem patient two: "I'm no better, but..."

Out of sight, out of mind

Patients also have a nasty habit of mentally focussing on particular symptoms, while completely ignoring others, that they may have laboured on the first visit. So, again when the question is asked "are you deriving any benefit from the treatment?" They forthrightly say "no!" Now, they probably have derived benefit in some way, but not in the way that they had expected; hence the need to question further and to certainly not immediately accept *their* assessment of the situation. Again, the initiative must be taken by the practitioner, by employing the same technique as in "Problem one"; that is to go over every single symptom again.

Problem patient three: "I'm definitely no better!"

Don't concede defeat before you check the files

More subtle again, is where even after extensive probing, there does not seem to be any change in any way, with any of the patient's illnesses, but there is change in what at the time of the first visit, seemed to be unrelated and unimportant symptoms: again, the importance of taking a comprehensive case history on the first visit, regardless of whether that information can be understood or directly related to the patient's reason for attending or not. The fact that these obscure symptoms have been initially noted and have subsequently improved, while the disease under treatment has not, is apart from anything else, encouragement for continuing treatment. Again, the need may be there to go over the whole case history again with the patient, as he may not automatically volunteer this information.

Deficiencies produce not only the illness but other symptoms as well.

Deficiencies produce not only the illness but other symptoms as well

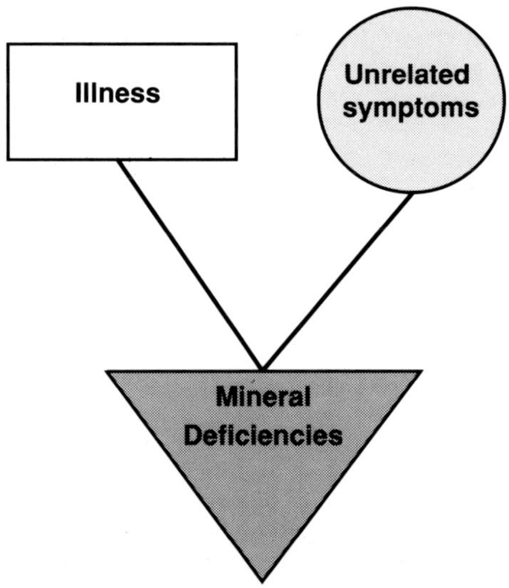

The rationale behind the mineral deficiency theory has a very logical and practical basis to it and one that also goes a long way to explaining some of the difficulties already cited in connection with patient management. For instance, the fact that, "Problem three" patient's illness had not improved in any way but unrelated symptoms had. Maybe those unrelated symptoms, are not as unrelated as they might have first appeared. Maybe those symptoms are in fact unrelated to the actual illness for which the patient is seeking treatment, but not unrelated to the deficiencies which have produced the illness. In other words, the one deficiency, or group of deficiencies, has produced not only the illness, but other symptoms as well.

Therefore, by carefully following the course of the symptoms visit by visit, often an indirect guide is established as to where the practitioner stands in his treatment programme. Philosophically we are reminded that it is individual symptoms that matter most and not the "label" of the disease.

The same deficiencies can produce more than one illness.

The same deficiencies can produce more than one illness

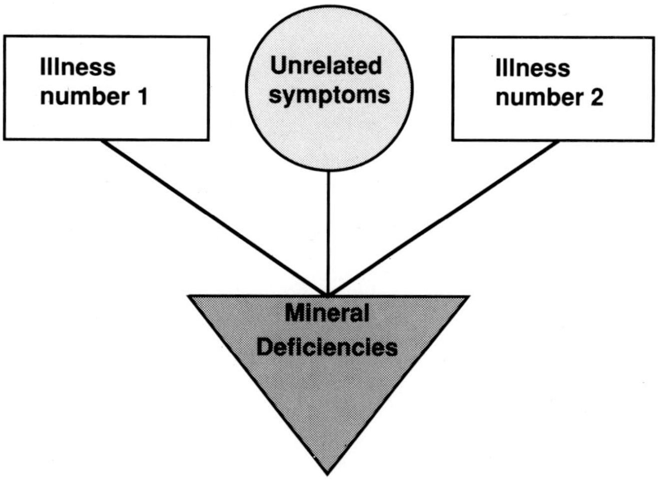

To extend the logic a little further. Apart from the principle, outlined previously, there exists the "One deficiency, many diseases principle", which is in fact the same thing, just extended slightly. This means that the same deficiency, or group of deficiencies, is quite capable of producing more than one illness in the same person. If we analyse the symptom picture of the typical chronic patient, we will usually find that the patient is not just suffering from one, but perhaps two and quite often even three distinct disease entities. The patient may have been driven to attend because of one particular illness, so if the practitioner adopts the often fatal "look only where the patient points approach", then the opportunity to learn more about the patient's deficiencies will be lost.

Connections can therefore be drawn between the patient's symptoms and the mineral deficiencies that underpin them, regardless of the number of illnesses. From a management standpoint, problems can again stem from not taking note of the total symptom picture and just focussing on the particular illness that the patient emphasises.

The same deficiencies can produce different illnesses in different people.

The same deficiencies can produce different illnesses in different people

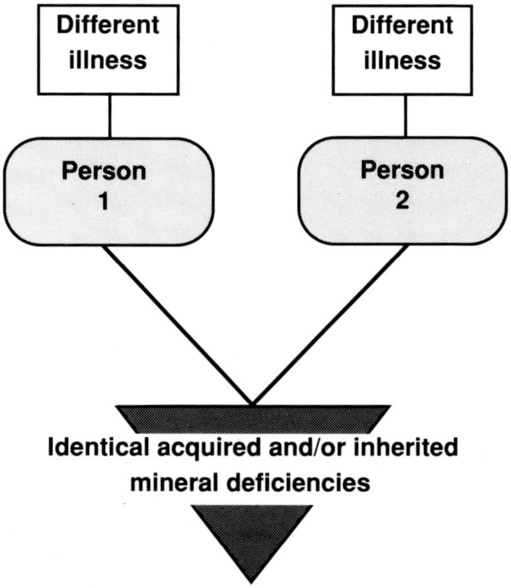

One man's headache is another man's bellyache

There is also a further interesting twist to the principle of the same deficiencies being capable of creating more than one illness. Although a certain group of mineral deficiencies will produce a particular disease in one person, the same deficiencies are quite capable of producing a totally different complaint in someone else. Genetic factors and acquired deficiencies through errors of lifestyle, are the major factors that influence this situation. It is reasonable to assume for instance, that members of the same family who share the same diet, will in time, acquire the same deficiencies, but not necessarily share the same illnesses. Clinically it will be observed, that many seemingly unrelated illnesses can be successfully resolved with exactly the same prescription, which is ample demonstration of this principle. It is also reasonable to assume, that members of the same family who share a common genetic pool, will be predisposed, regardless of external factors, to the weaknesses that those genes determine. Regardless of whether the deficiencies are created through genetic predisposition or diet, or both, there is no law that dictates that they must always produce the same disease.

With regard to the less tangible, genetic influence, this can best be observed when treating whole families. If the members of the family are assessed according to their own deficiency profile, rather than their illnesses, it will be observed that the resultant profiles are often identical. It will therefore be possible to establish the genetic links. not by illness, but rather by deficiencies. Thus it would appear then, that genetically acquired defects, do not only manifest in the familiar, immutable, absolute way, producing our hæmophiliacs, thalassæmias and polycystic diseases; but also in a way that predisposes us toward certain mineral deficiencies, which in turn dictate the specific nature of our disease.

Supplementary genes

When it comes to offering explanations as to causes for the inquiring patient, an understanding of this subtle predisposition toward certain mineral deficiencies, allows for answers that extend far beyond the simplistic principle that all deficiencies must be caused from poor diet alone. It also offers reasons why some patients must continually supplement with particular nutrients, regardless of good diet, if they wish to maintain the level of health and efficiency that they have come to enjoy. From the practitioner's point of view, it provides a reason why one person's illness can be remedied and remain remedied, because the illness was an acquired product of faulty lifestyle; and why another person must remain on a prophylactic dose, because their illness was a product of genetically determined defects. From a long-term management point of view though, there is no doubt, that the apparent absolute effect of genetic weaknesses may be modified through initially replacing mineral deficiencies and then ensuring their repleteness from that point on.

Winning the battle and losing the war

As mentioned previously, most new practitioners to mineral therapy, will worry unduly over initial results. Again for all the afore-mentioned reasons, the initial results may only prove to be the first, of many greater hurdles yet to come. In fact, those delightful first results may eventually reap a bitter harvest, if not for good management. Unlike many of its competitors in the race to satisfy the alternative health care consumer, mineral therapy very rarely produces an initial result, only to be followed by disappointment. Other forms of treatment often achieve quick and spectacular results, which intentionally or by default, has the effect of impressing the patient; but if this benefit cannot be sustained, or built upon, then any initial positive psychotherapeutic impact will soon be lost, perhaps along with the patient.

Putting aside all the more basic reasons why minerals are capable of producing a consistent and ongoing benefit; it is patient management more than anything else that will ensure that these benefits will continue through the patient's course of treatment and beyond.

Let's now look at some of potential hazards that can either make or break the treatment programme:

Response patterns and other ups and downs

Response patterns

Accepting that the majority of patients are going to respond to treatment; how are they going to respond and in what particular ways may the practitioner be required to guide that progress?

There are four basic individual response patterns that can be applied, and then there is an overall master plan (see "Putting it all together", on page 134), that must be established for each patient, if successes are going to outweigh failures. A few months of treatment will be required with most chronically ill patients, not only to establish if the treatment is going to be worthwhile, but to firmly categorise the patient into a particular response group.

Response pattern number one.

Too much too easy

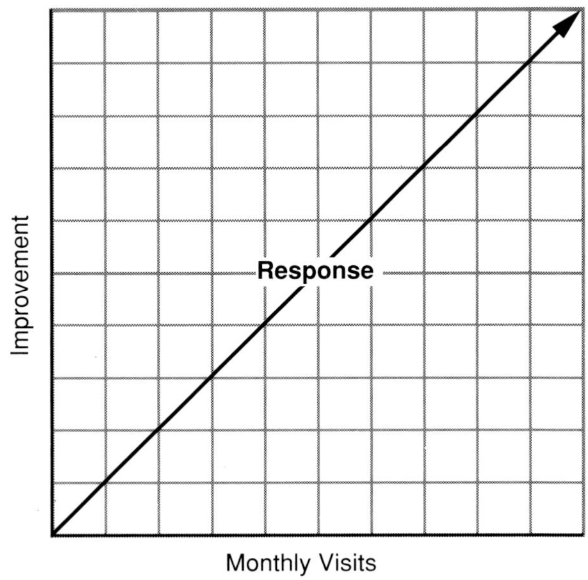

This first pattern is represented by the patient who shows results immediately and never looks back over the whole course of treatment. Whilst this may at first seem to be the most ideal of all the possibilities, it can still be fraught with difficulties. The fact that the patient has shown improvement on each subsequent visit, means that a point can be quickly reached where the patient makes a unilateral decision that he or she is cured. It would appear that for some patients, getting results quickly, can also mean, getting results too easily and therefore not properly appreciating what has actually been done for them. The abandoning of the treatment by the patient can either be by design or by default. The *by design* patient will make a conscious decision to stop the treatment because he believes he doesn't need to take it any more; while the *by default* patient just gets out of the way of taking it, because there is no longer any pain or discomfort to remind him.

From the practitioner's point of view it emphasises the importance of proper counselling along the way and not just taking the easy way out as a time saving ploy. The temptation is always there with the "easy patients" to cut corners and be lazy. Unfortunately, as with many other aspects of our lives, the ground we take the time to prepare now, determines the crop that we shall reap in the future. It is imperative that the practitioner, at the appropriate time in the treatment and according to the needs and understanding of the patient, prepare the patient for the possibilities that lie in the future. It should be emphasised to the patient that no chronic disease is established overnight, and that therefore a commitment to time, patience, and perseverance is going to be required to resolve the condition.

Response pattern number two.

80% out, for 20% in

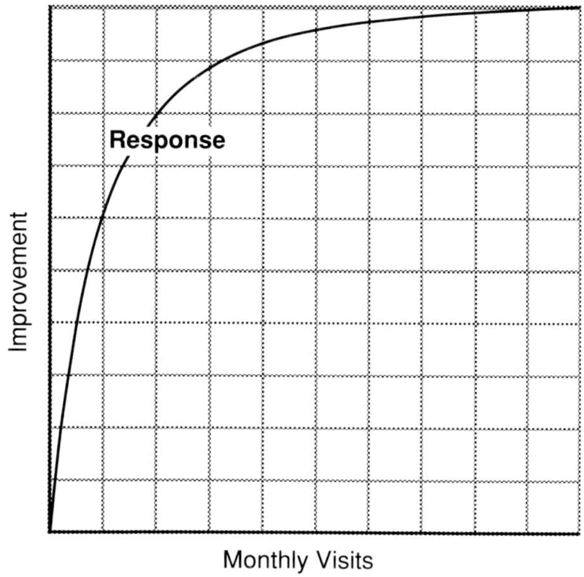

This response pattern, which is the most common (often with pattern number three superimposed upon it), represents almost a rule that can be applied to the course of most chronic illnesses whilst under treatment. Assuming there is no impediment to the course of healing, the progress is one of rapid initial improvement, followed by a tapering-off, rather than linear improvement all the way as in pattern number one.

The principle can be expressed by saying that a patient can be expected to receive 80% of the benefit in 20% of the time; and then spend the remaining 80% of the time chasing the last 20% of improvement.

The major problem associated with this response, is that as with the pattern one patient; results come too easily and are not appreciated for what they really are and with the patient quite likely to abandon treatment believing he's cured. Again, the patient must be made to understand, that the removal of the symptoms is not necessarily the removal of the cause. The symptoms associated with most chronic illness represent merely the tip of the iceberg, and in common with the iceberg, it means that there is still more than two thirds hidden from view. Time given by the practitioner to educate the patient is the only way to minimise the possibility, otherwise it's going to be pot-luck how the patient interprets the situation if it should arise.

Response pattern number three.

Now you see it, now you don't

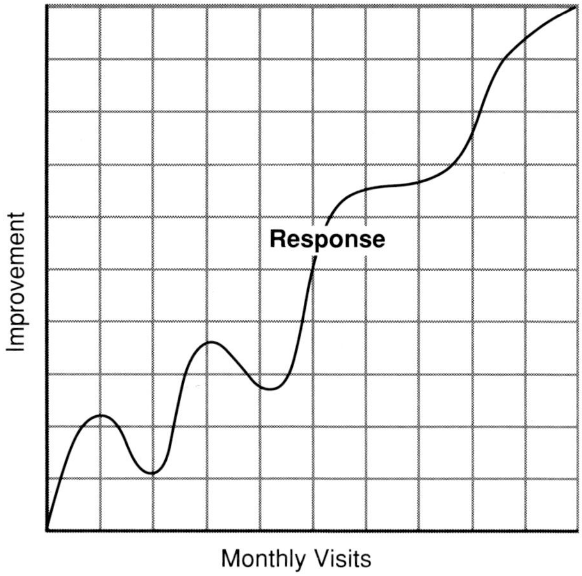

This response pattern which is most times superimposed over response pattern number one or two, will be seen to influence more than half the patients treated for a chronic illness. The management problems associated with this response, stem from its cyclic nature. Considerable improvement can be seen in the patient, then for the results to fall off but later to return to an even more pleasing level than they were beforehand. The patient, caught-up in this process, must be excused for often misinterpreting these events.

The misinterpretation takes one of two forms, with some patients even managing to combine them both. First, at the point where the initial flush of result falls off and is all but lost, the patient is convinced that improvement has gone forever and will never return. "What's the point in carrying-on, I may as well stop the treatment now." Secondly, at the point where the patient loses some or all of the initial benefit, he complains that, not only is he not as well as before, but that he is worse than he was when he first began the treatment. The patient will not only want to discard the treatment, but will also want to blame the practitioner for making his condition worse as well.

The timing of appointments can also have some bearing on these events. If the patient should coincidently enter a trough just at the time of an appointment, it will at least provide the practitioner with the opportunity to explain, but if it should occur between visits then that's another matter altogether. It is usual for most chronic illnesses to wax and wane, with the timing and magnitude of those cycles being dependent upon the illness, the individual patient and the circumstances connected with the patient's life. These are all factors that can be identified and considered by the practitioner when assessing a patient and determining a management strategy.

There is only one way to try and prevent these situations from arising, and that is through education. This means that the practitioner must draw the patient's attention to all the possibilities on the first consultation. The patient should also be encouraged to communicate any problems that he may have between visits via the telephone, otherwise he is just as likely not to return for his next scheduled appointment. There is no guarantee that these measures will circumvent the problem altogether, but generally, a better understanding leads to better compliance.

Response pattern number four.

More stops than starts

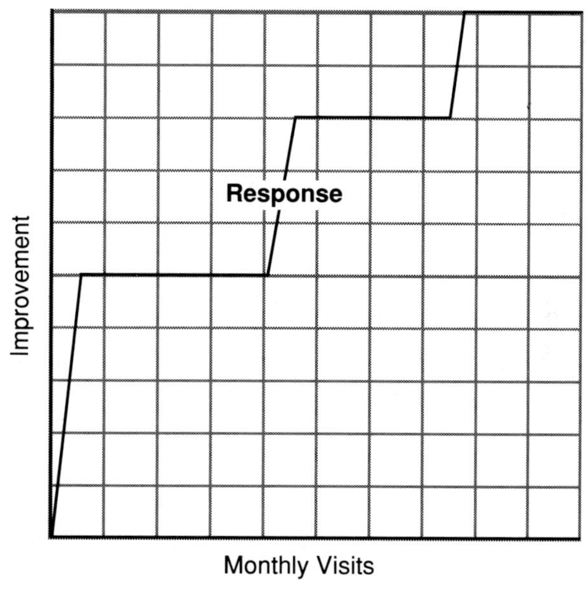

Fortunately only a minority of patients (about 10%) will fall into this pattern. The pattern is characterised by improvements, followed by long periods of no further change, sometimes lasting for a number of months.

As with response pattern number two, it is very easy for the patient to become convinced that he is not likely to derive any further benefit, or that he is back to where he was when he started. From the practitioner's standpoint though, it represents a dilemma, for following the first return visit, there may have been two or more consultations spanning a number of months, where the patient has shown no further progress. Credibility begins to wear thin and it would be quite understandable if the patient lost confidence and abandoned the treatment altogether. There is very little that even the experienced practitioner can call upon to change the situation, because every path seems to end in a cul-de-sac. However, what the practitioner must *not* do, is panic and begin chopping and changing the treatment. The patient's condition should have been monitored carefully, with the treatment being reviewed much earlier if a change was indicated. If any alteration is made to the treatment at this late stage, then it only introduces further complications. The first complication of course, is the one of credibility. If the patient has spent many months getting nowhere, then he is unlikely to agree to further treatment. Even if he does agree, or is talked into it, he may not follow it for very long. From the practitioner's standpoint, unless there is some blinding flash of inspiration that will lead he and the patient out of the present impasse, then it's probably better to suspend the treatment for the time-being. If the practitioner abandons the treatment rather than the patient, this should ensure that some command of the situation is retained. It is not uncommon for a patient, who, having reached the point of believing that he has not made progress, stops the treatment, only to find that his condition is subsequently worse. The practitioner should invoke this process, enlisting the patient's cooperation, so that at the very least the patient agrees to communicate the outcome of the suspension to the practitioner. If the patient does in fact see that his condition is worse when he stops the treatment, then he will resume the treatment of his own volition. This process clears the air, putting both the patient and the practitioner in the position of knowing exactly where they're placed.

Putting it all together.

A master plan of events

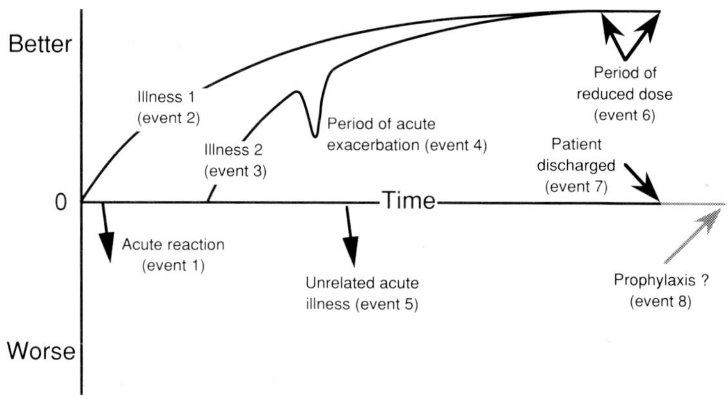

Having covered the general response patterns that apply to the chronic case, we should now look at the overall situation, putting together all the circumstances that may eventuate, from the time the patient begins treatment, until the time he is discharged.

As mentioned earlier, the typical chronically ill patient, usually presents with more than one illness, although he may only emphasise one. Let us then, follow the course of an imaginary patient who is under treatment for two chronic illnesses, but suffers a few unfortunate incidents along the road back to health. For simplicity the course of improvement for the chronic illnesses has been demonstrated as response pattern number two.

Acute reactions to treatment (event 1)

Acute reactions are induced by the treatment

The first event to note from the master plan diagram is the appearance of an acute reaction some few days into the treatment programme. An acute reaction constitutes symptoms that are induced by the treatment itself (see "Prescribing rules", on page 111). This event, although not occurring in every case, does occur sufficiently often that the practitioner should be versed in its management.

They have more to do with healing than with harm

An acute reaction should not be confused with the side-effects that are so often a feature associated with the technological drug. The acute reaction process has more to do with healing than it does with harm and is usually self resolving. From a management standpoint though, the fact that the process may be self resolving is of little consequence, if the patient has not been suitably informed beforehand. The sudden appearance of extra pain or discomfort will almost always be interpreted in the negative context. The form that an acute reaction can take, will be in either of two ways.

1. The sudden introduction of symptoms that the patient did not possess prior to treatment.
2. An exacerbation of the chronic symptoms under treatment.

Most times the induced symptoms take the form of minor discomforts, such as, flatus, indigestion, mild nausea, skin irritations or eruptions, headache and tiredness etc., and will usually occur within the first three days of treatment. If the illness under treatment is exacerbated, then of course the symptoms will pertain specifically to that illness. An example of this may be demonstrated by a patient who presents with arthritis, but complains that the joint pains are exacerbated within a few days of beginning the treatment; or maybe pains in joints where there were no pains before.

Management of the situation should be structured on two levels.

1. Education.
2. Intervention.

Education should first of all begin by alerting the patient to the possibility of a reaction prior to him starting the treatment, then by encouraging him to make contact in the event of any occurrence and of course, reassuring him if a reaction should arise.

Intervention (see page 111) will be what the practitioner does by way of management at the time that the reaction takes place. Usually this amounts to simply suspending the treatment for a few days until the symptoms settle down, and then resuming it again.

Acute reactions occur within the first few days of treatment

Acute reactions occur within the first few days of treatment, so the practitioner should realise that if the patient were to complain of unrelated symptoms or an exacerbation weeks or even months later, then it probably has little to do with a reaction to treatment. The correct interpretation of events at the time is essential, as the possibility exists for the practitioner to blame a reaction for the new symptoms, when in fact they are due to an unrelated acute episode (see page 137).

Even when new symptoms arise within the first few days, there is still the possibility that they are there for some other reason. Therefore, the practitioner should not automatically assume that any symptom that arises during that time, is definitely due to the treatment. Even if the symptoms abate when the treatment is suspended, it should also not be interpreted as proof that the treatment was responsible. Sometimes unrelated symptoms are labile, with the times of quiescence just happening to coincide with the time when the treatment was suspended. If there is any doubt in this regard, the treatment should be stopped and started at least twice. The normal course of events is for the reactions to settle almost immediately the treatment is suspended and certainly following a break of about three days. The symptoms do not usually return once the treatment is restarted following a three day break.

If on the rare occasion the reaction returns each time the treatment is re-introduced, then half, or even quarter dose should be tried for a time, before the treatment is returned to full dose. If this procedure should also fail, then an experiment should be conducted, by trial and error, to ascertain which particular mineral in the prescription is the offending item. If the mineral can be determined and removed from the prescription for a time, then the reaction will abate. It must then be left to the prevailing circumstances and the practitioner's discretion, as to when and if the mineral is re-introduced.

Unlike technological drugs and their side-effects, these acute reactions represent signs that the organism is working towards healing. Proof of this philosophy is that the continued taking of the treatment will completely remove those symptoms that the treatment induced (consistent with the "provings" of the homœopathic school of thought; see page 11, of the chapter "History"). This principle goes a long way to explaining why a remedy can induce symptoms where there were none, or cause an exacerbation of symptoms that the very same remedy would have been prescribed for anyway. This concept is often difficult to understand, for those not steeped in homœopathic philosophy, but a simple example may be given thus: potassium sulphate, as one of the minerals prescribed for the general symptom picture of a patient suffering from sinusitis, produces an improvement in the condition being treated, but at the same time induces other symptoms of, dry and flaky skin, which the patient didn't have beforehand (see pages 11-12).

Response path of chronic illness (events 2 & 3)

Events two and three from the master plan diagram indicate that the chronic illnesses do not respond simultaneously, with illness number two lagging behind. This example is common and highlights the need for the practitioner to keep in mind the three "problem patient" types that were detailed on pages 125-6. Although it is quite logical for each illness to respond in its own time, regardless that they may both stem from the same mineral deficiencies; this principle may not be apparent to the patient unless explained. In the clinical situation it will be observed that although the illnesses may not respond simultaneously, they quite often end up being resolved at approximately the same time. In terms of case-management, it is desirable if the practitioner can link both illnesses to the same deficiencies, because then hopefully, it will only be a matter of time and perseverance, before each illness is remedied. Unfortunately, it doesn't always work out that way, as all the patient's maladies may not be linked to the same deficiencies. Regardless, if there is reason to believe that the illnesses are linked to the same group of deficiencies, then that avenue should be exhausted first. If after one disease is remedied the other has shown no sign of change, then the whole case should be reviewed on the basis of present circumstances and a new prescription issued.

Unpredictable acute events

Because the patient will be treated over an extended period of time, it is quite likely that other related and unrelated episodes will arise that require the same attention to detail by the practitioner, as in the instances cited above. The two most likely occurrences are:

1. Acute episodes of a related nature (event 4).
2. Acute episodes of an unrelated nature (event 5).

Acute episodes are events that demand quick and proper interpretation and intervention

The related acute episode pertains to an exacerbation of the existing chronic illness (event 4); whilst the unrelated acute episode (event 5) is purely of a coincidental nature such as an infection etc. Neither of these events can be predetermined but their management at the time will have as much bearing on the overall outcome as a correct prescription does on the first visit. There is also the possibility that another unrelated chronic illness may arise during treatment, but this prospect won't be canvassed, as the general principles of management explained in this chapter, will apply equally to that situation.

The illness under treatment may undergo times of exacerbation

Chronic illness exacerbations (event 4)

Periodic acute exacerbations are a feature associated with many chronic illnesses. These factors must be considered in the treatment management for any patient where this process could occur. There are two ways to handle the situation should it arise.

1. To equip the patient on the first visit with treatment that will cover the times of exacerbation should they occur.
2. To wait until the need arises and prescribe at the time.

The first option cited is the one of choice if the circumstances are conducive. This opportunity will depend upon the actual illness being treated, the way the patient is being affected by the illness and the practitioner's experience in handling, not only the illness, but also these situations. If the practitioner has the opportunity to prescribe in advance (and that may simply mean an altered dose of the patient's regular treatment, see pages 117, 120-2), then the patient is equipped to handle the situation immediately, whenever the need should arise. This method also ensures better patient compliance when applied to the right patient. Before the practitioner offers this avenue though, the patient should be carefully assessed for his ability to understand and cooperate, otherwise compliance will be diminished rather than increased. If it appears to be too difficult for the patient to comprehend, then he should only be offered option number two, outlined below.

Even for an experienced practitioner, it is often impossible to anticipate the nature of future events at the time of the first visit. It would be unwise under these circumstances to formulate a treatment in advance that could be used at times of exacerbation. In this case, it is preferable for the practitioner to advise the patient to make contact if any significant change in his symptoms should arise. The treatment can then be reviewed in the light of what is happening to the patient at that time. For the inexperienced practitioner this represents an advantage, as the opportunity then exists to prescribe more accurately and to learn at the same time.

Regardless of whether treatment is offered in anticipation of an acute exacerbation, or prescribed at the time, the question will arise; "what does the patient do with his regular treatment?" In many instances, the treatment for the acute symptoms will represent no more than a modification in dose of the patient's regular treatment (see page 117). If the change is not too complicated and if the patient seems the type to be able to cope with the additional tablet load, then the regular treatment can be left in place. If on the other hand the changes to treatment need to be significant and the patient would interpret the changes to be too much of a burden, or if the practitioner needs a quick, clear and unambiguous assessment of the situation; then it is advantageous to abandon the regular treatment temporarily, only returning to it when the acute symptoms have been subdued.

The unrelated acute illness (event 5)

An unrelated acute illness has the potential to fool the practitioner

The unrelated acute episode can never be anticipated and is an event that hopefully, will never occur during the course of the patient's treatment. Realistically though, because the chronic case is going to be under treatment for some time, the likelihood of an unrelated illness arising is actually quite great. The management at the time should be along the same lines as for the acute exacerbation instance above, but with one exception. In almost every case, the regular treatment will need to be completely changed, with the patient putting aside his regular treatment, only resuming it when the acute illness has passed.

The acute unrelated illness will of course require the practitioner to assess the patient according to the symptoms occurring at the time and actually as if he were a new patient. It is a potentially dangerous mistake to diminish the importance of these symptoms, explaining them away as being related to the condition under treatment, or making a quick assessment of them over the phone; simply because the patient is already known to the practitioner. The patient may also, wittingly or unwittingly, be responsible for luring the practitioner into this trap; for, as the acute illness will usually arise between visits, he will seek free advice for the symptoms over the telephone. Assessment over the telephone for an exacerbation of the existing illness is one thing; but never for an unrelated acute illness!

Preparing the patient for discharge (events 6 & 7)

Discharging the patient

It is only when the patient's chronic condition has been completely cleared for a period of not less than two months, that the practitioner should even consider abandoning the treatment. At this point, for some of the management reasons already cited, the patient may unilaterally decide, or pressure the practitioner into deciding, that the treatment should be cut back or dispensed with altogether. If this action is taken prematurely, then the progress already made may be threatened and confusion with regard to the patient's true position will result. The principle must again be explained or reinforced to the patient; that the absence of symptoms, does not mean that the disease has been cured.

Don't drop the reins too soon

Unfortunately it is common practice for both the patient and the practitioner to slacken off once the symptoms have been checked. From the patient's standpoint, it is easy to understand, because once the symptoms have disappeared, there would seem to be no further reason to persist with the treatment. This attitude also has a lot to do with prior conditioning, with the usual orthodox medical attitude being to take a drug when the symptoms are there and dispense with it when they are gone; because, after all, the only objective is the relief of symptoms.

The out of sight, out of mind principle can also come into the picture when a patient is relieved of his pain and discomfort. In many instances, it is only while there is the reminder of things unpleasant, that the patient can be relied upon to keep up his treatment regimen. Once those reminders are gone, he just simply forgets, nothing intentional, stupid or devious, he just simply forgets.

At this point in the patient's treatment programme, the practitioner can also lose interest and become sloppy in his attention to detail. The novelty of the case can wear off and the passage of time can be responsible for blurring the original objectives. Although somewhat of a benign lure, this situation can nonetheless lead the practitioner into a deadly trap. If the practitioner should allow his interest to flag at this time, then a set of subtle, yet insidious events can bring about a breakdown of the whole treatment programme.

The patient's condition and compliance must be monitored conscientiously by the practitioner right the way through the programme, from day one to discharge. If the patient should become tardy with his medication, for whatever reason, and the practitioner does not make himself aware of the situation, then the effect will be far more complicated and confusing than it would have been if the patient had done the same thing early in the treatment. At this point, the effect of such tardiness is not going to be immediately evident as it would have been earlier in the treatment, so it is not going to be noticed by the practitioner either, unless he makes a conscious effort to explore the aspects of the total symptom picture and patient compliance on every visit.

As the diagram below illustrates, the longer the patient takes the treatment, then the longer he is likely to retain the benefits. It can be seen that the patient is rewarded many-fold for every month that he is required to persist. This process can also be seen to be a demonstration of the naturopathic principle of treating the cause, rather than merely the symptoms. If the cause was not being addressed, then the symptoms could be expected to return immediately each time the treatment was ceased, regardless of the time that the patient had been taking the treatment.

Loss of benefit following the premature withdrawal of treatment.

The longer the patient is on the treatment, the longer he will retain the benefit

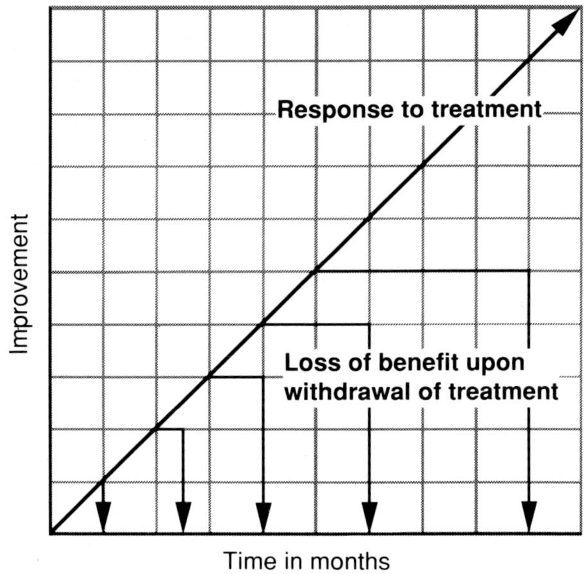

The patient may display no sign of regression as a result of his dilatory behaviour for some time, but if the treatment has been cut back or discarded prematurely, then eventually the original symptoms will break through. If this breakthrough does occur, it often comes with such speed and voracity, that it takes the patient and practitioner by surprise. The patient reacts by believing that all benefit has been lost, he's back to where he began and the treatment has probably done all it can for him. The practitioner, faced with the situation (that is if the patient bothers to return), is usually reduced to having to make excuses for what has happened.

Don't be made the scapegoat

This is a ridiculous situation and one that should be avoided at all costs. The scenario cited is only one of a number of less than satisfactory outcomes and simply serves to demonstrate how easy it is for the practitioner to be overtaken by events if he allows it. Generally speaking, the average patient of today, wants the greatest result for the least effort, and someone or something to blame if his desires are not fulfilled.

Assuming that none of these negative events have occurred, or if they have then they have been overcome, and the patient has been free from his original symptoms for at least two months, then the practitioner can begin the process of discharging the patient.

The patient should be instructed to take his next two months treatment at half the usual dose; i.e., sticking to the same regimen but reducing the actual dose. Reducing the dose of the minerals for two months, allows the practitioner to observe the patient under these new conditions, so as to ensure that there is no loss of benefit. If the patient's condition has remained asymptomatic throughout this time, then the treatment can be abandoned altogether; if not, then at least the practitioner can regain control of the situation before it gets too out of hand.

If there is any indication of a return of the symptoms, then the treatment should be immediately reinstated to full dose. The patient should also be briefed regarding this possibility and advised to promptly resume full dose, even before resuming contact with the practitioner. This return to full dose should be maintained for about two months, before again being reduced to half dose. If the patient continues to lose ground each time the dose is reduced, it usually means that considerably more time needs to be given to full dose treatment, or maintenance treatment needs to be considered.

The patient should be instructed that during the months following the completion of the treatment, he should continue to be watchful for any return of his original symptoms. Again he should be told to make contact immediately, or if he should have any of the original treatment on hand, then he should begin to take it again. If the practitioner withdraws the treatment in stages it provides the opportunity to keep control of the case and to learn through observation.

Prophylactic treatment

Maintenance treatment (event 8)

Following discharge there will always be those patients, who, once made well, do not remain well. If a patient regresses each time the treatment is abandoned, then this is probably a good indication that the patient will require a prophylactic dose to remain well. The criterion for establishing whether this is the case or not, is to apply the rule: that if following three attempts to abandon the treatment, the patient's symptoms keep returning; then this is fair justification for the establishment of a maintenance treatment programme. The reasons why three attempts need to be made before coming to this conclusion are.

1. As in dealing with acute reactions (see page 135-6), there may be other unrelated factors operating at the time, that cloud and confuse the issue, causing the patient and/or the practitioner to draw wrong conclusions.

2. If the treatment is tested in this way, it makes for much better compliance, because the patient can see for himself the direct effect of, and need for, the treatment.

To be or not to be?

The practitioner must avoid establishing a situation where the patient is obliged to follow a maintenance treatment programme, but where the patient has not seen a demonstration for that need. This is not to say that at times there will not be particular patients, who will actually request maintenance treatment, but generally speaking it is preferable that the patient be given the opportunity to see that need for himself.

In determining the maintenance programme, the practitioner will have to call upon his experience gained from dealing with the patient as an individual, the symptoms manifesting at the time and his technical knowledge as to the salts indicated by those symptoms. What actually constitutes maintenance treatment will generally fall into one of two categories. It must ultimately be left to the discretion of the practitioner though, as to which course of action will prove to be of most benefit to the patient.

1. A continuation of exactly the same regular treatment that the patient was taking, although at a reduced dose.

2. Selected elements from the patient's regular treatment at a full or reduced dose.

The conscientious and observant practitioner will discover with time, that *all* patients. if not *all* practitioners, would benefit from a maintenance program of minerals. Convincing others of this belief is the difficult part. It seems a shame that all around us there are people suffering needlessly though their own stupidity, prejudice, ego or ignorance. But, with the application of a bit of lateral thinking to this otherwise depressing situation we can be somewhat cheered, because life abounds with examples to demonstrate the fact that, pain is a much better teacher than pleasure!

Visit times; how long and how often

Appointment scheduling

Because the actual time that the practitioner will spend with a patient during consultation has to do with such matters as experience and the logistics of the practice environment, it is difficult to lay-down an appointment time that will be suitable for all situations. The time that a practitioner spends with a patient is also very much a personal matter. As a general guide though, approximately half an hour for a first visit and a quarter of an hour for a return visit would seem to be a workable routine for a practitioner with a receptionist and about double that time for one without.

The scheduling of appointments following the first consultation will have more to do with the nature of the illness under treatment than anything else. Follow-up contact for an acute case is obviously going to be required much sooner than it would be for a chronic one. Again, the practitioner's experience in dealing with these forms of illnesses is going to determine when that contact should be arranged. While it is impossible to propose an appointment plan for acute illness, the average chronic case seems to require monthly visits for the first two or three months and then bimonthly or quarterly visits after that. This initial routine of monthly reassessment is fortunate, as it allows the practitioner to monitor the case during it's most crucial phase, thus enabling him to adjust the treatment where required. In this regard, it is perhaps cautionary to reiterate two important points:

1. Because a patient has not responded during the initial months of treatment, does not mean that the existing treatment is inappropriate, but rather, that more time may be required.

2. Because a patient has not responded during the initial months of treatment is good reason to completely re-assess the case, effecting any required changes to treatment as soon as possible.

Chapter nine

Repertory of diseases

A clinical reference of diseases, with appropriate, and successful treatments listed, is what every practitioner dreams of, but in the real world no such system exists. Unfortunately, the principle of prescribing for the patient as an individual prevails and must take precedence over the "prescriptions for diseases" approach. Throughout the Repertory every attempt has been made to provide as much precise information as possible and still adhere to these principles, so that even where a practitioner finds the information wanting, at least he can be assured of being coaxed in the right direction.

Is the disease process more basic than we presently realise?

As the practitioner becomes experienced and relaxed about his prescribing, he will begin to see some very interesting phenomena; as certain mineral deficiency common-denominators, produce a particular illness, so too can those same deficiencies also be the cause of another, seemingly unrelated illness. The awareness of this fact suddenly confronts the practitioner with an amazing revelation and that is, that there is not a myriad of illness that must be treated and cured, by an equal number of approaches - but rather, certain root deficiencies that just manifest themselves in different ways.

The unity principle to disease

Once this principle is accepted, it is then the beginning of the development of mineral prescribing into an *art* . It is this understanding that equips the mineral prescriber far better than his counterpart practicing some other modality. He begins to see the *unity* of certain medically unrelated illnesses, which can often make treatment possible where treatment may not have been possible, or where the idiopathic nature of the illness precludes an understanding.

In this regard, the best value cannot be obtained from the Repertory by simply waiting for a patient to present with a particular illness, and then to look up a ready-made prescription. To understand the *unity* principle, the practitioner should read through the pages of the Repertory, from time to time, until there distils in his mind an understanding based upon this principle. The repertory will then be seen to be of far more value than first appearances may indicate.

Success through caution

Diseases are only listed where they lend themselves to predetermined prescriptions. There are obviously many other areas where mineral therapy could be applied successfully but these cannot be listed for that reason. Many medical symptoms are actually reflections of other causes and are therefore not illnesses in their own right. Symptoms such as; blood in the urine, vomit or fæces, difficulty in breathing and various types of pain, tumours or dystaxias, etc., are all considered to be areas, where for the sake of common-sense prudence, they have been omitted from the Repertory. This is not to say though, that mineral therapy cannot be considered in these conditions, but just that more information pertaining to the case should be obtained, before the appropriate treatment could be determined. As a practitioner gains experience, he will realise that the scope for application broadens, commensurate with his increased knowledge, experience and confidence.

How to use the Repertory

Some basic rules

To obtain the maximum value from the pages of the repertory, the following points should be observed:

1. That the prescription given for any disease or symptom is to be viewed as a general guide only.

2. That an individual patient may have particular symptoms or signs that will alter the prescription accordingly.

3. That where the group of minerals listed for a condition ends in a +, then the extra remedy(ies) to complete the prescription, must be gained from further questioning, particularly for "symptom qualifications".

4. That where acute conditions are concerned, the timing of doses is offered as general guide and may need to be adjusted to better suit the needs of the case under treatment. At times doses may need to be initially offered at intervals of only a few minutes, reducing the frequency immediately the symptoms respond. All tablets should be crushed or chewed and taken with hot water. The patient should be told to slosh the medicine around the mouth before swallowing.

5. Where suitable, the indicated salts may be applied to lesions topically as the powdered tablet, or mixed in an aqueous cream. These applications should be made twice daily. Burns and ulcers should be covered with a light gauze. The appropriate internal medication should be combined.

6. That all the other prescribing rules as listed on page 111, be observed.

The Repertory of diseases

A

Abortion	
Habitual	Where no reason can be found, SP, PP, MP (+ S, CF if cervical incompetence).
Threatened	PP, MP every 15-30 minutes (+ CF if time permits).
Abscess	PS, S + (PS, S every 2 hours to ripen). To heal following long suppuration, or if silica fails to resolve, change PS to CS.
Acidity, stomach	SP, PC, IP, MP (one of each every two hours for acute symptoms).
Acne	
Rosacea	PS, MP, S, CF, SP.
Vulgaris	Yellow heads, black heads, greasy skin PS, MP, S, CF or CS, + SP. White heads, blind pimples PC, IP, MP, S, CF, SP.
Adenoma	PC, MP, S, CF, SP.
Adhesion	PC, MP, S, CF, SP.
Aggression	Adults; PP, MP + usually SP. Children; PP, MP, CP + usually SP.
Agoraphobia	PP, MP. (With the PP, MP every 1-2 hours for acute symptoms).
Alcoholism	MP, PP + an Na salt.
Delirium tremens	MP every 15-30 minutes.
Allergies	all kinds. MP + a K salt + an Na salt. (Some chronic conditions also require S, and/or CF). With acute distress, or angioneurotic oedema, prescribe PS, PC, SS, + IP, a dose of each at least every 1-2 hours.

Alopecia	PP, MP, SCF, SP. (If pustulation or desquamation present, prescribe PS instead PP).
Alzheimer's disease	PP or PS, + MP + usually SP.
Amenorrhoea (primary or secondary)	PP + .
Amnesia	PP, MP +.
Anal fissure	CF, S +.
Anal fistula	CF, S +. (If suppurating + PS. If fistula won't heal CS +).
Anaemia (Hypochromic, microcytic)	CP, IP +.
Angina pectoris	MP +. Acute symptoms, 2 tablets chewed with hot water every 10-15 minutes.
Aneurisms	CF, S +.
Angioneurotic oedema	See "Allergies".
Anhidrosis	S +.
Anorexia nervosa	PP, MP +. (young adults + CP, IP) + usually SP. See also "Bulimia"
Anxiety	MP + (usually PP if associated with depression) +. Children; MP, CP +.
Appetite, poor	PP, MP + (with children or adolescents always CP; or CP + IP).
Arrhythmia	PP, MP + (but K. salt may be PS).
Arthritides	
Ankylosing spondylitis	S, CF, MP, PC, IP + (usually SP rather than SS and with the MP and PC, IP given at increased frequency for pain control).

Fibrositis	SP, MP, PC, IP, S, CF. (For acute symptoms give the SP, MP, PC, IP every two hours).
Gouty arthritis	(primary and secondary) SP, S, CF, PC, IP, MP. (SP, PC, IP, MP, every 2 hours for acute symptoms).
Osteoarthritis (Degenerative joint disease)	S, CF, MP + (usually SP and PC, IP). With acute pain and inflammation prescribe the MP, PC and IP every two hours.
Periarthritis	See "Osteoarthritis" above.
Pseudo-gout	See "Osteoarthritis" above.
Rheumatoid arthritis	S, CF, MP + a Na. salt + a K. salt. (For acute pain control prescribe the MP and the K. salt every 2 hours. If the K. salt is PC, prescribe PC, IP).
Scleroderma and SLE.	As for Rheumatoid arthritis, but if there is renal involvement with the disease, then discretion should be exercised with the K and Mg salts.
Spondylitis	See "Osteoarthritis" above.
Still's disease	See "Rheumatoid arthritis" above.
Asthma	Common basic prescriptions regardless of classification, as an example only: Children; PS, MP, CP, IP, SP. Adults; PS, MP, S, CF, SP. Acute symptoms; regardless of classification; PS, PC, MP, IP, one of each every 30 minutes as required. Mucus can't be raised PS, S +. Nervous, no expectoration, tight chest PP, MP +. White mucus PC +. Worse; damp weather SS, CP +. Worse; exposure to cold CP, S +. Worse; evening, night PS, S +. Yellow-green mucus PS +.

Atheroma	PC, MP +.
Atherosclerosis	MP, PC, S, CF + usually SP or SS.
Atrial fibrillation	PP, MP +.
Avascular necrosis	S, CF, MP, SP. (+ PC and IP if pain and inflammation) Some children also require the addition of CP to above prescription. See also "Osgood-Schlatter's disease" "Perthe's disease" and "Scheuermann's disease"

B

Barber's itch	PS +.
Basal cell carcinoma	PS, S, CF +.
Bed wetting	Children, nocturnal PP, MP, CP + usually SS. Aged, PP, MP, CF, SS.
Bell's palsy	PP, MP +. (For maximum effectiveness the PP, MP should be commenced immediately upon onset of symptoms, and given every 15-30 minutes).
Bilirubinuria	SS +.
Blackhead	See "Comedo" and "Acne".
Boils	PS, PC, IP, S, all every 2 hours. If lesion won't heal following above prescription, CS +.
Bouchard's nodes	See "Arthritides"; osteoarthritis.
Bone fracture	See "Fractures".
Bradycardia	PP, MP, CP, IP +.
Breasts	
Benign nodular	CF, S +.
Nipples crack	CF, S +.
Nipples infected	PS, PC, IP, all every 2 hours.

Bright's disease	See "Nephritis".
Bronchiectasis	PS, MP, S, CF + usually SP.
Bronchiolitis	See prescription for "Bronchitis".
Bronchitis	PC, IP, PS, all every 2 hours. Chronic, PS, MP, SP, CP, IP. White-clear mucus, PC. Yellow-green mucus, PS.
Bruises	PC or PC, + IP, all every 2 hours.
Buccal ulcers	PC, MP +. (For acute symptoms the PC should be given as PC + IP every 2 hours along with the MP and allowed to come in contact with the ulcer before swallowing).
Bulimia	PP, MP, SP.
Bunion	S, CF, SP. Pain; PC, IP, MP, all every 2 hours.
Burns	PC, IP, SS, MP, all every 2 hours. The PC and IP may also be applied topically to lesion twice daily as the powdered tablet, or mixed in an aqueous cream. Cover with gauze.
Bursitis	PC, IP, SS, all every 2 hours.

C

Callus, to promote	Children, CP, MP, SP. Aged, S, CF, MP, SP.
Candidiasis	PS, MP, SP. (With inflammation reinforce with PC and IP. Chronic conditions sometimes require S, or S + CF).
Capillary fragility	CF, S +.
Carbuncles	PS, PC, IP, S all every 2 hours. If lesion won't heal following above treatment, CS +.

Carcinophobia	PP, MP, SP.
Caries	CP, MP, S, SP, CF. See also "Dentition" and "Odontalgia".
Carpal tunnel syndrome	PC, IP, MP, S, CF + usually SS. Acute symptoms with pregnancy; PC, IP, MP, SS, one of each every 2 hours.
Cataracts	S, CF, PS, MP +. (To be effective the treatment must be commenced early).
Catarrh	White-clear mucus, PC +. Yellow-green mucus, PS +. Watery drip from nares, PS +.
Cellulitis	PS, PC, IP, all every 2 hours.
Cheilosis	CF +.
Chickenpox	PC, IP, PS, all every 2 hours.
Chilblain	CP, PC, IP, MP, SP. (CF, or S + CF if skin cracks).
Cholecystitis	PC, IP, MP, SP, all every 2 hours.
Cholelithiasis	PC, MP, S, CF, SP.
Circulation, poor	Young, CP, IP, MP, SP. Aged, CP (or S + CF), MP, PC, SP.
Claudication	PC, IP, MP, S, CF + usually SP.
Claustrophobia	PP, MP +.
Clots	See "Atheroma".
Coeliac disease	PC, MP (or PP, MP), + SP.
Colds	PC, IP, PS, all every 2 hours. Frequent colds; PS, MP, CP, IP, SP.

Colic	MP chewed with hot water every 10-15 minutes.
Babies	MP, CP, SP, 1/4 dose of each, crushed and given with each feed.
Biliary	MP, PC, IP, SP, one of each every 2 hours.
Children	Chronic condition; CP, MP + (often PP), SP. With the MP given every 1-2 hours at time of acute symptoms.
Uterine	See "Dysmenorrhoea".
Colitis	PP, MP + usually SP. (For acute symptoms prescribe the PP, MP every 2 hours). Ulcerative; PC, IP, MP, all every 2 hours.
Comedo	PS, S, SP. See also "Acne".
Concentration; lack of	PP or PS, + MP +.
Concussion (cerebral)	PC, IP, MP, SS, all every 2 hours.
Confusion	PP or PS, + MP +.
Conjunctivitis	PC, IP, both every 2 hours. If chronic PS, MP, SP.
Constipation	PP, MP, SS.
Contusions	PC, IP, both every 1-2 hours.
Convulsions (febrile)	PS, PC, IP, MP every 15-30 minutes at time of, or if threatened. PS, MP, CP, IP, SP to prevent.
Coryza	See "Colds".
Coxalgia	See "Arthritides"; osteoarthritis.
Cracked nipples	CF, S +.
Cramps	
Children	CP, IP, MP, SP.
Adults	As above, but S, CF in lieu of CP if associated with osteoarthritis.

Crepitation	See "Arthritides"; osteoarthritis.
Crohn's disease	PP or PS, + MP, S, CF, SP.
Croup	PC, IP, MP, all every 2 hours.
Cystitis	SP, PC, IP, MP, all every 2 hours.
Cysts (All types)	S, CF, PC + SP or SS.

D

Dandruff	PS, S, CF, SP.
Degenerative joint disease	See "Osteoarthritis".
Delirium tremens	See "Alcoholism".
Dendritic ulcer	See prescription for "Herpes".
Dentition	See also "Caries".
Delayed	CP, CF, S, MP + usually SP.
Enamel imperfect	CF, S +.
Febrile convulsions	CP, PS, IP, MP.
Non-febrile convulsions	MP.
Fever, red cheek	IP.
Gums pale	CP, IP.
Receding gums	CF, S +.
Teeth loose	CF, S +.
Teeth sensitive	CF, S, MP +.
Weak, chalky, rot easily	CP, CF, S, MP + usually SP.
Depression (endogenous or exogenous)	PP, MP +. (The PP, MP should be given hourly for acute symptoms).
Dermatitis	See "Eczema".
Desquamation; profuse	PS, MP, S, CF, SP.
Diabetes mellitus	SS, PC, MP.
Diarrhoea	PP, MP, SS.
Emotional	PP, MP, both every 2 hours.
After fatty food	SP, PC, MP, all every 2 hours.
Dilatations	IP, CF, MP +.
Discoid lupus	S, CF, PS, MP, SP.

Diverticular disease	PC, IP, MP, SP, CF.
Diuresis	MP +.
Dry mouth	PP +.
When anxious	PP, MP, both every 2 hours.
Duodenal ulcer	SP, PC, IP, MP. (One of each every 1-2 hours for acute symptoms).
Dupuytren's contracture	PC, MP, S, CF, SP.
Dysmenorrhoea	
Uterine colic	MP, CP every 1-2 hours with hot water. (If pain has been a regular feature of periods, symptoms should be anticipated by commencing the increased dose a day or so before the flow begins).
Haemorrhagia	PC, IP, MP, all every 2 hours.
Depression	PP, MP, both every 2 hours.
Oedema	SS +. (In acute conditions give every 2 hours).
PMT/PMS	See "Premenstrual tension".
Dyspareunia	MP, PP +.
Dyspnoea	See "Emphysema".

E

Earache	See "Otitis externa", "Otitis media", and "Otitis interna".
Ecchondroma	S, CF +.
Ecmnesia	PP or PS, + MP +.
Eczema	Typical prescription: PS, MP, CP, IP, SP. Dry sloughing in flakes PS, S, CF +. Dry serous exudate PS +. Emotional factors PP, MP +. Infantile CP +. Itchy vesicles PC, IP, MP +. Skin fissures CF +. Weepy PS or SS +.

Emesis (cyclical in children)	PP, MP, CP, SP.
Empyema	PS, S, PC, IP, all every 2 hours. If lesion refuses to heal once pus has found a vent, change PS to CS.
Emphysema (pulmonary)	PS, MP, S, CF, SP. (With acute distress, prescribe the PS and MP every 2 hours).
Encopresis	Children; PP, MP, CP, SP. Aged; PP, MP, CP or CF, +.
Endometriosis	PC (or PC + IP if flooding or pain) + MP, S, CF, SP or SS.
Enuresis	
Nocturnal	Children; PP, MP, CP, SS. Aged; PP, MP, CP or CF, + SS.
Diurnal	PP, MP, IP, SS.
Enterobius vermicularis	SP, CP, 2 tablets of each with each meal.
Epicondylitis	PC, IP, MP, all every 2 hours for pain. PC, IP, MP, S, CF, SP for chronic condition.
Epilepsies	MP + a K. salt + an Na. salt.
Epistaxis	IP every 2 hours. CP, IP, MP, SP for chronic conditions
Erysipelas	PS, MP, PC, IP, SP.

F

Fainting	See "Syncope".
Fasciitis	MP, PC, IP, S, CF, SP.
Fat intolerance	SP, PC, MP.
Febrile convulsions (Children)	CP, PS, IP, MP.

Fever	PS, PC, IP, all every 1-2 hours.
Fibroid (uterine)	PC, S, CF, MP + usually SP.
Fibroma	See "Cyst".
Fibrositis	See "Arthritides".
Fissure	CF +.
Flatulence	SP, PC, IP, MP. (If symptoms are acute, prescribe all minerals every 30 minutes while symptoms last).
Flatus	MP +. (If emotional reasons or spasms, prescribe PP, MP every 1-2 hours).
Flu	PS, MP, PC, IP, all every 2 hours.
Flushing	PS, MP +.
Fractures	Children CP, MP, SP. Aged S, CF, MP, SP.
Frozen shoulder	S, CF, MP, PC, IP, SP. (With the PC, IP and the MP every 2 hours for pain control).
	G
Ganglia	S, CF + usually MP, PC (and IP if pain) + SP or SS.
Gastric reflux	See "Pyrosis".
Gastritis	SP, PC, IP, MP. (With increased dose of all if acute).
German measles	PC, IP, PS, all every 2 hours.
Gingivitis	PC, IP, S, CF +.
Glandular fever	SP, MP + a K. salt + usually CP, and IP.
Glaucoma	PC, MP, S, SS.

Globus hystericus	PP, MP +.
Gonorrhoea	PS, PC, IP, MP, SP, all every 2 hours. If condition not resolved after above, change PS to CS.
Gouty arthritis	See "Arthritides".
Growing pains	CP, IP, MP, SP. (Some conditions may require S and CF).
Gumboil	S, PS, PC, IP, all every two hours.

H

Haemorrhoids	CF, S, MP, + PC and IP if itching and bleeding +.
Hair	Ends split S +. Premature loss PS (PP, MP if associated with depression) + S, CF +. Oily PS +.
Halitosis	PP, MP, SP.
Hayfever	See "Allergies".
Haygarth's nodes	See "Arthritides"; rheumatoid arthritis.
Head	Crawling sensation MP and/or CP. Scalp sore if hair touched PP and/or IP.
Headaches	Cotton-woolly; fuzzy PS +. Migraine PP, MP +. (See also "Migraine"). Pressure feeling MP +. Come on in stuffy or smoky rooms PS +. Tension/worry PP, MP +.
Heberden's nodes	See "Arthritides"; osteoarthritis.
Hepatitis	SS, PC, IP, MP. Two hourly dose of each while acute symptoms last.
Hernia	CF, S +.

Herpes	
Simplex (type 1 and 2)	For acute stage, PS or PC, + IP, MP, SP or SS, depending upon the symptom picture, with a 2 hourly dose of each. For chronic, recurring condition, usually PS alone, or PS, MP, SP.
Zoster	For acute stage, PC, IP, SS, MP, every 2 hours. For later stage, PP or PS, + MP, SP (+ sometimes S or CF).
Hiatus hernia	PC, IP, MP, SP. (Once condition is stabilised, S, CF should be added to prescription).
Hives	See "Urticaria".
Homesickness	PP, MP +.
Hydraemia	SS +.
Hydrocele	CF, S, SS.
Hyperactivity	PP, MP +. For acute symptoms, give doses of PP and MP hourly.
Hyperaemia	IP.
Hyperchlorhydria	SP, PC, IP, MP. Two hourly dose of all if symptoms acute.
Hyperemesis gravidarum	For acute symptoms, SP, PP, MP, all every 1-2 hours.
Hyperkeratosis	See "Keratosis"
Hyperpyrexia	PS, PC, IP, all every 1-2 hours.
Hypertension	
Atherosclerosis	MP, PC + usually SP or SS.
Anxiety	Or where no other reason can be found (essential), PP, MP +.
Oedema	SS (sometimes double dose) + usually PC and MP.
Hyperthermia	PS, PC, IP, dose of each at least every 1-2 hours.

Hypoglycaemia	PP, MP + usually SP.
Hypotension	PP + (If associated with anaemia CP, IP) +.
Hypoxia	PS, MP, IP.

I

Illusions of the senses	MP + usually PP or PS +.
Immunodeficiency	PS or PP, + MP (if stress related) + CP, IP, SP.
Incontinence	See "Enuresis" and "Encopresis".
Indigestion	SP, MP, PC, IP, all every 1-2 hours.
Infections	
Viral	PS, PC, IP, all every 2 hours.
Bacterial	PS, PC, IP (+ S to promote discharge if indicated). Prescribe one of each every 2 hours.
Fungal	PS, MP +.
Frequent colds, etc.	PS, MP, CP, IP, SP.
Infectious mononeucleosis	SP, MP + a K. salt + usually CP, IP.
Infertility	
Female	PC, IP, MP, S, CF, SP. For psychogenic causes, or where no organic reason can be found; PP, MP, SP, CP, IP.
Male	Where no organic reason can be found PP, MP, SP.
Inflammations (local)	PC, IP, both every 2 hours.
Influenza	PS, PC, IP, all every 2 hours.
Insomnia	PP, MP. To be taken with hot water at bedtime.
Irritable bowel syndrome	PP, MP + usually SP, with 2 hourly doses of the PP and MP at times of exacerbation.

J

Jaundice (hepatocellular or cholestatic)	SS, MP, PC, IP.

K

Keratosis (hyper)	S, CF + usually PC and SP.
Keloid	See "Scar tissue".

L

Leucorrhoea	PC, IP, SP with 2 hourly dose of each if acute and scalding.
Lichen (various forms)	PS, MP, S, CF, SP.
Ligamentous weakness	S, CF, MP, SP (+ PC and IP if inflammation).
Lipoma	PC, MP, S, CF, SP.
Lupus (discoid)	SP, PS, MP, S, CF.

M

Manicdepressive psychosis	PP, MP + usually SP, with 2 hourly dose of the PP, MP during acute depressive or manic phases.
Mastitis	PC or PS, + MP, SP. (PC and IP every 2 hours if acute). If there is pus discharge that does not resolve, change PS to CS.
Metrorrhagia	PC, IP +.
Memory, poor	PP or PS, + MP +.
Menopause	See "Flushing" and "Depression".
Menorrhagia	See "Dysmenorrhoea".
Migraine headaches	PP, MP + in most cases but can be PS, MP +.

	Headache can often be aborted if PP, MP is given in hot water every 5-10 minutes at prodromal stage.
Moniliasis	See "Candidiasis"
Morning sickness	See "Hyperemesis gravidarum".
Motion sickness	PP, MP, SP, all every 1-2 hours.
Motivation, lack of	PP, MP +.
Mouth, dry	PP.
Multiple sclerosis	PP or PS, + MP, SP, S, CF.
Mumps	PC, IP, both every two hours.
Muscle spasms	MP every 15-30 minutes for acute pain.
Myasthenia gravis	PP, MP +.
Myocardial infarct	MP, PP, both every 5-10 minutes crushed in hot water.
Myofascial pain syndrome	SP, MP, PC, IP, S, CF. (For acute symptoms give the SP, MP, PC, IP every two hours).
Myokymia	MP, PP, with the MP every 30 minutes if acute.
Myxoedema	PP, MP, SS +.

N

Narcolepsy	PP, MP +.
Nausea, fat intolerance	PC, SP, MP (Dose of each every 2 hours if acute).
Nephritis	PC, IP, MP, CP, SP. Acute glomerulo; PS, PC, IP, all every 2 hours.
Nettle rash	See "Urticaria".

Neuralgia	Children, acute MP and CP every 2 hours. Chronic PP, MP +. Acute paroxismal MP every 15-30 minutes with hot water.
Neurasthenia	PP, MP +.
Neurodermatitis	See "Eczema".
Neuroses (All types)	PP, MP +. Acute symptoms; PP and MP, every hour.
Nipples; cracked	CF, S +.
Noise, sensitive to	PP, MP +.
Nose bleed	See "Epistaxis".
Nostalgia	PP, MP +.
	O
Obsessional neurosis	See "Neuroses".
Odontalgia	MP, IP, both every 15-30 minutes for pain. Boring pain, worse at night, CP. Febrile convulsions and infections during teething, CP, PC, IP, MP, SP. Gums bleed, spongy, receding and have bright-red seam, PP +. Root abscess, PS, S, PC, IP, all every 2 hours. Toothache with red cheek and fever, worse, hot drinks and pressure on tooth, better from cold applications IP, SS.
Oedema (All types)	SS (increased dose in acute cases) + PC +.
Oligomenorrhoea	PP, MP +.
Orbital neuralgia	MP every hour. If associated with depression, add PP.
Orchitis	PC, IP, PS, all every 2 hours.

Osgood-Schlatter's disease	S, CF, MP, SP. (+ PC, IP and MP every 2 hours if acute inflammatory pain) Children/young adults also require the addition of CP to above prescription.
Osteitis deformans	See "Paget's disease".
Osteoarthritis	See "Arthritides".
Osteochondritis	See "Osgood-Schlatter's disease" "Perthe's disease", and "Scheuermann's disease".
Osteochondroma	S, CF +.
Osteomalacia	SP, CP, MP, S, CF.
Osteomyelitis	SP, MP, S, CF, PS. (For acute symptoms prescribe PS, PC and IP every 2 hours).
Osteoporosis	SP, CP, MP, S, CF.
Osteoma	CF, S +.
Osteoid	PC, IP, S, CF, MP +.
Osteomalacia	See prescription for "Osteoporosis".
Otalgia	See "Otitis, externa, media and interna".
Otitis	
Externa	PC, IP, both every 2 hours.
Media	PS, MP, CP, IP, SP. Acute symptoms PC, IP, PS, all every 2 hours.
Interna	PS, PC, IP, all every 2 hours.
Otorrhoea	PC, IP, PS, all every 2 hours.
Otosclerosis	S, CF +.
Overuse syndrome	See "Repetitive strain injury".
Oxyuriasis	SP, CP, 2 tablets of each with each meal.

P

Paget's disease	PC, IP, MP, S, CF, SP. (With the PC, IP, MP every 1-2 hours for pain control).
Pallor	CP, IP +. (+ PP if associated with depression).
Palpitation	PS or PP, +. With anxiety/depression PP, MP +. With anaemia CP, IP +.
Palsy, Bell's	See "Bell's palsy".
Paralysis	PP, MP +.
Paranoia	PP, MP +.
Paresis	PP, MP +.
Parkinsonism	PP, MP +.
Parotitis	PC, IP, both every two hours.
Paronychia	PS, S, CF. (For acute symptoms prescribe PS, S, CF, PC, IP, all every 2 hours).
Pelvic inflammatory disease	PC or PS, + MP, IP +.
Peptic ulcer	SP, MP, PC, IP.
Periarthritis	See "Arthritides"; osteoarthritis.
Pericarditis Adhesive or fibrinous	PC, IP, both every 1-2 hours. PC, IP, S, CF, MP, SS.
Periods	See "Dysmenorrhoea" and "Amenorrhoea".
Perthe's disease	S, CF, CP, MP, SP.
Pharyngitis	PC, IP, both every 2 hours.
Phlebitis	PC, IP +.
Phobia (all kinds)	PP, MP +.

Phosphaturia	CP, SP.
Photophobia	PP, MP +.
Piles	See "Haemorrhoids".
Pilonidal sinus	PS, PC, IP, all every 2 hours.
Pleurisy	Dry; PS, PC, IP, all every 2 hours. Wet; PS, PC, IP, SS, all every 2 hours.
Pleurodynia	SP, MP, PC, IP, S, CF. (For acute symptoms give the SP, MP, PC, IP every two hours).
Pneumonia	PS, PC, IP, SS, all every 2 hours.
Polyarteritis	PC, IP +.
Polyarthritis	See "Arthritides"; rheumatoid arthritis.
Polymyalgia rheumatica	Usually SP, MP, PC, IP, S, CF. (with a 2 hourly dose of the MP, PC and IP for acute symptoms).
Polyneuritis	MP, PP +. Acute paroxysms; MP and PP, every hour as required.
Polyuria	Aged PP, MP, CP or CF, + SP or SS. Children CP, PP, MP, SP or SS. With anxiety PP, MP every 2 hours. From exposure to cold CP, MP.
Post-nasal catarrh	White mucus PC +. Yellow-green mucus PS +. Watery PS +.
Pre-eclampsia	SS, PC, MP, all every 2 hours as required.
Premenstrual tension	PP, MP, SP. (If oedema give SS instead of SP). At ovulation time and just prior to menstruation prescribe PP and MP every 2 hours. See also "Dysmenorrhoea".

Proctalgia	In absence of pathology; PP, MP +.
Proctitis	PC, IP +.
Prolapse	CF, S +.
Prostatic hypertrophy (benign)	PC, MP, S, CF + usually SP.
Prostatitis	PC, IP, PS, all every 2 hours.
Pruritus (Essential)	PP, MP, both every 1-2 hours for symptomatic relief. Check for underlying cause before prescribing additional remedies.
Pseudo-gout	See "Arthritides".
Psoriasis	PS, MP, S, CF, SP.
Ptosis	PP, MP.
Pyelitis	PC, IP, PS, all every 2 hours.
Pyogenic infections	See "Infections".
Pyorrhoea	PS, MP, S, CF, SP.
Pyrexia	PS, PC, IP, all every 1-2 hours.
Pyrosis	SP, PC, IP, MP, all every 15-30 minutes for acute pain.

Q

Quinsy	PS, PC, IP, all every 1-2 hours.

R

Raynaud's disease	MP, PS or PP, + S, CF or CP, + IP + usually SP.
Reflux; gastric	See "Pyrosis".
Repetitive strain injury	PC, IP, MP, S, CF, SP. (with 2 hourly dose of the PC, IP and MP at times of exacerbation).
Rheumatism	See "Arthritides".

Rheumatoid arthritis	See "Arthritides".
Rhinitis	PC, IP, PS, all every 2 hours. See also "Allergies".
Ringworm	See "Infections; fungal".
Rosacea	PS, MP, S, CF + an Na salt.
RSI	See "Repetitive strain injury".
Rubella	See "German measles".
	S
Scalp	Crawling sensation MP and/or CP. Dandruff PS, S, CF, SP. Oily PS +. Sore to touch PP and/or IP.
Scar tissue	S, CF, PC + usually SP.
Scheuermann's disease	S, CF, CP, MP, SP. (+ PC, IP and MP every 2 hours if acute inflammatory pain)
Schizophrenia	PP, MP + (with hourly dose for acute symptoms).
Schlatter's disease	See "Osgood-Schlatter's disease".
Sciatica	MP, PC, IP, all every 2 hours.
Scleroderma	See "Arthritides".
Seborrhoea	PS +.
Senility	PS, MP, S, CF, SP.
Sensitivity to noise	PP, MP +.
Septicaemia	PS, PC, IP, all every hour.
Shingles	See "Herpes zoster".
Sinusitis	PS, MP, S, CF, SP. Acute episodes; PS, IP, PC, all every 2 hours.

Sjogren's syndrome	PC, MP, IP, S, CF, SS.
Skin	
Cracking	CF or CP, + S +.
Dry	PS or SS +.
Flaking	PS +.
Heals slowly	S, CF +.
Oily	PS +.
Premature aging	CF, S, PP, MP + SP or SS.
Sloughing (desquamation)	See "Desquamation".
Somnambulism	PP, MP +. (Children + CP).
Spasms	See "Muscle spasms".
Spondylitis	See "Arthritides"; osteoarthritis.
Sterility	
Female	SP, PC, IP, MP, S, CF. For psychogenic causes, or where no organic reason can be found; PP, MP, SP, CP, IP.
Male	Where no organic reason can be found PP, MP, SP.
Still's disease	See "Arthritides", Rheumatoid arthritis.
Stomatitis	PC, IP, MP, S, CF, SP.
Sycosis barbai	PS +.
Syncope	PP, MP at time of. (CP, IP, PP, MP, SP for chronic symptoms).
Systemic lupus erythematosus	See "Arthritides"; SLE.

T

Tachycardia	PP or PS, + MP +. (CP and IP if associated with anaemia).
Tearful	See "Depression".
Teething	See "Dentition".

Tendonitis	See "Tenosynovitis", "Repetitive strain injury" and "Epicondylitis".
Tenesmus	PP.
Tenosynovitis	PC, IP, MP, S, CF, SP. (with 2 hourly dose of the PC, IP and MP at times of exacerbation).
Thread worms	See "Oxyuriasis".
Thrombosis	PC, IP, MP, all every 2 hours for acute symptoms. Add SS to above prescription if oedema present.
Tic	PP, MP +. (Children + CP).
Tic douloureux	PP, MP +. (For acute pain PP, MP every 15-30 minutes in hot water).
Tinea	See "Infections fungal".
Tinnitus	PP, MP, SS.
Tongue	Burning PS +. Bleeding/cracked CF +. Ulcerated, see "Ulcers".
Tonsillitis	Acute PC, IP, PS, all every 2 hours. Chronic PS, MP, CP, IP, SP. If tonsils continue to suppurate and won't heal following above CS +.
Toothache	See "Odontalgia".
Torticollis	Acute; MP, every 30 minutes. Chronic; MP, PP +.
Trichomonias	PS, PC, IP, SP, all every 2 hours
Trigeminal neuralgia	See "Tic douloureux".
Tuberculosis	CP, PS, S, MP, SP. Acute symptoms, PS, PC, IP, all every 2 hours. Open lesions, if above prescription fails to heal, CS +.

U

Ulcerative colitis	See "Irritable bowel syndrome".
Ulcers;	
Buccal	PC, MP, S, CF, SP. (For acute symptoms PC, IP and MP, every 2 hours, chewed with warm water and letting the minerals come in contact with the ulcers for as long as possible before swallowing).
Duodenal/Gastric	SP, MP, PC, IP + often S, and CF. (For acute pain or melaena, prescribe the PC, IP, MP every 2 hours).
Herpetic	See "Herpes".
Suppurating	PS, S, PC, IP. If lesion fails to heal, change PS to CS.
Varicose	PS or PC, + IP, MP + SP or SS (+ S and CF if intractable).
Urethritis	See prescription for "Cystitis".
Urticaria	PC, MP + usually SP. (For acute symptoms PC, IP, MP, all every 2 hours).
Uterine prolapse	CF +.

V

Vaginitis	See "Trichomonias"
Vaginismus	MP, PP +. (+ IP if vagina hot and dry).
Varicella	See "Chickenpox".
Varicose veins	PC, MP, S, CF + usually SP. (For acute symptoms prescribe PC, IP and MP every 2 hours.
Ventricular arrhythmia	PP, MP +.
Vertigo	PP +.

Vomiting	See "Emesis".
	W
Warts	PC and SS; or PP, MP, SP.
Water-brash	See "Pyrosis".
Weepy, depressed	PP, MP +.
Whitlow	See "Paronychia".
Wry neck	See "Torticollis".

Bibliography

Ashmead, D., ed. Chelated mineral nutrition in plants, animals and man. Springfield. Ill: Thomas, 1982

Boericke, W. Boericke, O., ed. Homœopathic materia medica. Philadelphia: Boericke and Runyon, 1927

Boericke & Dewey. (1914) The twelve tissue remedies. Calcutta: Roy Publishing, 1963

Bowen. Trace elements in biochemistry. Academic Press, 1966

Callinan, P., & Fisher, L. Celloid prescribers' reference. Sydney: Blackmores, 1985

Dixon, M., & Webb, E. Enzymes. New York: Academic Press, 1979

Dunne, L. Nutrition almanac. 3rd Ed. New York: McGraw Hill, 1990

Eichhorn, G. L., & Marzilli, L., ed. Advances in inorganic chemistry. Amsterdam: Elsevier Biomedical Press, 1979

Emslie-Smith, D., et al., ed. Textbook of physiology (BDS). 11th Ed. Edinburgh: Churchill Livingstone, 1988

Fisher, L. Mineral compounds and human disease. Sydney: Blackmores Books, 1978

Friedman, J. "Naturopathic treatment and childhood behavioural disturbances". Canberra: Report of the committee of inquiry into chiropractic, osteopathy, homœopathy and naturopathy. Appendix 16. Australian Government Publishing Service, 1977

Ganong. Review of medical physiology. 10th Ed. Lange, 1981

Guthrie, H. A. Introductory nutrition. St. Louis: Times Mirror/Mosby College, 1989

Guyton, A. Physiology of the human body. 5th Ed. W. B. Saunders & Co, 1979

Haehl, R. (1922) Samuel Hahnemann; his life and work. New Delhi: B. Jain, 1989

Harrison & Hoare. Metals in biochemistry. Chapman & Hall, 1980

Hahnemann, S. (1833) Organon of medicine. 6th Ed. New Delhi: B. Jain, 1988

Krupp, Chatton, & Werdegar. Current medical diagnosis and treatment. Los Altos, Ca.: Lange, 1988

Loewy & Siekevitz. Cell structure and function. 2nd Ed. Holt, Rinehart, & Wilson. 1971

Lovelock, J. Gaia, a new look at life on earth. Oxford: Oxford University Press, 1988

MacLeod, J. ed. Davidson's principles and practice of medicine. 13th Ed. Edinburgh: Churchill Livingstone, 1981

Mitra, B. Tissue remedies. 5th Ed. Calcutta: Economic Homeo Pharmacy, 1983

Osterberg. Williams ed. Introduction to bio-inorganic chemistry. Thomas, 1976

Phipps. Metals and metabolism. Oxford: Oxford University Press, 1976

Schüssler, W. (1885) Biochemic treatment of disease. New Delhi: B. Jain, 1989

Schüssler, W. Biochemic pocket guide with repertory. New Delhi: B. Jain, 1989

Shannon, S. A complete repertory of the tissue remedies of Schüssler. Calcutta: Roy Publishing, 1978

Smith, R. "Mineral deficiencies in plants". Paper; conference: Better health through mineral nutrition, Utah, 7-9 Feb. 1980

Taylor, R. Medicine out of control: the anatomy of a malignant technology. Melbourne: Sun Books, 1979

Index

Notes